DAKINI POWER

Twelve Extraordinary Women Shaping the Transmission
of Tibetan Buddhism in the West

Michaela Haas, PhD

SNOW LION

BOSTON & LONDON

2013

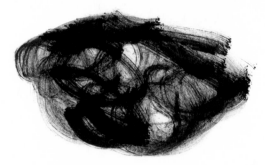

Snow Lion
An imprint of Shambhala Publications, Inc.
Horticultural Hall
300 Massachusetts Avenue
Boston, Massachusetts 02115
www.shambhala.com

9 8 7 6 5 4 3 2 1

First Edition
Printed in the United States of America

∞This edition is printed on acid-free paper that meets the
American National Standards Institute z39.48 Standard.
♻ This book is printed on 30% postconsumer recycled paper.
For more information please visit www.shambhala.com.

Distributed in the United States by Random House, Inc., and in Canada by
Random House of Canada Ltd

Designed by Gopa & Ted2, Inc.

Library of Congress Cataloging-in-Publication Data

Haas, Michaela, 1970–
Dakini power: twelve extraordinary women shaping the transmission of
Tibetan Buddhism in the West / Michaela Haas, PhD.—First Edition.
pages cm
ISBN 978-1-55939-407-9 (pbk.)
1. Buddhist women—Biography. 2. Women teachers—Biography. I. Title.
BQ850.H33 2013
294.3'92309252—dc23
[B]
2012037891

Dakini Power

CONTENTS

The Karmapa

FOREWORD

THE PATH to enlightenment and liberation which the Buddha taught was for all sentient beings, for women as well as men.

In the past there were many great women practitioners such as Mahāprajābatī Gautamī, who was both Sakyamuni Buddha's adoptive mother and the first woman to be ordained into the sangha he established. Buddhist texts also refer to female Arhats. Equal practice opportunities were given to both men and women, and the four pillars of the house of Buddhism include ordained nuns and lay women.

I am heartened to read the accounts in this book of the achievements of women teachers from different schools of Buddhism: it is a celebration of the contribution which female practitioners have made throughout Buddhist history and which they are continuing to make.

Unfortunately, influenced by the views and customs of the time, too many societies have put too much emphasis on the differences between men and women, and this has led to discrimination against and unequal treatment of women in many religions, including Buddhism.

My heartfelt prayer is that women such as these are the trailblazers; their efforts will lead to a fresh recognition of the unique insights and qualities of female spirituality, and wider acknowledgment of women practitioners and teachers.

17th Karmapa Ogyen Trinley Dorje
Dharamsala, Himachal Pradesh, India
3rd November, 2012

Special Thanks

To my soul mate who loves me unconditionally and continues to believe in me when I don't. Without your emotional and practical support, I could not have written this book. This book is for you, and for all lovers who stand by their partners no matter what.

To my mother and father who never understood why their only daughter left her five-star TV career to sit in caves in the Himalayas and search for God knows what all over Asia. This book is for you, and for all parents who keep loving their children even when they seek adventures out of the ordinary.

To my teachers, male and female, wild and playful, who continue to challenge me in unexpected ways. This book is for you, all teachers and all students, all who keep finding and who keep searching with open mind.

Dakini (SANSKRIT):

FEMALE MESSENGER OF WISDOM

—

PREFACE

M ANY OF US dream of exchanging our day-to-day responsibilities
for a heartfelt life full of purpose, but few of us ever get around
to doing something about it. The women in this book are the exception.

What drives a young London librarian to board a ship to India,
meditate in a remote cave by herself for twelve years, and then build
a flourishing nunnery in the Himalayas? How does a surfer girl from
Malibu become the head of the main international organization for
Buddhist women? Why does the daughter of a music executive in Santa
Monica dream so vividly of peacocks one night that she chases these
images all the way to Nepal where she finds the love of her life? These
are some of the fascinating biographies in this book: twelve stories of
courage, determination, and wisdom.

The women featured in *Dakini Power* are universally recognized as
accomplished practitioners and brilliant teachers, and they bring fresh
insights into Buddhism in the West. This volume focuses specifically
on contemporary teachers of Tibetan Buddhism, both Westerners and
Asians, who teach in the West.

All twelve women followed their intuition against all odds, made dramatic decisions, and sometimes had to fight for their survival in order
to lead the lives they envisioned. All of them were criticized at one point
or another—for being too conservative or too rebellious, too feminist
or not feminist enough—yet they pulled through with immense bravery.
What inspiration these women's stories offer modern spiritual seekers!

Some of these teachers, such as Dagmola Sakya, Tsultrim Allione,
and Elizabeth Mattis-Namgyel, are mothers and were struggling to

raise their children while working and carving out time for their spiritual path. Others, such as Tenzin Palmo, Pema Chödrön, and Karma Lekshe Tsomo, were born in busy hubs of the West but then decided to become nuns, exchanging their English birth names for Tibetan ordination names. A few, for example, Dagmola Sakya and Khandro Tsering Chödron, reveal fascinating glimpses into pre-Communist Tibet before the Chinese takeover catapulted them into exile. Chagdud Khadro,[1] Thubten Chodron, and Sangye Khandro were raised in the West, and an inexplicable urge sent them on rickety overland buses through Afghanistan and Pakistan to India. Conversely, Khandro Rinpoche, one of the very few female Tibetan incarnate masters, was born and trained in India but then flew to America to investigate the crazy Western mind. Roshi Joan Halifax joined the civil rights movement and was involved in the counterculture of the sixties before finding her calling in assisting the dying. She is a Zen priest, included in this book because of her extensive ties with Tibetan teachers and core Tibetan practices.

Originally, Khandro Tsering Chödron's life story was meant to be the opening chapter for this book, but sadly she passed away during my research. The last chapter of this volume now stands as a farewell tribute to her, outlining her heritage as the lessons we can learn from the life and death of a highly realized practitioner.

ROLE MODELS, REFORMERS, RADICALS

Rarely do we meet someone who touches us deeply to the core, who embodies a profundity of wisdom that actually changes us. For me, the women in this book are such outstanding masters. They are all highly educated, savvy women. Some of them have published books that I recommend you read. But what I find most inspiring is how they live Buddhist wisdom in everyday life, how they carry themselves not only on the teaching throne but in personally challenging situations, how they deal with the messy stuff—death, divorce, betrayal, and loss.

What can we learn from these women? How do they handle the cultural differences? How do they deal with the more controversial aspects of Buddhism? The Westerners among them risked alienating their families and closest friends by steeping their lives in a foreign culture. Often, this necessitated radical life changes; sometimes they risked their lives. What did they find on their journey? Was the price they paid worth it to them?

While I hold a doctorate and am a trained journalist, I am also a student of the dharma.* My intention is to honor the lives and accomplishments of these female pioneers of Buddhism in the West, not least because they seem to have bridged gaps that many, including myself, struggle with. I have found strength and courage in their friendship and teachings.

Both as an academic and as a journalist, I have been trained to report "neutrally," but this is not a neutral, "objective" book. In the two decades I have worked as a writer, I have also learned that objectivity is an impossibly distant goal anyway, because our biographies inevitably color our experience. To state upfront that my interest is personal and close to my heart is simply more honest. Each chapter is based on personal meetings with the teachers, some of whom I have known for many years. Sometimes they directed me to teachings they have given in other places, and I showed respect for their time by not prolonging interviews with questions they had answered elsewhere. I honored requests to exclude some personal material and adapted some sections to safeguard the identity of sources whose political situations were precarious. My notes at the end of each chapter give fuller details.

This book is a labor of love. Though their true essence cannot be captured with mere words, it is my aspiration to pay homage to these remarkable women and to offer them the respect they deserve for following their dreams all the way. I sincerely apologize if I have made any errors or misrepresented their work in any way.

---

*Dharma (Sanskrit; Tib. chö) here refers to the Buddha's teachings. The word has a wide range of meanings which include truth, path, and phenomena.

A LIFE-CHANGING JOURNEY

My introduction to Buddhism began in the autumn of 1996 when, after a serious health crisis at age twenty-six, I took three months off from my hectic life as a reporter and booked an around-the-world ticket to India, Sri Lanka, the Maldives, and Bhutan. The Maldives were for diving with sharks, India for yoga and markets, Sri Lanka for oil massages, and Bhutan—well, that tiny Himalayan kingdom just randomly popped up because a friend had praised it as a "really exotic destination," hard to get into. That was enough to trigger my curiosity. I knew very little about Buddhism at the time, but I heeded the friend's advice that the Bhutanese didn't fancy ignorant hordes of tourists. They demanded that their state religion be taken seriously. Only Buddhists would be allowed to enter the most sacred, coolest temples, he said. Before boarding the tiny propeller-plane to fly across the Himalayas, I dutifully sat down on the beaches of the Maldives to study a dry Buddhist art guide. The joyful, golden meditator in the cross-legged lotus posture was the Buddha, easy to figure out. The daredevil with the trident and the funny hat was called Padmasambhava, revered as the pioneer of Tibetan Buddhism. I memorized the name of the peaceful naked white lady with the lotus in her left hand as Tara, the female Buddha of Compassion.

Though I had always been fascinated by Buddhist ideas, I wasn't interested much in a deeper meaning. I was collecting exotic memories. Unexpectedly, in Bhutan, the drawings of the dancing deities came alive. The vibrant paintings in the secluded temples spoke to a deeper place in my heart. Something within me connected to the explosions of colors and mantras I encountered while trekking. My mind shifted into an acute awareness that I had never known, a firsthand glimpse of what Tibetans call "the nature of mind"—the naked simplicity of awareness beyond concepts. With the solid walls of my old perception cracked beyond repair, I couldn't have gone back to my old life even had I wanted to. I came as a tourist; I left as a pilgrim.

Unable to figure out what exactly had effected this transformation, I was too captivated to write this off as a tourist mirage. My mind had been touched deeply enough to inquire what this unique wisdom culture was all about. Why were there so many deities, what insights were these extensive libraries holding? I was intrigued by the Tibetan teachers I met. They were tough but playful. They accepted no nonsense, but their faces were covered in soft smiles. A joyful fearlessness radiated through their powerful presence, which was radically different from the nervous edginess of my news desk. They knew something I had to know. Mind is the creator of both happiness and suffering, they said, and we can learn to emancipate ourselves from the uncontrollable shift of outer events by getting to know our mind and its nature. I did go back to the newspaper, but during my next assignment in Asia, I faxed my resignation from a rundown Nepalese post shack to my dumbfounded boss: "Thank you for all your support. I'm not coming back."

I became deeply interested in the unique Tibetan science of the mind. Just sitting down for a simple twenty-minute meditation session, I soon realized that my notion of having control over my own mind was masking a deeper disability—emotions and thoughts percolate up continuously, churning the mind beyond command. The Buddha's teachings contain a stunning promise: that we all can regain the driver's seat if only we pay close attention—and if we realize that there is no driver to begin with. The still-revolutionary insight of the Buddha is that we are what we think—that reality is what we create in our mind, and that there really is no limit to the depth of mind's potential. Within weeks, I signed up for a course of Buddhist philosophy in Kathmandu, the Nepalese capital, studying Tibetan and Sanskrit. In my spare time, I trekked the mountains, tried to sit crosslegged in remote monasteries overlooking the Himalayas, and felt the happiest I'd ever been.

Before my life-changing experience in Bhutan, when I was still living in Europe, I thought I was on top of the world. On the surface everything was going great and I thought I had it all. Still, a nasty fact kept nagging at me like a small stone in my shoe, no matter how hard I tried to ignore it: I wasn't happy. I was, in fact, depressed. How could that be? I knew for a fact that a more prestigious job, a handsomer boyfriend, a higher paycheck would not provide more happiness. The first Noble Truth the Buddha taught spoke to that profound unsatisfactoriness that I experienced in my very fortunate life: "Life is suffering," he had said, 2,500 years ago, and now I recognized that the first Noble Truth wasn't just talking about starvation in Somalia or cancer diagnoses but compassionately describing a fundamental fact of life.

Even more importantly, Buddhism offered a complete path to accomplish what my work as a journalist had failed to do: to reduce suffering. I had been very clear from the start why I wanted to become a political journalist. Changing the world was my goal. Growing up with loving parents in an idyllic village in Bavaria, with barely 250 inhabitants, three farms, one church, and one pub, I was intensely aware how privileged my existence had started out, and I swore to use my writings to give a voice to those who didn't have one. Yet, admittedly, my project of changing the world was progressing more slowly than I had hoped. Social change did not happen quite as fast as I wrote about it. My youthful enthusiasm for making the world a better place, one word at a time, was flagging.

Buddhism, then, offered a revolutionary alternative: The bodhisattva ideal in Tibetan Buddhism is that of a warrior who compassionately seeks liberation not for himself or herself but for the sake of all sentient beings. And liberation from suffering, a promise of the Buddhist path, was primarily a matter of the mind, an internal revolution, so my imperative shifted from exposing corrupt governments to exposing the corruption of my own mind.

Thus seventeen years ago I rather abruptly exchanged my prime real estate in Munich for a sparse bedroom on a rooftop in Kathmandu. I moved in with a Tibetan family that had just escaped from the Chinese terror and dove into this foreign new world wholeheartedly. I still continued to work as a reporter for TV and print—but my focus had shifted. I sent just enough stories to the glossy magazines from India, Nepal, and Bhutan to finance my studies and retreats. Surprising even myself, I was not deterred by the unfamiliar teachings on reincarnation and the nature of mind; on the contrary, they finally provided answers to the questions I had entertained since I was a child: How did we get here? What is the purpose in life?

When the spiritual leader of the Tibetans, His Holiness the Fourteenth Dalai Lama, gives public talks in the West, often the first thing he stresses is that the attendees should not readily leave their birth religion. As a newly minted Buddhist who had grown up Catholic, this advice puzzled me. But a decade deeper into the path, after I had moved back to Europe, the gaps between Western and Asian culture became more obvious to me, and I got a firsthand taste of how challenging the task was to have a foot in both worlds. Unexpectedly, my academic research sharply brought to the forefront the friction between rational analysis and religious faith, even in a tradition that prides itself on being based on logic.

The deeper I delved into the study, the faster was I approaching a predetermined breaking point, an inevitable collision of my Western upbringing and traditional Asian culture. As a woman in a patriarchal tradition, an academic in the midst of a religion that requires devotion, I felt myself brushing up against many questions, challenges, and demands that I found hard to juggle.

Surely other women have encountered similar challenges, I thought, and yet they have followed through, not pulled out. I sought out their stories at a low point in my life, when I was battling a chronic illness and struggling with some of the more outrageous aspects of Tibetan Buddhism. Transplanting an ancient tradition from remote caves in Asia to the megalopolis of Los Angeles where I live now comes with built-in growing pains. It is a tensile test, probing both the flexibility of our minds and the strength of a tradition. The answers I received from these teachers span the entire spectrum of possible solutions, from the heartfelt conservative assertion that the wisdom tradition really does work exactly as it did a thousand years ago if practiced properly, to progressive calls for reformation.

To meet these women gave me courage and inspiration, new insights and enthusiasm. I hope that by meeting them in this book, you will be inspired in the same way: to let go of old fears, explore new paths, and listen to the whisper of your inner voice with confidence.

DAKINI POWER

INTRODUCTION:

THE DAKINI PRINCIPLE

"Whether male or female, there is no great difference. But if a woman develops the mind of enlightenment, her potential is supreme."[1]
—*Padmasambhava, pioneer of Vajrayana Buddhism in Tibet*

TIBETAN BUDDHISM offers a unique premise: that to be a woman can actually be favorable on the path to spiritual realization. Women, so the eighth-century trailblazer of Buddhism in Tibet reasoned, are better equipped to realize the wisdom of the teachings. Modern teachers have echoed this sentiment. As the Western nun Tenzin Palmo comments, "Many lamas* have said that women make superior practitioners because they are able to dive into meditation much more easily than males. This is because many males are afraid of dropping the intellect, especially monks who have been studying for a long time. To suddenly just let that go and be naked in the meditational experience is frightening for them, whereas women seem to be able to manage it naturally."[2]

A female embodiment of enlightenment is called a *dakini* in the ancient Indian language of Sanskrit. But what exactly is a dakini? Dakinis are elusive and playful by nature; trying to nail them down with a neat definition means missing them, since defying narrow intellectual concepts is at the core of their wise game. I listened to the teachers in this book when they shared their understanding.

"To me the special female quality (which of course many men have

---

*Lama (Tib.; Skt. *guru*) is the Tibetan term for a Buddhist master. It could literally be translated as "high mother" or as "unsurpassed."

as well) is first of all a sharpness, a clarity," says Tenzin Palmo, who has vowed to attain enlightenment in a female body. "It cuts through—especially intellectual ossification. It . . . gets to the point. To me the dakini principle stands for the intuitive force. Women get it in a flash—they're not interested in intellectual discussion which they normally find dry and cold with minimum appeal."[3]

As Khandro Rinpoche, whose very name literally means "precious dakini," points out: "Traditionally, the term *dakini* has been used for outstanding female practitioners, consorts of great masters, and to denote the enlightened female principle of nonduality which transcends gender." Khandro Rinpoche defines the authentic dakini principle as "a very sharp, brilliant wisdom mind that is uncompromising, honest, with a little bit of wrath." This, to me, is a very exact description of the qualities of the teachers who are featured in this book. Despite their gentleness and humor, I experience many of the female teachers as direct, sharply intelligent, radical, and courageous.

The dakini principle must not be oversimplified, as it carries many levels of meaning. On an outer level, accomplished female practitioners were called dakinis, and it is in this sense that the term is used in the title of this book. But ultimately, though she appears in female form, a dakini defies gender definitions. "To really meet the dakini, you have to go beyond duality," Khandro Rinpoche teaches, referring to an essential understanding in Vajrayana that the absolute reality cannot be grasped intellectually. The Tibetan word for dakini, *khandro*, means "sky-goer" or "space-dancer," which indicates that these ethereal awakened ones have left the confinements of solid earth and have the vastness of open space to play in.

Practitioner-scholar Judith Simmer-Brown differentiates four levels of meaning:

> On a secret level, she is seen as the manifestation of funda-
> mental aspects of phenomena and the mind, and so her power
> is intimately associated with the most profound insights of
> Vajrayana meditation. In this her most essential aspect, she
> is called the formless wisdom nature of the mind itself. On

an inner, ritual level, she is a meditational deity, visualized as the personification of qualities of buddhahood. On an outer, subtle-body level, she is the energetic network of the embodied mind in the subtle channels and vital breath of tantric yoga. She is also spoken of as a living woman: she may be a guru on a brocaded throne or a yogini meditating in a remote cave, a powerful teacher of meditation or a guru's consort teaching directly through her life example. Finally all women are seen as some kind of dakini manifestation.[4]

Thus, dakinis appear in many forms. "The dakinis are the most important elements of the enlightened feminine in Tibetan Buddhism," says American teacher Tsultrim Allione.[5] "They are the luminous, subtle, spiritual energy, the key, the gatekeeper, the guardian of the unconditioned state. If we are not willing to invite the dakini into our life, then we cannot enter these subtle states of mind. Sometimes the dakinis appear as messengers, sometimes as guides, and sometimes as protectors."

PLAYFUL, SEDUCTIVE, AND WILD

You might walk into a Tibetan Buddhist temple such as Tsultrim Allione's Tara Mandala in Colorado and encounter an abundance of female figures: Prajnaparamita, the embodiment of "transcendent wisdom," might sit in perfect meditation posture on a lotus, holding up a loose-leaf text of the wisdom sutras.* Tara, the female buddha known as the "One who Liberates," sits with one leg stretched out indicating that she is ready to jump up and help beings whenever needed. Her seven eyes watch the visitors with a calm but penetrating gaze. "The extra eyes of mercy enable her to see and save suffering beings from misery,"[6] says Dagmola Sakya, who reports having visions of her. "Tara . . . is the mother of all beings who cares for them as though each was her own

---

*Discourses ascribed to the Buddha.

child."[7] Tara and Prajnaparamita are both referred to as mothers of all buddhas, since the "Awakened Ones" are born from wisdom.

For lack of a better word, in English these buddhas are usually called "deities." Yet, literally, the Tibetan word *yidam* means "holding the mind." Unlike in other religions, such as Christianity or Hinduism, these archetypes of enlightenment are not externally existing entities whose blessings are invoked. Rather, deities in Vajrayana Buddhism are manifestations of mind the practitioners evoke to purify neuroses and connect with a deeper level of awareness. Some of them are depicted as serene and peaceful like Tara and Prajnaparamita. Others, such as Vajrayogini, manifest as wrathful and fierce, flashing their fangs, baring their naked breasts and vaginas in a wild dance, and destroying ignorance without hesitation. Because dakinis are said to break through blockages and obstacles, they are often associated with an uncomfortably fierce demeanor. "There is the aspect of compassion, embodied by Tara; then there is the mother figure and its aspects of love. But then, in the tantric tradition, there is the wild aspect of the dakini, untamed, and free, belonging to no man," Tsultrim Allione explains.[8] "Dakinis have a quality of playfulness, expressing emptiness and pulling the rug out from under you. This feminine quality of seduction and play makes you insecure and yet open."

Tibetan Buddhists were not the first to meet the dakinis. Like many elements of Vajrayana, the dakinis emerged first in the Indian tantras,* and those, in turn, had partly drawn on ancient pre-Aryan goddess traditions. When tantra originated in India, the dakini was seen as wrathful and often described as a blood-drinking flesh eater who lived in charnel grounds or cemeteries, challenging the yogis to explode their fears. After Buddhists adopted tantric ideas and tantric Buddhism migrated to Tibet in the eighth century, this image softened somewhat. A gentler, more sensual and accommodating female image emerged, one that nurtured and sustained the practitioners; though that enticing figure

---

*Tantra (Skt.; Tib. *gyü*) literally means "thread" or "loom." Here it refers to the class of esoteric literature and practices that originated in India in the early centuries CE. In relation to Tibetan Buddhism the term "tantra" is used for the later esoteric texts as distinguished from the sutra texts that are ascribed to the historical Buddha Shakyamuni.

could still instantly resort to more dramatic, wrathful means when the peaceful approach of seduction didn't work. This enigma is embodied in Vajrayogini, who is often called the chief of dakinis. Usually depicted as an attractive teenage girl, naked except for a few bone ornaments, she glances invitingly while also swinging a curved knife, ready to cut through ego clinging without warning.

"INFERIOR BEINGS" IN TIBET

The Himalayas were always a nursery for highly accomplished female practitioners and to some extent still are. The yoginis* might live in remote hermitages or nunneries as devoted practitioners, or as the wives, mothers, or daughters of famous teachers. Students often sought their advice informally, but women rarely wrote books, sat on high thrones or assumed lofty titles of their own. "There were certainly many great female practitioners in Tibet," says Tenzin Palmo. "But because they lacked a background of philosophical training, they could not aspire to write books, gather disciples, go on Dharma tours, and give talks. When we read the histories, we will notice that nuns are distinguished by their absence. But this doesn't mean they weren't there."[9]

Promising young males in the Himalayas were usually isolated from the distractions of daily society in order to undergo a rigorous course of study and retreats, but less attention was paid to their female counterparts. While iconic archetypes of feminine enlightenment were erected on shrines, few women in Tibet were actually emboldened to follow in their footsteps. Despite the encouraging quote of the pioneer of Tibetan Buddhism that women's potential to attain liberation is supreme, most Buddhist cultures throughout the centuries perceived women as lesser beings. The few encouraging statements are outnumbered by plenty of passages in the writings attributed to Padmasambhava and other masters that lament the hardships of womanhood. Commonly used Tibetan words for woman, *lümen* or *kyemen*, literally mean "inferior being" or

*Derived from the Sanskrit word *yoga*, literally "union," *yogini* is a Sanskrit term for a female practitioner dedicated to the spiritual path, mostly in the Hindu and the Buddhist traditions.

"lesser birth." Some orthodox masters doubt to this day if women can attain realization at all, and age-old liturgies have women pray for a better rebirth in a male body. As Dagmola Sakya's biography illustrates, even contemporary women often were denied access to basic education, for one does not need these skills to bear children and herd the cows. One of my Tibetan friends, the only sister of four renowned Tibetan teachers, does not even know her birthday, because her parents deemed it not important to note down the day as they did with her brothers. Khandro Rinpoche describes the prejudices she encountered when she attempted to study advanced philosophical texts.

In Asia, almost always men were the ones who sat on thrones, made important decisions, and were recognized as incarnations, while mostly women would do the laundry and the cooking. As British abbess Tenzin Palmo points out, "I find it puzzling, in a way, that a third of the male population in Tibet became monks, . . . yet there were very few nuns."[10] When asked about the reasons, some traditional teachers respond that men were simply more interested in religious studies, but this omits economic facts: monasteries were often well supported by the government as well as the local population, equipped with excellent schools and colleges. The few nunneries, by contrast, were mostly in extremely remote locations, thus cut off from support by villagers, not bankrolled by governments nor major sponsors, and without adequate teachers. To this day nunneries in Asia usually lack the resources the monasteries get and some of the nuns who escape from Tibet cannot even read or write.

SECOND-CLASS NUNS

One of the reasons for the difference in support is that the Tibetan tradition does not know full ordination for women. When Buddhism traveled from India into Tibet, apparently the quorum of twelve fully ordained nuns required for bestowing full ordination never reached Tibet.[11] There are singular accounts of fully ordained Tibetan women, such as the Samding Dorje Phagmo (1422–1455), who was once ranked the highest female master in Tibet, but we know very little about the exact circumstances of their ordination.[12] So currently full ordination is not an option for women in the Tibetan tradition, thus rendering nuns inferior. In fact, the Tibetan word for nun, *ani*, with which the nuns are commonly addressed, does not actually mean "nun" but simply "auntie," whereas Tibetans know a host of honorific terms for monks. In order to receive full ordination, Tibetan Buddhist nuns have to travel to countries where the Chinese ordination lineage is available. "But most Tibetan nuns can't afford to travel to Hong Kong, Taiwan, or Korea," says Tenzin Palmo, "and even if they did, from the nuns' point of view, they want to be ordained in their own tradition, in their own robes, by their own teachers or the Dalai Lama!"

Thus even the eminent Khandro Rinpoche, whose life and accomplishments as one of the very few female rinpoches* is featured in the first chapter, is technically a novice.

His Holiness the Fourteenth Dalai Lama has stated publicly that he supports full ordination for Tibetan nuns, but that he cannot make the decision alone; the monks' community would have to endorse such a move. To underline his stance, the Dalai Lama gave a group of senior Western bhikshunis† 50,000 Swiss francs to research the complex task of bringing full ordination to Tibetan nuns. The Committee on Bhikshuni Ordination, with Tenzin Palmo and her friends Pema Chödrön, Karma Lekshe Tsomo, and Thubten Chodron, continues to present its findings and suggest solutions.

THE FIRST FEMALE PROFESSOR

The Dalai Lama has spoken out many times about the need for resolving the issue. "Two thousand five hundred years ago, . . . the Buddha was preaching in . . . a male-dominated society," he stated in an interview.[13] "If he stressed feminist viewpoints, nobody would have listened to him. . . . The important thing is that now, for the past thirty years, we have worked to change that." The Dalai Lama acknowledges that many nuns are very sincere but have been given no chance to ascend to the highest

---

Rinpoche (Tib.), pronounced "rin-po-chey," literally means "precious." The title is bestowed on eminent teachers out of reverence.
†Fully ordained nuns.

ordination level. "This has made me somewhat uncomfortable, especially since the Buddha gave equal opportunities to women. But we, even as followers of Buddha, neglected that. In the last few centuries, we completely neglected the quality of religious studies in nunneries." The Tibetan leader has emphasized that conditions are improving with the same levels of studies now available to women. Until very recently, the nuns were unable to attain the title of *khenpo* or *geshe*—the Tibetan equivalents of doctors and professors. Why is that? Because the absence of full ordination in the Tibetan lineage does not allow them to study the full geshe curriculum, which includes the entire monastic code (Skt. *vinaya*).

The Dalai Lama personally founded and supported the Institute for Buddhist Dialectics near his seat in exile in Dharamsala, North India, waiving some of the traditional requirements for female students. In April 2011, he awarded the geshe degree to a Western nun. This is a historical first in many ways: geshe degrees are traditionally conferred in the major monasteries on monks after twelve or more years of rigorous study in Buddhist philosophy. Despite not being fully ordained, German-born novice Kelsang Wangmo (formerly Kerstin Brummenbaum) was finally rewarded for mastering sixteen years of strenuous study in highest Buddhist philosophy. "It was difficult to be the only woman," Kelsang Wangmo says. "It was very lonely, because the monks didn't want to hang out with a nun." The Dalai Lama had advised her to study a slightly altered curriculum instead of the full Vinaya, but her all-male classmates thought the situation was absurd. While she couldn't attend the Vinaya classes in person, her fellow students sneaked her the recordings so that she could listen to them after all. "Also, my classmates were taking turns teaching the lower classes, but as a nun I could not officially teach the junior monks," Kelsang Wangmo says, referring to a passage in the monastic code that does not allow nuns to teach monks, but adds, resolutely upbeat: "All this is changing now, and my teachers have been very supportive. We must not give up. If I can do it, anybody can do it."

STEPPING OUT OF THE SHADOW

While a multitude of male Tibetan teachers have gained international recognition, one can count on one hand the female outliers who have been fully trained to give empowerments and teachings in the West today. Therefore it is no coincidence that only three teachers of Tibetan origin are featured in this book. The biographies of Khandro Rinpoche, Dagmola Sakya, and Khandro Tsering Chödron testify how incredibly rare it was for women to access the same education and training as their male counterparts because of the patriarchal background. While many of the women have stood in the shadow of their male counterparts (often their husbands, fathers, or teachers), and while it is somewhat uncommon for them to step out of that obscurity by putting their own biography in the spotlight, this is the logical next step in women taking their seat as Buddhist teachers. It is the intent of this book to make the luminous qualities of these women known, including their challenges and doubts, which in the Tibetan tradition are usually not discussed frankly.

QUEENS, NUNS, AND YOGINIS

Traditionally, life stories of female Buddhist masters were rarely told. Apart from the biographies of a few noteworthy exceptions, we know little about the female adepts of Tibet. Take Tulku Thondup's wonderful *Masters of Meditation and Miracles*, for example. One reads more than three dozen impressive narratives of the most important lineage masters in the Ancient Tradition (Nyingma) of Tibetan Buddhism, yet apart from Padmasambhava's five consorts, only one woman master is among those honored: Jetsun Shugseb Lochen Rinpoche (1852–1953). An outstanding practitioner and founder of a vibrant nunnery in Tibet, she is one of the very few female masters who initiated her own reincarnation lineage. Like many of her fellow nuns, even this exceptional master prayed to be reborn in a male body to find better circumstances for pursuing the path in the future. (Ironically, her male reincarnation has abandoned religious life to study in Beijing.)[14]

Of course, there must have been countless more realized female practitioners, meditating unflinchingly despite poverty and discrimination. As Tenzin Palmo points out, "One can only admire them; they were intrepid. They went to remote places, to caves up in the mountains, and they practiced and practiced. They were wonderful. But of course one never hears about them, because nobody wrote their biographies. Nobody considered it important to write the biography of some woman. It is not evident from the texts that there were many, but we know that there were."[15] Tsultrim Allione found the lack of biographies so pressing that she researched the stories of historic Tibetan yoginis in her book *Women of Wisdom*: "We need to have models for enlightenment for women. We need to be able to see the female body as a vehicle for enlightenment. In the absence of these models, women often feel that they don't have the capacity for full awakening in this very lifetime."[16]

ANCIENT METHODS FOR THE MODERN WORLD

With Buddhism the fastest growing religion in many Western nations, an increasing number of Westerners are deeply fascinated by the teachings of the Buddha and his very practical, applicable methods. Scientific research has proven that Buddhist meditation significantly helps in reducing stress and anxiety while increasing well-being and happiness. I have seen intense transformation in top executives of various religious backgrounds who came to my seminars to learn the art of sitting still, coupled with the profound science of compassion that the Buddha uncovered. This then is one of the questions that guided my interest in this book: What do the age-old teachings of the Buddha have to offer for women and men in our modern world?

In most Buddhist countries throughout Asia, the task of spiritual realization is carried out by "professionals," as Tenzin Palmo calls them.[17] Monks and nuns devote themselves full time to study and practice, without the "distractions" of family, job, and mortgage. In some countries, it is considered a must that at least one of the children in a family opts for monastic life. Yet in the West, where Buddhism is now taking root, comparatively few wish to get ordained. Rather than isolating themselves in remote mountains, working moms, accountants, and CEOs are looking for ways to turn their everyday lives into a meaningful path. Tenzin Palmo has observed that traditional teachers sometimes make a distinction between "spiritual practice on the one hand and everyday life on the other."[18] She remembers how once a frustrated working mother complained she did not have much time for spiritual practice and asked the advice of a traditional Tibetan teacher, "What should I do?" The lama replied, "Never mind, when your children are grown up you can take early retirement and then you can start to practice."[19]

I haven't heard such a statement from the female teachers in this book. Several of them are mothers; many have worked "ordinary" jobs as cleaners, school teachers, or translators before being recognized as outstanding Buddhist teachers. All of them are careful to acknowledge that practice means awareness in every moment, whether sitting on a meditation cushion, loading a washing machine, or coordinating an executive meeting. "Spiritual practice is everyday life, not just sitting on the cushion, meditating," says Dagmola Sakya, a mother of five boys. "Every move, every word, every thought is practice. Dharma is in daily life." And Zen priest Roshi Joan Halifax emphasized at a recent TED conference, "Women have manifested, for thousands of years, the strength arising from compassion, in an unfiltered way, unmediated, in perceiving suffering, as it is. They have infused societies with kindness. They have actualized compassion through direct action."[20]

A SEA CHANGE IN THE WEST

Every time Buddhism migrated from its place of origin in India to other countries, whether Sri Lanka, Burma, Japan, China, or Tibet, the philosophy, customs, and rituals transformed as well. Not surprisingly, Buddhism's relocation to the West comes with a sea change of emphasis and culture.

In Tibet, practitioners holed up in caves, sometimes for decades. In the West, teachers reach thousands instantly by streaming their wisdom on podcasts. In the Himalayas, women rarely got equal access to education. In the West, women demand to be acknowledged in the many leadership roles they assume. In many Asian Buddhist communities, open dissent is unthinkable, while in academia, critical discourse is crucial. In the traditional monasteries, nobody would have dared to spar with a teacher who presents a literal interpretation of the mystical lore. In the West, fact-checking is deemed pivotal. "The Eastern pattern is more toward seeking harmony," Roshi Joan Halifax has observed. "The Western pattern is to seek transparency."

Yet maybe of all these changes that we are watching Buddhism undergo in the West, the most momentous may be that women are insisting on playing an equal role. More and more women are now rising as teachers in their own right who understand their responsibility: to invigorate and bolster women to hold up half the sky as spiritual seekers and teachers. As feminist Buddhist scholar Rita Gross points out, "The single biggest difference between the practice of Buddhism in Asia and the practice of Buddhism in the West is the full and complete participation of women in Western Buddhism."[21] The Dalai Lama has acknowledged this by pointing out that his next incarnation could be a woman. Why not? What's the big deal?

"The lamas can't ignore this any longer," says Western nun Karma Lekshe Tsomo whose life story is featured in this book. "In most dharma centers, look into the kitchen—all women. Look into the offices, who does the administration? Mostly women. Who does the driving and organizing, the cleaning and the correspondence, the shopping and managing? Mostly women." That women then also become teachers and abbesses is only a natural evolution.

Like mirrors, their biographies sharply reflect larger issues, such as the current transformation of Buddhism in the twenty-first century and the role women play in this endeavor as prime agents. This perspective was in line with the advice my teacher, Dzigar Kongtrul Rinpoche, had given me for the book: "Biographies are good," he said, "but they won't have much impact unless you don't gloss over the issues." Which issues? "You have to ask the women what the issues are," he responded, and this is what I did. One nun surprised me by candidly summing up the issues with two words: "Sex and sexism." So we ended up talking not only about meditation and compassion, but also about power and abuse, seclusion and seduction, logic and faith, devotion and rebellion.

Jetsun Khandro Rinpoche in Amsterdam.
Photo by Diana Blok. © Diana Blok

1: JETSUN KHANDRO RINPOCHE

A NEEDLE COMPASSIONATELY STICKING
OUT OF A CUSHION

---

*A young Tibetan uses her unique status to empower
women in the East and West*[1]

TO CONDENSE MORE energy in five feet two is impossible. Like a high-powered, nimble, compact car, Khandro Rinpoche glides through the Verizon Center in Washington, DC at top speed. With the resolute gestures of a seasoned choirmaster, she directs 175 volunteers, shepherding them into a smiling army of ushers. For almost a week they have been working around the clock to make the Dalai Lama's groundbreaking visit to the capital a smooth success. Lack of sleep never slows Khandro Rinpoche down. "Being available; helping whenever, wherever, whomever" is how she defines Buddhism in action. Without a sign of hesitation the sturdy nun jumps to relieve a fatigued volunteer by grabbing a cookie box out of his hands, quickly dispensing the blessed wafers herself. "You can do fifteen thousand people in eleven minutes," she assures her troops, pats a bleary-eyed helper on the back, and comfortingly strokes the cheek of a panicked student.

Why is Khandro Rinpoche then taking her place in the back of the arena, framed by a flock of nuns, and not installing herself on the brightly illuminated stage next to His Holiness and the dozens of other high-ranking Tibetan masters in their best robes? "The stage is where all the well-behaved people sit," she explains with a twinkle. "I like to observe people and interact. In the back, you hear and learn a lot about what's *really* going on." Besides, she needs to be able to wield her iPhone and dash off to rescue the complex maneuver of distributing fifteen thousand red protection cords. Her alert, dark eyes monitor the scene with a laser-focused yet spacious awareness.

The rearmost benches at the Verizon Center provide a fitting snapshot of what Khandro Rinpoche is all about: making a difference without making a fuss; being of service while escaping the limelight. "Service" might be the word she uses most, and rather than just preaching, she lives it. "She used to be like an AK47, just boom boom boom, getting things done," her sister Jetsun* Dechen Paldron quips. "She thinks she has mellowed out, but while she might have become more focused, she is still just so much energy one person almost cannot contain it."

Khandro Rinpoche jetsets tirelessly between her late father's monastery and her own two nunneries in India, her American headquarters in the Shenandoah Mountains in Virginia, and an ever-increasing number of Buddhist communities who are keen to benefit from her sharp acumen. As if that weren't enough, she also spearheads an unusually large count of social projects—from taking care of abandoned lepers, seniors, and stray dogs in India to planting trees in Virginia. "You cannot benefit beings by being an island on your own," she said in a radio interview.[2] "It is an uphill task getting out of a society so preoccupied with self-cherishing."

TRAILBLAZER UNDER SCRUTINY

Jetsun Khandro Rinpoche is one of the very few fully trained female rinpoches in the Tibetan tradition. This unique position grants her more freedom and impact than some of the male teachers. Women, especially, are drawn to her strong warrior-like presence. "It is unusual to see a woman who is so at ease with power," one American nun observes, "and who uses it, but with kindness, never falling into the traps of a power trip."

Yet Khandro Rinpoche's unmatched stature comes with a heightened sense of scrutiny. Aware that she was closely watched from a young

*A highly honorific Tibetan title of reverence for an accomplished female practitioner or a noble woman of high status.

age onward, she decided early on not to shy away from the role of a
trailblazer but to march ahead boldly. "If I mess up, I could mess it
up for a lot of women," she admits frankly, echoing the sentiments of
many female CEOs. "As a woman, you can accomplish a hundred things
perfectly, and then you make one mistake and everybody goes, 'See, she
can't do it.' That would affect not only *my* path but the confidence in
Tibetan women." There is no need to worry, for the opposite is true.
Her undaunted pioneering work has ensured a ripple effect for women,
especially nuns, throughout Asia and the West.

Khandro Rinpoche has learned the craft of developing and shar-
ing Buddhist wisdom almost from the crib. She was born in 1968 as
Tsering Paldron (The Lamp of Glory and Long Life), the daughter of
Sangyum* Kusho Sonam Paldron and the Eleventh Kyabjé Mindrolling
Trichen, who was the head of the Ancient School[†] of Tibetan Buddhism.
At the age of twenty-nine, her father had escaped the Chinese grip in
1959 by fleeing to Kalimpong, a sleepy former British hill station in the
Lower Indian Himalayas. By the time his first daughter was born, he
was immersed in the immense task of reestablishing the eminent Mindrolling monastery in exile. Khandro Rinpoche's upbringing exemplifies the fate of the second generation of Tibetan refugees: she has never
been to Tibet, has never seen the elegant brown stone monastery that
used to be the ancient home of her lineage. "I have applied many times,
been denied many times," she says matter-of-factly.

All but eight of the once-flourishing six thousand Tibetan temples
and monasteries were reduced to rubble during the so-called Cultural
Revolution in the sixties. Though some have been rebuilt since, Communist China tightly restricts the number of monks and nuns who once
made up a sixth of the entire population. Even just possessing a picture
of the Dalai Lama can provoke imprisonment in one of the forced labor
camps. With the massive transportation of millions of Han Chinese
into the Tibetan areas, the remaining five to six million Tibetans are
now a minority on their own turf. While the traditional practices of cir-
cumambulating holy shrines and reciting powerful mantras are largely

*"Sacred consort"; honorific Tibetan term for a high lama's wife.
†The Nyingma (Tib.) School traces its beginnings to the late seventh century.

being suppressed in the land of their origin, these ancient rites are being revived and taught anew to an eager generation of young students in the West. Inadvertently, the Chinese have instigated the worldwide spread of Tibetan Buddhism, ensuring a much more vigorous global revival than the Tibetans ever imagined.

RIGHT HERE, RIGHT NOW

In addition to shouldering responsibilities at the Mindrolling monastery in India, Khandro Rinpoche is also nurturing this shoot of Buddhism in the West. This afternoon, after the Dalai Lama ends his program in Washington, the volunteers grab salads on the run and rush to hear her teach. The conference hall at the Hilton that had originally been booked for her talk quickly turns out to be too small for the two thousand-plus attendees who want to meet her in person, so the organizers relocate her to the back end of the massive Verizon Center. She arrives with an impressive all-female entourage, including her younger sister, several of her nuns, and a cloud of volunteers. Khandro Rinpoche is the shortest, yet she is clearly the driving force, the center of the typhoon.

"Isn't it wonderful to see a female rinpoche, for a change?" asks one of the organizers, American nun Tenzin Lhamo. In response, the entire audience erupts in cheers and applause. Khandro Rinpoche's topic is *bodhichitta*. Bodhichitta is a Sanskrit term that means "awakened heart," the altruistic wish to attain enlightenment for the sake of all sentient beings. Khandro Rinpoche immediately pulls the idea from the realm of theory into the heart. "We are not working with a Sanskrit or Tibetan term here, we're working with ourselves, and not in the future, but right here! Ask yourself," she demands, "as a human being, am I living a life that is dedicated to increasing happiness for myself and others?"[3]

For an hour and a half, Khandro Rinpoche shines her brilliant knowledge, in eloquent flawless English. She never glances at any notes. What the historical Buddha taught could not have been more straightforward, she says: "If you want something, simply create the causes. If you don't want something, don't create the ground for it." Yet, she jokes, it only took 2,500 years to turn this easy recipe for happiness into "the most complicated philosophy on earth." Why? Because, for the life of us, we don't want to give up our self-cherishing. Our constant attempts to exempt ourselves from this simple logic of altruism necessitated the later explosion of practices, mantras, a colorful pantheon of deities, philosophies, and texts. Each was designed to convince us that our particular style of self-cherishing will not lead to happiness for ourselves or others.

A "SPIRITUAL" FLASH MOB

Khandro Rinpoche distills the rich, intellectual philosophy into a down-to-earth call for action. Starting with loving-kindness for oneself, one expands one's heart with the very vast vision of fostering ultimate happiness for all sentient beings. She throws in resonating, full belly laughs and jokes to make the phenomenal task of enlightening all sentient beings more appetizing. "You'll never understand genuine compassion if you're not joyful," she admonishes her audience. "Some people mistake loving-kindness for posing as a doormat. Joyfulness is the ability to appreciate something good in the day, in yourself, in others, in your home, in your work. That makes you more open."

What Khandro Rinpoche has observed from her vantage point behind the scenes is fuel for her dharma talk. Just the evening before, the serene crowd suddenly morphed into a mob trampling over one another in a frenzied effort to grab the last of the remaining empowerment* substances. "It's very nice that you like the idea of loving-kindness," she softens the forthcoming blow, "but I'd love it if your fondness for loving-kindness wasn't restricted to reading about it."

People might have expected a more saintly, gentle talk from a young nun, but Khandro Rinpoche pulls no punches. "Let's put aside attaining enlightenment for the sake of all sentient beings for a moment," she quips. "Let's get down to it: Can we at least for one week behave like

---

*In Tibetan Buddhism, empowerments (Skt. *abhisheka*; Tib. *wang*) are vital ceremonies that transmit the blessings of the lineage and authorize students to engage in the practice of specific deities and texts.

people who are receiving the most profound teachings from His Holiness the Dalai Lama?"

Silence. The crowd now shifts uneasily. Busted.

Tenzin Lhamo, who practiced psychotherapy for almost thirty years, likens Khandro Rinpoche to a skilled doctor who intuitively finds the raw spot, "presses on the point where it hurts until you feel the healing, and then lets go. She's just *nailing* it."

A HOTHOUSE FOR WOMEN MASTERS

Khandro Rinpoche often laughs, but she rarely smiles. Her gaze is not unkind, but it is uncompromising. Her voice is not cutting, but it invites no objections. What she demands of her students is not impossible but surely challenging: mindfulness in action, all the time. "She watches with laser-sharp attention," one of her students says, "and if she catches you being unkind, she will be on it." She might point out a slip by teasing a student in front of the group. "I'm strict," she admits. "If you want to break through the layers and layers of students' stubbornness, the antidote has to be much more powerful." Yet a profound compassion shines through her vivacity. "A lot of people are intimidated by me," she admits. "There is a decorum, a hierarchy." She keeps a little distance too. Unlike other teachers, she never socializes with students. "The teacher-student relationship requires a very delicate handling. As a teacher, you have to carry the confidence and the trust." She likens herself to "a needle in the cushion, someone who always keeps things uncomfortable, so that complacency does not creep in."[4]

At a recent teaching in Pittsburgh someone asked why her tradition was called "mind rolling."[5] Khandro Rinpoche picked up an incense box produced by the monks of her monastery. Indeed, the label sported a gap between "Mind" and "rolling." She got a good laugh out of this misunderstanding. "They are three different words, where *min* means 'ripening,' *drol* means 'liberating,' and *ling* means 'place,'"* she clarifies the Tibetan. "The literal translation would be 'the garden of ripening and liberation.'"

*Pronounced "min-dro-ling."

This spiritual nursery has proven to be a hothouse for women masters. The Mindrolling lineage, one of the six great traditions of the Ancient School, is one of the rare Tibetan traditions that do not distinguish between male and female heirs. Right from the beginning in the sixteenth century, lineage founder Terdak Lingpa* emphasized the need for women to train as practitioners and teachers, not the least because he admired his own mother as an exceptionally realized meditator. Consequently he empowered his daughter, Jetsun Mingyur Paldron,† along with his two sons, as lineage holders. His daughter ended up rebuilding Mindrolling Monastery after the Dzungar Mongols' invasion, hence saving the lineage with its texts and treasuries from early extinction. Her inspiration has continued, emboldening many women to practice and teach within this lineage. Thus Khandro Rinpoche arrived into this life with an open invitation to follow their example.

"As the firstborn, there was some pressure," Khandro Rinpoche admits. "You always have that thought of belonging to this unbroken line of great teachers. In the shrine room, I look at the murals, and not only do I see the buddhas and bodhisattvas, but there is my aunt, my great-aunt, my grandfather, and so on, all looking at me."

Embodying thirteen hundred years of wisdom

When she was ten months old, her father took her to see his close friend, the Sixteenth Karmapa,‡ in Sikkim. The Karmapa recognized the baby as an incarnation of Khandro Urgyen Tsomo, better known as the Great Dakini of Tsurphu. Despite her widespread fame, only fragments of her

---

*Rigdzin Terdak Lingpa (1646–1714), a teacher and student of the Fifth Dalai Lama, was renowned as a great treasure revealer and established Mindrolling Monastery in Central Tibet in 1676.
†Jetsunma Mingyur Paldron (1699–1769) was said to have mastered many of the most advanced practices by the age of fourteen. She became an accomplished lama in the Kagyü tradition of Tibetan Buddhism. For a detailed account of her life, see Khandro Rinpoche's website: mindrollinginternational.org/mindrollinghistoryproject.
‡The Sixteenth Gyalwa Karmapa, Rangjung Rigpa'i Dorje (1924–1981), was the head of the Karma Kagyü lineage of Tibetan Buddhism and the abbot of Tsurphu Monastery in Central Tibet. In 1959, he escaped with 150 students and many of the monastery's most sacred relics to Bhutan. At the invitation of the King of Sikkim, he established Rumtek Monastery, his new seat in exile, in Sikkim in 1966.

biography have survived. She was the consort of the Fifteenth Karmapa, Khakyab Dorje (1871–1922), and is credited with extending his life for several years through her mastery of practice. After the Karmapa's passing, she remained at Tsurphu Monastery in retreat, widely revered as an awe-inspiring hermitess. "She was loving and compassionate, full of devotion, and with an unfathomable spiritual depth," wrote Tulku Urgyen Rinpoche (1920–1996), who met her in Tibet. "She was a very special being, a true dakini. She spent almost all her time in retreat practicing and reciting mantra, and reached a profound level of experience and realization. This is not hearsay; I can bear witness to it myself."[6]

While she was dying, she indicated to her students that she would be reborn in the northeast of India. Her description fit Khandro Rinpoche's birthplace in Kalimpong. The Great Dakini was even deemed to be an incarnation of Yeshe Tsogyal, the consort of Padmasambhava, the wild trailblazer of Tibetan Buddhism. This would make the present Khandro Rinpoche a direct offshoot of the earliest Buddhist pioneers in Tibet. Thus her students revere her not only as a forty-three-year-old nun but as the embodiment of thirteen hundred years of wisdom.

DECEPTIVE TITLES

The first time I attended a teaching with Khandro Rinpoche, sixteen years ago in France, the resident master introduced her as an emanation of Yeshe Tsogyal, the female buddha Tara, *and* Vajrayogini. Khandro Rinpoche laughs off these grand labels: "Oh yes, they name every female deity they can find. It is very kind of them, very kind, maybe too kind."

What does it mean to Khandro Rinpoche to be regarded as the scion of these great women masters? "These titles can be deceptive," she cautions. "People are overly preoccupied with titles, being more fascinated with the packaging than the content. This is dangerous." Khandro Rinpoche sighs. "Every time they find a nice woman, they call her a dakini. It depends on your realization whether you deserve that title or not."

Khandro Rinpoche prefers to resort to logic: in Tibetan Buddhism, realized masters are believed to have the choice to reincarnate in a form and place where they can be most helpful. "Buddhist philosophy is com-

Khandro Rinpoche at age eleven with her father, Kyabjé Mindrolling
Trichen; her mother, Sangyum Kusho Sonam Paldron; and her younger sister,
Jetsun Dechen Paldron, in India. Photo courtesy of Mindrolling International

pletely founded on the law of causality and interdependence," Khandro Rinpoche explains. "In the case of reincarnations, or *tulkus*,* they
generate the aspiration to continually benefit sentient beings, and this
aspiration controls their rebirth. Therefore the tulkus have always been
regarded with great veneration, because absolute compassion brings
them back to benefit sentient beings constantly." When she questioned
her late father, himself a recognized tulku, she learned that an authentic

Tulku (Tib.), literally "emanation body," here refers to the reincarnation of a great
master who intentionally takes rebirth in order to benefit beings. The Tibetans began
identifying direct reincarnations of their deceased masters in the twelfth century.

reincarnation "has less obscurations, so you have less homework to do in terms of purifying obscurations. The mind is clearer, more refined; learning comes easier and faster; their knowledge is greater."

The recognition was especially tricky in her case, because several distinct lineages* in Tibetan Buddhism follow slightly different practices. She was born into a Nyingma family but recognized as a Kagyü dakini. "Mindrolling is a family blood line; they get a bit possessive about the eldest in the family," she says, albeit with a smile. "There was some hesitation: We're not gonna give the firstborn to the Kagyüpas!" Yet according to Khandro Rinpoche the Kagyü nuns are "very headstrong, very stubborn women." They would proclaim it far and wide that the Mindrolling daughter belonged to them, repeatedly pressuring the Sixteenth Karmapa to recognize the child. So, at the age of three, the Karmapa formally enthroned Khandro Rinpoche, personally supervising her education up to the time of his death in 1981. He suggested she should learn English, foreseeing her genius for spreading the dharma in the West.

A NAUGHTY TOMBOY

From the age of three Khandro Rinpoche was clad in brocade, seated on thrones, and offered prostrations. "Because I was the eldest, my father really loved me, some would say he spoiled me," Khandro Rinpoche admits. The rambunctious tomboy took advantage of her liberties, knowing full well that there was hardly anything she could not get away with. "I was a very, very naughty girl, pampered, a troublemaker." She would skip school, roam the village streets with her gang, brush up against other kids in brawls. She playfully clenches her fists, mimicking what her miniature self must have looked like: wild, angry, mischievous. "My mother always thought I didn't appear like the elegant, dignified Jetsunma kind." Khandro Rinpoche's mother grew so worried her little

---

*There are five main traditions within Tibetan Buddhism: Nyingma, Kagyü, Sakya, and Gelug, plus the pre-Buddhist Bon tradition that has since transformed itself into the fifth branch of Tibetan Buddhism.

rebel would become uncontrollable that she packed her off to a strict British-style boarding school, run by Catholic missionaries. "Everything I am today I owe to my mother," Khandro Rinpoche says. Unabashed emotional gratefulness rings in her voice. "I find in her and in my sister my greatest critics, because they would never let the tulku syndrome get into my head."

Triumphing in the Bible competition

Her keen intellect and natural curiosity made Khandro Rinpoche a straight-A student, even in unfamiliar Christian territory. Attending Sunday Bible school could score extra marks, so she learned the Bible by heart and came first in the Sunday school New Testament memorization competition. "It was fun!" she exclaims. After two-and-a-half years in the boarding school, her parents became concerned their future lineage holder might lose sight of her spiritual heritage and brought her back home. For more than a decade, she, her mother, and her younger sister lived as the only women among five hundred monks in the monastery that her father and mother had rebuilt in exile. In the mornings she attended a Catholic convent; at noon her father would wait for her with lunch; in the afternoons her tutors drilled her in rituals and philosophy.

She does remind me of her father, who was also her root guru and clearly the most important figure in her life. She tenderly calls him "His Holiness" or "Kyabjé"* when she remembers him as someone "who did not do things to be polite. He did not do sweet talk. If he could keep it short, he would keep it short."[7] A majestic lion of a teacher, Mindrolling Trichen Rinpoche could be intimidating. Instead of gently tossing a silk scarf over my head as most masters do, I remember his yanking my ponytail hard when I came to see him for a blessing one day in Nepal, as if to emphasize: You need to wake up!

"We have all inherited the famous Mindrolling temper," says sister Jetsun Dechen Paldron. "You have to know the difference between

---

*"Lord of Refuge"; a Tibetan term of enormous reverence for a highly realized teacher, often translated into English as "His Holiness."

anger and wrath. Anger is sticky—there is you and I, hurt, and neurosis. Wrath just means pointing out that something that should have been done, hasn't been done, but your love for the other person doesn't change. Rinpoche might be wrathful but never angry. She likes to say it as it is, but she is the kindest person I have ever known. Sometimes I think she's too much of a softie. And she's immensely generous. My mother was worried she would give away so many things she would drive us bankrupt."

UNFIT FOR LIMITLESS COMPASSION

As a child Khandro Rinpoche overheard discussions about discrimination against women, "but I thought it must happen elsewhere, certainly not here. Wherever we went, my sister and I were loved so much, the monks hardly even let our feet touch the ground." Yet when the teenager ventured out to attend courses at other monasteries, her radar picked up on things previously unnoticed. Since her mother was adamant that "we had to earn things on our own merit, not on the ticket of being the great Trichen's daughters," Khandro Rinpoche would often go to teachings without revealing her identity.

Outside of the protected sphere of her family monastery, she encountered "many, many difficult situations, both personally and as told by others. Sometimes situations were comical, often sad, occasionally abusive." She realized, "Yes, indeed, there are masters who have very traditional ideas about what women are, what they are capable of, where they are allowed to sit, which teachings they can receive." Khandro Rinpoche insists that her closest teachers whom she considers truly realized, such as her father, the Karmapa, or Dilgo Khyentse Rinpoche,* "made it crystal clear that girls and boys are valued the same. I never encountered any concepts about gender discrimination on that level." Dilgo Khyentse Rinpoche even refused to start important ceremonies

*Kyabjé Dilgo Khyentse Rinpoche (1910–1991), born in Dergé in East Tibet, was the head of the Nyingma lineage and regarded as one of the most eminent Dzogchen masters of the twentieth century.

until the girls were present. Yet patriarchy runs deep in Tibetan society and in the day-to-day dealings with tutors and monks, she was provided with plenty of opportunities for practicing patience. "What bothers you more than the discrimination is the patronizing attitude—not being taken seriously as a human being." Khandro Rinpoche reached a tipping point when, at seventeen, she visited a monastery to receive teachings on the *Thirty-seven Practices of a Bodhisattva*, one of the classic texts on how to generate unlimited compassion. The teacher barred her from entering. Receiving these teachings would be a waste of time, he explained, since women were incapable of developing bodhichitta.

This ban is particularly ironic here, for the *Thirty-seven Practices* evokes the Tibetans' all-time favorite role model for limitless compassion—mothers.

> If all your mothers, who love you,
> Suffer for time without beginning, how can you be happy?
> To free limitless sentient beings,
> Give rise to awakening mind—this is the practice
>   of a bodhisattva.[8]

Abashed and "very upset," Khandro Rinpoche turned to her father for advice. Mindrolling Trichen Rinpoche recalled that his own mother had encountered the same problem. What did her grandmother do? Khandro Rinpoche asked. She had sat outside of the monastery walls, just close enough to hear the teachings. So Khandro Rinpoche did the same. Sitting outside of the temple, where the monks toss their shoes, she received teachings on how to foster compassion without discrimination.

The image of her sitting by the smelly shoes is haunting. I imagine she must have weighed her options. Staying away would have changed nothing. Getting into an argument, not something she was afraid of, would have made matters worse. But backing down would imply a silent consent that women were incapable.

Rather than choosing attack and blame, she fortified her own mind with patience. In the end, Buddhism is about working with your own mind, not everybody else's mind. "Sincerity, as I was taught by my parents, is on your own merit. You have to go through a whole process of working with your mind." Yet a decision was slowly ripening during these teenage years: "Something has to be done."

"HITLER" ON THE THRONE

The constant doubt whether women were as capable as men irritated her. When she started to take more responsibility at her father's monastery, she found that "monks did not always take orders lightly from a girl." The sweet and smiling approach didn't cut it. Khandro Rinpoche toughened up. "In some ways you had to be very uncompromising, and that didn't sit well with their laid-back attitude." The monks nicknamed her "Hitler." While they piously bowed low to her up front, they would mimic the Nazi salute behind her back. Khandro Rinpoche took it lightheartedly: "It was all done in good fun."

She shuttled back and forth between the newly built Mindrolling monastery in Dehra Dun and her predecessor's nunnery, Karma Chö-khor Dechen, in Rumtek, Sikkim. The more time she spent with the nuns, the more she wanted to join them—a decision that shocked her family. "As the firstborn, they would have preferred for me to marry, get a child, and lead a family life, because the Mindrolling lineage is a family line." Her own reasoning was different: very aware of the women's situation, she wanted to devote her life to furthering their educational opportunities. Her family countered with convincing arguments: There are already many nuns, why do you have to do it? Or, you don't have to be a nun to help women. All true, she concedes, but her heart had already decided. After all, she jokes, interrupted by another round of belly laughs, "Who could have married me anyway? The poor man!"

Tulkus are usually given little liberty in making their own decisions. They are put through an elaborate, rigid training program from a young age onward, more often than not with the help of a whip. While the young incarnates are revered for their potential, individualism is an unknown concept. "Maybe I was given more freedom because I was a girl," Khandro Rinpoche ponders, yet she still had to make the ordination idea "palatable to a lot of people." Nobody knows the exact date of her vows, because she sneaked them in slowly, in stages, between ages seventeen and twenty-four. First her silky, long black hair shrank to shoulder length "because it was more practical," then to a bob "because of the heat in India." Khandro Rinpoche indicates with her flat palm how the haircut ascended higher and higher. An incident in the Mindrolling family a few generations earlier had reenforced the traditional belief that cutting the hair of a realized master will shorten his or her life span. As she always did when in doubt, Khandro Rinpoche consulted her father. She recalls, "He would *laugh and laugh* about it. 'Listen to everybody's advice,' he said, 'respect that everybody has their own reasons for their beliefs, and ultimately do what you think is right. Otherwise, if you always make decisions according to what other people want you to do, you will never be happy.'"

WHO NEEDS HAIR?

One afternoon, the nuns were getting their bimonthly shave from the local barber, and Khandro Rinpoche got in line. Not really paying attention, the barber energetically shaved off a broad patch of hair from her neck to the top of her head. Khandro Rinpoche leaped at the chance: "Shave the whole thing off!" A fifteen-minute family panic ensued at the sight of the newly bald teenager, "but apart from hair nothing changed that day."

"If someone needs *hair* . . ." Instead of completing the sentence, Khandro Rinpoche points to her sister, Jetsun Dechen Paldron, who appears at our table in the back of the Verizon Center with a question as if on cue. Her thick black hair falls to her shoulders. Lanky and beautiful, she is always dressed in stylish silk dresses or modern suits. The two are a commanding duo. One tall, one short; one fashionable, one ever in the same crimson robes. "She is the person I trust the most," Khandro Rinpoche attests and admits to relying heavily on her sister's feedback and support. "People give me a lot of credit, but she is really the key person who keeps all our projects in the East and West very stable."

Unlike Khandro Rinpoche, her younger sister was a calm and gentle girl. Shortly after Jetsun Paldron's birth, their father suffered a stroke.

For many months, before her mother left to spend most of the day at the hospital, she would tie the baby onto the seven-year-old Khandro Rinpoche's back. When the mother came home at night, she would find the two asleep, cuddled together. "She is a big mother hen," her sister says about Khandro Rinpoche, "and I am her ultimate chick." The sisters rarely spend more than a few months apart. "She is my big sister but also my teacher, my boss. I look up to her and admire her," Jetsun Paldron says. "Her integrity is unfailing. We don't agree on everything, but her words and deeds always match." Jetsun Paldron sees supporting her sister as her main task in life. "When our father passed away in 2008, everybody disintegrated—except her," Jetsun Paldron says. "She emerged as the wise person who held us all together." Now married to an American, Jetsun Paldron has assumed increasing responsibilities in the Mindrolling lineage, especially for archiving and translating the precious teachings. Both lay claim to the same meticulous traditional training, sharp-witted intelligence, and an unwavering dedication to preserving the teachings. And Khandro Rinpoche jokingly puts the responsibility for continuing the family line on her sister as well. "She has hair, she can have babies."

Confident, dynamic leaders

Khandro Rinpoche's biography interweaves highly exceptional components for a Tibetan woman: an injection of limitless self-confidence by her parents, full training in all aspects of Tibetan ritual as a tulku, paired with Western-style education and the freedom to make her own choices.

In her early twenties she headed to America for a crash course in Western thinking, methodically researching the Western mind as a scientist would study a strange animal. From visiting juvenile delinquent centers to conferring with Zen masters about their strategies for establishing Buddhist communities in the United States, she set about taking in a whole new world with the same zeal she brought to Bible studies. "You have to understand," she says, "growing up in a monastery I had no idea about Western life, things like prisons or business." Heeding her mother's wish for a broad education, she studied journalism, homeopathy, and business management for a few years—clearly being groomed as a future ambassador of Tibetan Buddhism.

But why are there not more women like her, not more female rinpoches? This is probably the question she gets asked most frequently.

Khandro Rinpoche points out that there were many realized female practitioners in Tibet, "but they stayed away from the great monasteries, the powerhouses." Even if they did not assume lofty titles or hold court in monasteries, the Tibetans revered them. She considers her own mother "probably one of the most realized teachers alive. You see that some of the great teachers' wives are extraordinary in their realization, capability, and love. They never put themselves forward, but in their demureness they were very courageous, helpful, and brave." She stresses several times that the Tibetans' reverence for the great dakinis is "not based upon their association with a teacher, being married to them, or being their daughter, but on their own merit and realization." At the same time, she agrees that the need for female teachers is immense. Educating and empowering women is at the core of her work. "Maybe I can help put a little bit of plaster in the cracks here and there," she quips. "There is very little I can do individually, but I can be a medium through which more women become confident, dynamic leaders."

Historically, the Mindrolling nuns gathered at Samten Tse (Peak of Meditation) nunnery in Tibet that had been founded by Khandro Rinpoche's previous incarnation. Both the monastery and the nunnery survived the attacks of the Chinese army heavily damaged and with a reduced number of ordained. Khandro Rinpoche was longing to continue the tradition in exile. She had no money, and again, her parents came to her support. In 1993, her mother sold almost all her family jewelry so that Khandro Rinpoche could start her own nunnery in Mussoorie in the Shivalik Hills of the Indian Himalayas, naming it Samten Tse Retreat Centre after its Tibetan original.

"DON'T SHAVE OFF YOUR COMMON SENSE!"

There Khandro Rinpoche did get babies after all: she adopted two little girls whose Tibetan families could no longer care for them. "I *love* children," she says enthusiastically, and while she considers all her nuns as her extended family, she did want to care for a few as her own. Kunzang Chödron, now sixteen, came to Khandro Rinpoche at eight months old; Yeshe Chödron, now nineteen, was left at Mindrolling by her family as a toddler to become a nun. "It was not really her calling to ordain at so young an age, so we let her grow up and decide by herself," says Khandro Rinpoche. Both girls live with Khandro Rinpoche's mother at Samten Tse when Rinpoche is traveling. "It gives my mother the vibrancy to have two headstrong teenagers to look after, *again*!" she jokes.

Khandro Rinpoche does not really have a home, but Samten Tse is where she feels most comfortable, "because that's where all my nuns are." Uniting the many diverse streams of her training, Khandro Rinpoche envisioned "a very experimental place, Western and Eastern women, nuns and lay, living together." She describes the center as "extremely vibrant with wonderful, strong women." In addition to passing on the traditional rituals, Khandro Rinpoche actively educates them toward financial independence, bringing in trainers for business management, sometimes even martial arts. She tells new nuns: "Don't shave off your common sense with the hair!" When Khandro Rinpoche notices that they are insecure in a restaurant, she might get everybody dressed up for formal dinner and etiquette training, thus "jolting them out of their hesitancy. The idea is that they get traditional as well as Western education and become confident, capable leaders. Sometimes as a woman you have to be proud." Her sister seconds this approach: "We don't want to be seen as 'special case women.' Every woman should have the opportunities we had."

In her late twenties and thirties, Khandro Rinpoche started pondering how women are responsible for their own development and for obstructing it. "A lot of women talk about having equal rights, nuns being allowed equal seating with the monks, and so forth." While she considers these issues very relevant, she has learned that "respect can never be demanded. Acknowledgment might be given upon demand, but it is never sincere." When feminist Buddhists approach her complaining about the shortage of female role models, she might throw the issue back

Khandro Rinpoche during a visit to France.
Photo by Volker Dencks. © Volker Dencks

at them: "Does the teacher you dream of have to be a woman? If so, will you want to spend as much time as possible with her? Our wants and wishes never end."[9] She has found her own way of balancing the demands and prejudices that come her way: "If being a woman is an inspiration, use it. If it is an obstacle, try not to be bothered." Khandro Rinpoche stays clear of becoming the poster child for Buddhist feminists. "There is no need for aggression or for sadness about discrimination. One just works harder, works harder," she repeats the last two words several times. "This is what I would like women to know—you need a lot of patience, you have to work toward it, and if you are really serious about equal qualities of women, then you have to work by example."

THE TRAP OF FEEL-GOOD BUDDHISM

Though Khandro Rinpoche downplays her own significance, her influence both in the East and West can hardly be overstated. In 2003, when Khandro Rinpoche founded her first center in the West, Lotus Garden, in Stanley, Virginia, she soon invested six Western teachers, four of them women. One of them is Rita M. Gross, probably the most noted and outspoken feminist Buddhist scholar. Gross acknowledges "that the presence of female teachers is really the key issue. If there are not many women teachers present, it is a clear sign of patriarchy. Khandro Rinpoche is very empowering to her female Western students because of her example."

Because Buddhism is still new, "working with Westerners is like working with a flexible mold, you can still shape them," Khandro Rinpoche beams. "Rinpoche does not discriminate between her Western students and her nuns," her sister has observed. "She gives them the same training, the same scoldings, the same schedule." After growing up in a monastery where everybody's full-time job was Buddhism, Khandro Rinpoche had to slowly adjust her expectations of what working lay parents can deliver in the West. "You can let go of self-cherishing by sitting in a humid cave for fifteen years and developing arthritis, you can do it by shaving your hair and living in a monastery, or you can do it right here, in the middle of Washington, DC." She enthuses about "the refined intellect, remarkable exertion, and devotion" of her hundreds of Western students, "but"—here comes the but—"while their view might be altruistic, the inclination is very oriented toward their individual path, *my* path, *my* practice, *my* progress." The culture of individualism is hard to break. "Therefore I emphasize that they have to be able to work together, create a community, offer service wherever and whenever it is needed, *especially* when there is no reward." One of the teachers she entrusted, Jann Jackson, a sixty-one-year-old former therapist, speaks with the deepest appreciation about receiving "uncompromising feedback that really stings. Then I go back and ask myself: Is there a grain of truth in it? It is the ultimate act of kindness to love us enough to not let up when she sees a gap between the teachings and our conduct. The result is a quality of being thoroughly processed. She does not want to fall in the trap of catering to the Western desire for 'feel-good Buddhism.'"

REFUGE AND RAPE

Venturing into the West also triggered a different stance to Khandro Rinpoche's early feminist approach. "It wasn't the discrimination from the men but the naïveté of the women that struck me. How much *we* are responsible—are we going to be so awestruck, so insecure, so indecisive, so emotional that we throw out all logic?"

Traveling in the West, she was shocked to hear repeated accounts of sexual abuse. She reached a turning point when giving teachings in Germany, where a woman in the audience was in tears. When Khandro Rinpoche investigated, the woman blurted out she had been raped. "By a Buddhist teacher." At a refuge* ceremony the teacher had told her to come later to the swimming pool, alone, naked. "Did you go?" Khandro Rinpoche asked. "Yes, I went," the woman responded. In recalling the story, Khandro Rinpoche shakes her head and asks, "What happens to common sense?"

An initial impulse might be to blame the teacher who had the audacity to misuse the sacred refuge vow for taking advantage of a trusting, naïve student. Yet Khandro Rinpoche does not take the route of blame. I have never heard her speak out in public against male teachers who abuse their position with sexual advances on admiring students. "She probably knows that ranting and raving doesn't change this," her student Rita Gross says.

"I speak about it very openly with my nuns and my Western students," Khandro Rinpoche emphasizes. "There are issues we have to address honestly, directly, while keeping in mind both sides of the story. Sometimes there is abuse, sometimes there is an abuse of the abuse. Making a big stance on it is always very tricky, because people can misunderstand the context. Hearing about it may create unnecessary confusion that may lead a person away from the dharma. It is a very discouraging topic."

No shortcut to enlightenment

Now we are in blustery terrain. Sexuality is a precarious, easily misunderstood topic in the Vajrayana. Unlike other Buddhist traditions that tread on the safer path of renunciation, Vajrayana embraces sexuality as a powerful means of transforming neuroses. Of course, this risky busi-

---

*The ceremony that marks one's formal entry into the Buddhist path.

ness comes with the heightened danger that charlatans might employ it as a pretense for indulging in their passions. A number of abuse allegations have rattled the Buddhist communities both in the East and West. Conventional standards of appropriate behavior are routinely waived for high-ranking teachers who are regarded as the embodiment of Buddha's brilliance, thus sanctioning even unconventional actions as enlightened deeds.

In the context of Vajrayana then, how would Khandro Rinpoche define sexual misconduct?

Her answer is clear-cut: "Study the Vinaya!"* Though the Vinaya is traditionally the codex for the ordained, Khandro Rinpoche insists that it is crucial study material for laypeople as well. "It provides a very strict and clear code of conduct, what is allowed and not allowed. If you study it, you can identify when someone manipulates and misuses the teachings, and then students can ask questions. There is a lot of goodness in questioning. If it does not make sense, question it! When we find careless ethical conduct, we need to ask, why is this happening?"

Breaking monastic vows obviously constitutes a serious offense for ordained teachers, but how can we define sexual misconduct for teachers who have not taken vows?

"Every teacher has at least taken the lay vows and the bodhisattva vows," Khandro Rinpoche retorts. "Apart from the obvious misconduct of using force, taking advantage of your own position and the naïveté of a student is abuse and very painful to see. Abuse is when there is pretense, conceit, or lying. Pretending someone has more realization than they actually have and thus misleading the student is very, very harmful. There is no shortcut to enlightenment," she states, "and anyone who offers one should be treated with suspicion."

Yet, I probe once again, how can a student, especially a beginner, judge whether a teacher is truly realized or just bluffing with charisma?

Khandro Rinpoche acknowledges that "the Buddhist teachings give a lot of freedom for each individual, so we cannot really enforce one statement on everybody, we have to look at the situation." Again, she

---

*Vinaya (Skt.; Tib. dulwa) here refers to the Buddhist code of ethical discipline.

refers to her father's advice. Whenever she spoke with him about the topic, "he always said, the solution is education. When you educate people well, you are giving them the tools to make their own decisions." Khandro Rinpoche has adopted that credo for herself: "There is nothing that education cannot change." Rinpoche's father also suggested keeping dharma centers small in number in order to build relationships deeply rooted in mutual trust. "He said anytime you go into places where you don't know everybody by name, then you are not able to train them properly."

A CLOCKWORK OF KINDNESS

Khandro Rinpoche's way of working with her students is therefore extremely personal. "It's the complete opposite of trying to magnetize thousands of students," says Jann Jackson, who has been her student for almost twenty years. "When students are dazzled by her charisma and ask if they can become her student, she might say, 'That's lovely. Why don't we watch each other for the next twelve years, and then let's see?'"

I observe that personal one on one at the Verizon Center. During the hours we talk, others swoop in with requests at least twenty times. She repeatedly jumps up and gives every person exactly what they need: a blessing for an adoring American girl, a good-natured slap on the back for a volunteer, a hearty teasing for her coordinator who forgot to pick up his cell phone, travel directions for her sister, empowering advice for an insecure young mother, a ceremonial white scarf for a fellow Tibetan lama, a hug for a young nun—all unfolds like one choreographed ballet of compassionate efficiency. I see a precise clockwork of kindness in action, never tiring, never missing a beat. Despite the many who vie for her attention, she does not get flustered. She stays completely present and unfailingly returns to our conversation by completing the sentence exactly at the point where she got interrupted. One of her student-teachers, Helen Berliner, compares the spectacle to "the Bolshoi Ballet. She is the general, pairing rigorous discipline with nurturing, and in the end, unlike a dance performance, it gives you a higher purpose to reach for."

When the Dalai Lama thanks the volunteers this afternoon, he remarks that he has rarely seen such an efficient, warm crowd of helpers working together so smoothly. Khandro Rinpoche eagerly passes on the compliment to her team: "It's all because of *you!*" she cheers on her team. "No, it's all because of *you!*" her students retort. In a hilarious stand-off, the students and their teacher throw the responsibility for the success back and forth at each other, until they all erupt in laughter. It's been a good day. She has been of service. And only a few people have noticed that she was in the back seat, driving.

Dagmola Kusho Sakya during a visit to Malibu.
Photo by Amy Gaskin. © Amy Gaskin

2: DAGMOLA KUSHO SAKYA

FROM THE PALACE TO THE BLOOD BANK

How a village girl from East Tibet became a princess,
then a laboratory worker and a mother of five, and finally
the first female Tibetan teacher in America[1]

NEXT TO THE thirty-million-dollar houses of movie stars and Hollywood producers, Dagmola's simple elegance is all the more striking. Of all places, I meet this dignified Tibetan lady on the beach in the
legendary Malibu Movie Colony. Sitting on the wooden deck of her best
friend, eighty-two-year-old lawyer and artist Carol Moss, Dagmola's
wide-brimmed blue sun hat hides the grey streaks in her pinned-up,
black hair that she never cuts. The blue and yellow flowers on her sky-
blue silk blouse and her chocolate-brown traditional wraparound dress
match the ocean and the sand, as the waves of the Pacific roll in behind
her. Her kind eyes sparkle vividly, as she leans forward, reviewing the
string of catastrophes that catapulted her out of her palace in Tibet
into modern-day America. She was the first Tibetan woman ever to
immigrate to America. It never fails to impress me how true practitioners come out of devastating events with even more compassion and
empathy. Hard to imagine a face that could look softer, warmer, more
loving. Dagmola's smile can light up any room full of people.

Her high cheekbones and graceful posture give her an unusual
beauty, even in her late seventies. Her age does not slow her down; on
the contrary. She just got back from teaching in Mexico and is off to a
weekend gathering in New York, sneaking in work on the sequel to her
autobiography, all the while taking care of her husband, Dagchen Rin-

poche, and their monastery in Seattle. Now she is catching a rare break at the Pacific to visit her eldest son. In a way, no location could illustrate more starkly the extremes Dagmola's life encompasses: seventy-seven years ago, when Dagmola was born in a tiny hamlet without electricity or running water on the other side of the planet in Tibet, the Malibu Movie Colony started to become a ritzy hangout for Hollywood icons such as Gloria Swanson, Bing Crosby, and Gary Cooper.

Her full title reads Her Eminence Dag-Yum Kusho Sakya, which denotes her high-ranking status as the wife of one of the most eminent masters in the Sakya* tradition, Dagchen Rinpoche. *Dag* refers to the first syllable of her husband's name, *Yum* means "consort," *Kusho* is a title of reverence. However, in the face of her disarming cheerfulness, friends and students quickly do away with formality and lovingly call her Dagmola. She is one of only two senior Tibetan ladies who were recognized as outstanding teachers after settling in America and who now travel internationally to teach and bestow empowerments just as they had learned in pre-Communist Tibet. The other one is her husband's cousin, Her Eminence Jetsun Kusho Chimé Luding.[†2] Dagmola readily admits that if she had stayed in Tibet, she probably would never have started teaching. "In Tibet, they respect yoginis very much, but the people want teachings from the lamas," she says humbly. "With so many great teachers around, what did I have to add?"

"YOU MUST TEACH!"

Yet in the West, Dagmola's students left her no choice. Female practitioners, in particular, feel inspired by her warm presence and flock to her for advice. After she first came to America in the sixties, she was translating for her uncle, the renowned Dezhung Rinpoche (1906–1987),[3] an ordained monk. When women asked for advice about rela-

---

*The Tibetan name *Sakya* literally means "grey earth," since the first Sakya Monastery was built in the unique grey landscape of southern Tibet near Shigatse. The Sakya school, one of the five main Buddhist lineages in Tibet, developed during the eleventh century.
†Jetsun Kusho Chimé Luding, born in 1938, is the elder sister of His Holiness the Sakya Trizin, the head of the Sakya lineage.

tionship quarrels or sexual problems—topics traditionally not raised with ordained teachers—he felt deeply uncomfortable and referred such questions to his niece. Thus more and more Western students came to rely on her wisdom. One especially persistent female student, urging her to teach more publicly, even went on a letter-writing spree behind Dagmola's back, requesting teaching authorization for her from the finest of Dagmola's teachers: Dilgo Khyentse Rinpoche, Kalu Rinpoche,* Sakya Trizin,† Chögyam Trungpa Rinpoche,‡ and many more. As one enthusiastic response after the other rolled in, Dagmola still wasn't running out of excuses. "When she brought all these letters, it didn't mean anything to me, because lamas kindly say 'yes' to everything; they cannot say 'no,'" Dagmola explains laughingly.

Yet in 1978 traditional teachers empowered her in chorus, when Dilgo Khyentse Rinpoche was visiting the Shambhala Mountain Center in Colorado. The most renowned teacher of his era, his presence commanded awe. Dagmola and her husband, Dagchen Rinpoche, as well as Chögyam Trungpa and a dozen other fine teachers, had flown into the remote mountain site by helicopter. The impressive phalanx of masters was gathered around a table, singing and joking, when a student approached Dagmola with a question about the teachings. She hesitated, saying, "Look, there are so many great teachers here, you should ask one of them." Trungpa Rinpoche overheard the conversation and burst out: "Answer! Answer!" Then he turned to the circle: "I think Kusho Dagmola should teach! So many Westerners, especially women, like to receive teachings, and she is the most qualified, because she received so many teachings." Dagmola recalls feeling extremely embarrassed. In Asia, such a scene would have been unthinkable. Yet all the lamas joined in unison: "Yes, yes, of course, you must teach!"

The event is significant because that student in the Rocky Mountains is not the only one who feels much more comfortable approaching Dag-

---

*Kalu Rinpoche (1904–1989), born in Kham, East Tibet, was an eminent master of the Shangpa Kagyü lineage.
†His Holiness the Forty-first Sakya Trizin (b. 1945) is the head of the Sakya lineage.
‡Chögyam Trungpa Rinpoche (1939–1987), born in Kham, fled Tibet in 1959 and became one of the most successful pioneers of Tibetan Buddhism in the West.

mola than one of the high-ranking male teachers. With her disarming amiability, Dagmola immediately cuts through the finely woven net of hierarchy and protocol that often surrounds traditional lamas. After our first meeting some years ago, she heartily hugged me good-bye, and in her firm embrace my mind simply fell apart, into a state of utter peace.

EVERY BREATH IS PRACTICE

When even her beloved uncle, Dezhung Rinpoche, asked her to teach, Dagmola finally recognized that there was a genuine need for her insight. Her experience as a working mother of five sons resonated with many students. Since she worked in the laboratory of an enormous hospital, many doctors, healers, and nurses sought her advice on problems like burn-out and stress. She did not need to put herself in their shoes—she knew the challenges only too well. Many students found her counsel so profoundly helpful that they came back for more. "I think it is important in the West that women can talk openly to other women and help each other," Dagmola has realized. "Tibetan lamas like my uncle never had any experience of ordinary life. They might have received many teachings, but they do not always quite connect to women's issues." Dagmola reasons that women have a softer heart, "because we're the ones bearing the children. Men might be more powerful, but sometimes they don't listen."

Dagmola's eldest son, David Khon, echoes this sentiment: "The lamas are usually brought up quite removed from society. My father comes from an aristocratic family. That does not mean that he is incapable, but he always had other people to take care of finances or the household. Look what Dagmola did: caring for us children, doing the whole household, and making a living. She had to figure all this out on her own as a refugee!"

Dagmola refuses to make a strict distinction between child care, kitchen chores, and office work on the one hand and the spiritual path on the other. "Spiritual practice is everyday life, not just sitting on the cushion, meditating. Every move, every word, every thought is practice. Dharma is in daily life." Though the term "Buddhist" has become a household word in the West, Tibetans hardly ever use it for themselves. Dagmola draws great meaning from the original Tibetan name for practitioners: "*Nangpa* literally means 'insiders.' This indicates the path is about ourselves, looking inward at our own mind instead of searching for meaning outwardly."

In addition to teaching at Sakya Monastery in Seattle, where she lives, Dagmola also guides small but thriving centers in Arizona, California, Hawaii, and Mexico. "I am only sharing my own heart experience," she emphasizes. "I am not a lama or powerful; just think of me as a good friend." But with her own husband now traveling less at age eighty-two, she has stepped in and really become a prime agent in establishing Buddhist teachings in the West. "There are not many old teachers left who experienced the culture in Tibet firsthand. Our closest friends are gone now, so it is important for me to share." After she had written down her life story about her years in Tibet—an unusually bold move for a Tibetan wife—the Dalai Lama personally urged her to write about the second half of her life as well,[4] suggesting that the experiences of the first Tibetan immigrant in America would be inspiring for many.

"DON'T ROCK THE BOAT!"

Dagmola did not give her first formal teaching until the midnineties, not least because her full-time job plus her five children barely left any leisure. It was Carol Moss, her friend in whose Malibu house we're meeting, who organized the memorable debut in her living room. When they met for the first time at the wedding of Dagmola's eldest son in Los Angeles, the two hit it off instantly, like two sisters reuniting after a long separation. "There was this brilliant woman," Carol Moss recalls, "clearly capable and eager to teach, but everybody was tiptoeing around it." When Carol, a long-time student and sponsor of Buddhist teachers, announced Dagmola's first teaching at her house in Brentwood, the prospect caused quite a stir. Carol remembers it as "an *extremely big deal*." Dagmola's firstborn son, David Khon, begged Carol to keep things low key. According to Carol, "He kept saying, 'Don't rock the boat! Don't rock the boat!'"

Dagmola prepared her first talk meticulously, taking extra care to pronounce every syllable correctly, without the slightest fault. "She was terrified of making a mistake in the presence of some Tibetan attendees," says Carol Moss. "She knew they would then gossip and scold her husband: Can't you rein in your wife?" But of course, all went splendidly; soon students were asking for more. Carol recalls a White Tara empowerment that Dagmola gave in the Malibu Library the year after. "We could only fit in seventy-five people, but 135 came. We had to turn people away. It was the most special event. During the empowerment we would stay with the Tara mantra,* just singing it for a long time. There was clearly a presence of light in the room that everybody felt. I have never experienced anything like this."

Immense pride rings in David Khon's voice when he compares his mother's current success to the first half of her life: "Buddhist societies are very patriarchal. If we had stayed in Tibet, she could not have become a teacher in her own right. She would just always have been Dagchen Rinpoche's wife. If you walk into any temple or monastery, even today, women sit in the back. They are not mistreated or denigrated, but girls don't get to go to school, and because they don't have education, they don't become teachers. With Buddhism coming to the West, I see so much potential for new teachers now."

THE ONLY GIRL AT SCHOOL

A combination of the most unlikely circumstances enabled Dagmola to become one of the first Tibetan women ever to teach in the West. Little in Dagmola's early years foretold her later career. In fact, nothing would have seemed a more unlikely feat for a little village girl in the remote area of East Tibet, since she was not born into a rich or aristocratic family. Her birth province, Kham,† is home to a special, fearless people: the Khampas, proud warriors with long, often braided, hair,

---

*Consecrated syllables, believed to be imbued with the deity's blessings.
†Kham is one of three regions traditionally considered to constitute Tibet. Since the Chinese takeover it has been divided between Sichuan and Yunnan provinces and the Tibet Autonomous Region.

easily recognizable by the red or black tassels woven into their braids. Their daredevil spirit and passion for fast horses, coupled with their deep understanding of the land and respect for nature, reminds me of Native Americans.

Nestled between two mountain ranges, on the banks of the river Tha, her village was home to about thirty-five families, mostly farmers. Some of the mountains nearby never quite lost their snow blanket, for Dagmola "a constant reminder of the deities we believed dwelled there."[5] From the five elements that make up nature—earth, water, wind, fire, space—up to the most majestic Himalayan mountain ranges and their inhabitants, pious Tibetans regard everything as sacred.

This part of East Tibet was already under Chinese jurisdiction when Dagmola was a child and her father was of Chinese origin, but apart from the occasional Chinese officer passing through and demanding bribes or a night with a woman, her village was not too bothered by the Chinese influence. Back then, Dagmola was known as Sonam Tsé Dzom, "the Unity of Merit and Long Life." Though disappointed that their only child was not a boy, her parents loved her dearly, expecting her to carry on the family line. Her father staffed a Chinese government office in the city of Jyekundo; her ingenious mother, Püntsok Drolma, labored hard to harvest the fields and manage the household while her husband worked in the city. The family lived in a three-storey, square-shaped building made of mud and stone, nicknamed the "Yellow-House Nest." Three rows of prayer flags whispered their prayers into the wind from the nearly flat roof. On the first floor, their best horses were kept at night, while goats, sheep, and cattle slept in the barn adjacent. On the second floor, family life revolved around the kitchen with the big open stove that was fueled by dried yak dung. The third floor featured three bedrooms, an open area, and an elaborate shrine room with traditional paintings of deities, loose-leaf prayer texts, and an altar from which the smell of burning butter lamps wafted through the house day and night. Dagmola was too little to fathom whether the Chinese-Tibetan marriage got strained by the political pressure, but when Dagmola was five years old, her father was reassigned to a post in China. Her mother decided not to follow him there. Dagmola recalls her last memory of him: he carried his only daughter in his arms all the way to the ferry that would take him away. She never saw him again. Much later she heard that he fell into the hands of the Communists, was put under house arrest, and disappeared.

FLYING HOUSES WITH WINGS

Dagmola's uncle, the learned Dezhung Rinpoche, must have seen her potential early on. As the head of the family, he ordered her mother to send her to school. That was a first: Dagmola was the only girl in her village to attend the small monastic school. In Tibet education was invariably linked with religion. The monasteries functioned as the centers of learning; they had the teachers, libraries, and printing presses. Only due to her uncle's insistence did Dagmola learn reading and writing with the monks. Starting at the age of eight, two years later than the boys, she soon caught up and became an enthusiastic and proud student. Her classmates teased her relentlessly about being a girl, while her girlfriends pitied her, for what was she, a village girl, going to do with all this useless knowledge?

"I really didn't think I was different than the boys, but I got into lots of trouble with this attitude!" Dagmola recalls. "Girls were not important in Tibet at that time. This was very difficult for me." She was not treated equally in the all-male environment. Little things that marked the difference burned themselves into Dagmola's memory. For instance, when the monastery received gifts of food, money, or candy—a very rare treat in Tibet—the boys received their share, but not Dagmola. She remembers crying when watching the monks munch raisins or sweets. But Dagmola received something else, which was even rarer for a girl in rural Tibet: a healthy dose of self-confidence. Her uncle Ngawang, in particular, kept telling her that she was special. He listened attentively when the little girl told him about her visions. She dreamed of flying through the sky "in small houses with wings," visiting "strange-looking people with white hair in big cities with giant buildings." Decades later she recognized that she had foreseen her airplane trip to America.

The villagers gossiped that Dagmola's family was "treating her like a tulku, but she's not." In the afternoons, she learned household work, dairying, working the fields, spinning her quota of yarn with her grand-mother. When an angry yak skewered her with his horn and pierced her cheek, leaving a gash to the right of her mouth, the villagers took it as a bad omen for the spoiled girl. Everybody was worried that her beauty might be ruined, as that would make her unfit for marriage, and what else was she going to do?

Dagmola paints the picture of a hard-working but carefree child-hood, full of little adventures with her pony and her loyal four-horned pet sheep, watched over by a solicitous uncle whose colorful visitors from all of Tibet sparked her curiosity about other parts of the country. She was only vaguely conscious of the Communist Revolution that took place in 1948 and 1949 in neighboring China. The medium of the Tibetan state oracle prophesied that by 1950, Tibet would face chal-lenges it had never seen before.

Unaware of the volte-face ahead, her family took Dagmola, then fif-teen, on a pilgrimage to the holiest places of Central Tibet—a highlight of any Tibetan's life. Mounting her horse for what was meant to be a year-long trip alongside her mother, aunts, and uncles, guarded over by their mighty Tibetan mastiff, their party of forty had no bad omens about the arduous journey that would turn their life upside down.

After months of riding, warding off snow, cold weather, and avid admirers along the way, Dagmola arrived with her family in Sakya, the seat of the once vastly powerful Sakya lamas. With the help of the Mongol Khans, the Sakyas had ruled over most of Tibet in the early part of the second millennium. Dagmola confesses being disappointed that Sakya really lived up to its name: "There were no trees, no greens, everything was grey. I just thought, 'Ohhh, this is no good!'" But Dag-mola's disappointment soon gave way to excitement.

ROMANCE AND INTRIGUE

Dagmola immensely enjoyed the company of twenty-year-old Jigdal Dagchen Rinpoche,* the designated heir to his father's throne at the

---

*At the time Dagmola met him, he was just called Jigdal Rinpoche. The title Dagchen was conferred on him later, after his father's passing. Tibetans often have several names and

Puntsok Palace. His long black pony tail, his mastery on horseback, his quiet, noble demeanor—all appeared so attractive! They played card games together or roamed in the wild mountains on picnics. Dagmola remembers feeling "flushed, warm, and nervous" when he touched his forehead to hers—an intimate gesture a master like him would usually only make towards another high lama or close family. "[He] was very generous, fun, and . . . much more casual than I ever dreamed," Dagmola remembers. "He was carefree and had a sense of humor that I enjoyed."[6] They kept their innocent courting secret for months, knowing that his parents would severely disapprove.

Royal marriages are often gambits in a political power play rather than questions of the heart. As is the custom in much of Asia, marriages are usually arranged by the parents, often many years in advance, with the help of astrological charts. Girls, especially, had no say in the choosing of their husband. In fact, Dagmola had already been promised to a handsome heir of an estate in East Tibet, and Dagchen Rinpoche's marriage with a princess from Sikkim had been pledged. The simple village girl from East Tibet would not be considered an appropriate candidate by any standards. Yet observers could not fail to notice how the two glanced at each other, and palace servants started to gossip and spy.

After a garden party, sitting on a bench in the palace garden, Dagchen Rinpoche surprised Dagmola by asking her outright for her hand. "If your mother and uncle give their consent, will you marry me?"[7] Torn between longing and fear, Dagmola turned him down. "I like you," she said, "but I want to go home."[8] Despite her love for Dagchen Rinpoche, she was terribly homesick and could not wait to see her friends in Kham. "In the moonlight, I could see that he was both hurt and surprised," Dagmola recalls. "Hundreds of girls would have snapped up the chance to say yes."[9] According to legend, Dagchen Rinpoche's ancestors had descended from heaven as representatives of the Buddha. Dagmola cared for Dagchen Rinpoche but felt that "in our case the geography was wrong. . . . Under no circumstances would his parents accept me as part of their family. . . . Yet each time I saw him I felt closer to him."[10]

titles, and in order to keep confusion to a minimum, he is here continuously referred to as Dagchen Rinpoche, the name by which he is most commonly known today.

Dagmola underestimated Dagchen Rinpoche's determination, and she too longed to be with him. They became inseparable. Dagmola could not illustrate the way courtship worked back then more clearly than by describing the way Dagchen Rinpoche requested permission from Dagmola's uncle. Her fiancé "placed the message on . . . five sheets of thin wood edged in red, with a designed cover and bottom also in red. The message was written on a coating of powder. All this formed a kind of elegant layered box, together with a decorated band of leather and silk. . . . An auspicious day was selected, and the message was delivered by a Sakya government secretary."[11]

Dagchen Rinpoche's parents were thoroughly dismayed. They told their son—through messengers—to forget about the whole thing. By custom Dagchen Rinpoche did not approach his parents directly, even though they lived in the same palace and saw each other every day. Messengers were sent back and forth with auspicious scarves draped around scathing notes. The family even offered Dagmola money to buy her off. But neither Dagchen Rinpoche nor Dagmola budged. "They wanted someone who was the daughter of a high-ranking official, or a princess, or someone very learned. I was none of this. Dagchen Rinpoche then told his parents that if he could not marry me he would become a monk. So that did it!" Remaining celibate would have entailed a terrible loss of face for his parents, since their eldest son was supposed to carry on the lineage. It took months of back-and-forth diplomacy, polite threats, and secret rendezvous, before the parents finally realized they had no choice but to relent.

A TWENTY-POUND HEADDRESS

The wedding invitations finally could be sent in early March 1950. While Dagmola gained custom-tailored robes for her new life as a princess, in faraway Beijing Mao Zedong* had gained victory over China,

*Communist leader Mao Zedong (1893–1976), often referred to as "Chairman" Mao, founded the People's Republic of China in 1949. His authoritarian regime boasted of significant modernization but was also responsible for horrific torture, famine, and persecution, which cost the lives of tens of millions of people.

Dagchen Rinpoche and Dagmola Sakya with their three older sons in Lhasa, 1959, shortly before their escape. Photo courtesy of Sakya Monastery

forcing his Nationalist adversaries to retreat to Taiwan. While the whole town of Sakya prepared for the weeklong wedding, Mao prepared thousands of his troops to move further into East Tibet. While Dagmola learned to wear the elaborate headdress, a twenty-pound crown of corals, turquoise, and gold, her neighbors back home prepared to hide their valuables for fear of the plundering Chinese. Homesick Dagmola eagerly awaited each letter from her family, who had returned to East Tibet without her. Since her family downplayed the imminent danger in order not to worry her, Dagmola had no inkling of the sweeping changes the new rulers would force on her life.

Mao Zedong's People's Liberation Army had started to amass its troops at the Tibetan borders as early as 1949, but the Tibetans were slow to take notice. At that time, there were only ten transmitter radios in the whole of Tibet—no post office, no newspapers, no telegrams, no television.[12] News spread the old-fashioned way—on two legs or four legs, either via fast-running monks or yaks. Tibet's lack of communication helped advance Mao Zedong's plan to extend his "heavenly empire" before the majority of Tibetans were on alert. The first thing Mao's Red Army accomplished was the amazing feat of building a truck road through the hostile mountains. The Chinese pretended the new roads were to help the Tibetans, but of course, the concrete was mainly poured to enable thousands and thousands of trucks to carry Chinese soldiers deeper and deeper into the mountain ranges.

THE LOTUS THAT BRINGS FORTH MANY SONS

While the Communist army besieged East Tibet, Dagmola was under a different kind of pressure—the expectation to produce a son. "It is said in the history of Sakya that the wives who will bear sons are chosen by the deities. So it must have been a protective deity that somehow chose me," Dagmola says. During the wedding, Dagmola received the name Jamyang Pema Palgyibutri, which she translates as "the Deity of Wisdom, the Lotus That Brings Forth Many Sons." Dagmola remembers how her father-in-law "gave me blessings and special pills. If you don't have a son, they might bring a second or third wife." She frankly admits that dealing with the hostile in-laws "wasn't easy."

Now she was part of a historic family. "Heavy responsibility for religion, tradition, and western Tibetan culture were mine at age sixteen," she writes in her autobiography. "How fortunate I was to have a kind and generous husband, who had demonstrated his devotion by fighting fiercely against the highest odds to win me."[13] After all, Dagmola was still a teenager, immature and childish even in her own admission. To this day, she still has a playful and vivacious streak, and I can just see her hatching innocent pranks. In February 1951, she gave birth to her first child, a baby girl. Her husband's family did little to hide how disappointed they were. "Although I still was young and there was plenty of time for male offspring, I felt something of a failure."[14] The little girl, constantly sick from the start, only lived for three months.

OPEN RIVALRY

Dagchen Rinpoche's father had died only weeks earlier, and the whole family was mourning. With the head of the dynasty gone, the space was wide open for family rivalry. Dagchen Rinpoche's mother schemed for her second-born son to seize the throne. "From the day of his birth my husband had been trained to be the next Trichen,"* Dagmola remarks.[15] "To us it was unthinkable that the second in line would be her choice." Dagmola can't hide a suspicion that her "unsuitable" marriage to the family heir might have been a factor in the strife for the throne that broke out after the patriarch's death. "There was some resentment obviously caused by me. I was never to be accepted fully by my mother-in-law, it seemed, for being a Khampa and not from one of Lhasa's noble families. This intrigue left my husband and me heartsick and unbelieving. It was even more of a shock because the two brothers were close and had never been rivals. . . . It was a very unhappy time."[16] Dagchen Rinpoche's brother did not want to participate in the rivalry against his brother and opted for ordination as an exit strategy. Finally, a rival palace won the fight for political and religious control of the Sakya school. Dagchen Rinpoche lost his bid to become the head of the tradition.

Instead he fulfilled his wedding promise to take his wife on what was meant to be a two-year trip to her hometown. Just before their departure, Dagmola realized she was pregnant again. Traveling through rugged terrain might not be easy for anybody, but could any expecting mother these days imagine riding on horseback and on yaks for many months, dressed in their finest, wearing a twenty-pound headdress? If not near any monastery, they would put up their tents. The locals greeted Dagmola and her husband with much devotion and curiosity when the party stopped along the way. One of the highlights was meet-

*Lit. "Great Throne," a Tibetan title for the Sakya leader.

ing the Dalai Lama at his summer palace in Lhasa. Shy Dagmola had an audience with the then seventeen-year-old spiritual and political leader. Dagmola remembers being immensely nervous. She also saw her first automobile, her first red tomatoes, and well-armed Chinese soldiers.

The closer they came to East Tibet, the more difficulties the party encountered with Chinese posts. In the midst of traveling, at a monastery near Jyekundo, Dagmola gave birth to her first son. Later he chose the name David, but at birth he was named after the Buddhist deity of wisdom, Manju Vajra in Sanskrit, which Dagmola affectionately shortened to Minzu-la. Soon after, Jamyang Khyentse Chökyi Lodrö,* one of the most revered Tibetan masters of the twentieth century, recognized Minzu-la as the incarnation of Dagchen Rinpoche's father. Traditionally, Sakya sons are always born again into Sakya families. "When a Sakya lama dies, we don't search for his incarnation outside the family," says Dagmola. "They come back to us anyway."

In a silk-covered sedan chair, carried by a monk on horseback, Minzu-la was escorted into Dagmola's hometown. Dagmola was overjoyed to recognize all the familiar faces of childhood companions. What a difference between her stately arrival now and her departure only a few years before!

Before long her husband, Dagchen Rinpoche, was asked by the Dalai Lama to accompany him to meet Mao Zedong in Beijing in 1954. Dagmola and her baby son moved into the room of Jamyang Khyentse Chökyi Lodrö's wife, Khandro Tsering Chödron. For almost a year, they studied and practiced together, and became best friends. Khandro and Dagmola participated in the empowerments and teachings usually reserved for male reincarnations. With a small group of women, they even practiced the sacred physical and breathing exercises of Tibetan yoga together. "Although we women wore only one pant-like garment, extending from the waist to the knee [with a bare chest], we never became cold, with a dozen of us in the small room, all exercising," says Dagmola. "It was an entirely new experience for me. The goal of the program, based on ancient Buddhist teachings, was to cleanse the

---

*1893–1959. See also chapter 12.

circulatory system . . . and balance functions of the body and mind.
. . . I struggled to keep from giggling. We were grunting and making
funny noises as we stretched and bended. Tibetan women traditionally
didn't do this exercise in a group. I tried to remind myself that this
was dharma practice, but the scene was too humorous. My problem
was compounded because [Khandro] also was a giggler. Together we
were bad examples."[17] Even now, so many decades later, Dagmola still
shakes her head with regret that she didn't make better use of these
extraordinary teachings.

Meanwhile, in Beijing, Mao Zedong tried to charm the Tibetan del-
egation with exotic foods, luxurious living quarters, and propaganda
films. Dagchen Rinpoche was present when Mao famously promised
the Dalai Lama that the cultural and religious freedom in Tibet would
remain untouched*—a promise that would be breached many times
over in the years to come. Mao's deep aversion to religion also became
obvious. It was during these meetings that Mao uttered his famous
statement, "Religion is poison." Dagchen Rinpoche was not fooled by
the charade. When he learned that his mother had passed away, he had
a convincing reason to excuse himself, and hastily returned to his wife
in East Tibet to perform the traditional rituals for his mother. Soon after,
Dagmola got pregnant again. They called their second son Kunga Dorje,
which could roughly be translated as "Joyous Thunderbolt."

ESCAPE IN DISGUISE

Due to his unique firsthand knowledge, Dagchen Rinpoche was keenly
aware of the danger the Chinese represented. In 1955, the Chinese called
a meeting in Beijing and made it mandatory for all important masters
from East Tibet to attend. Khyentse Chökyi Lodrö set an example of
how to respond to the call—disguised as a simple monk on pilgrimage,
he clandestinely escaped west to Central Tibet. "Khyentse Rinpoche's
move made us realize the impending danger. How long would we be

*In 1951 this promise had been written down as part of the famous "Seventeen-Point
Agreement for the Peaceful Liberation of Tibet," but by 1954 the evidence that the agreement had been a ruse was already apparent.

free to come and go at will?"[18] says Dagmola. A letter from Khyentse Chökyi Lodrö ended with the greeting that "we will see you in Lhasa," a hint for Dagmola and her husband to speed up their return. At ten weeks old, their newborn was considered sufficiently mature to travel the long way back from East Tibet.

Fights between Tibetan guerrillas and Chinese soldiers broke out all around them. This time, they chartered Jeeps and got shot at several times. But when Dagmola's younger baby got sick with pneumonia, the Chinese decided to turn this crisis into a showcase for their modern methods and insisted on admitting the little boy and his mother to their hospital in Dartsedo, a large town on the Tibetan-Chinese border. In a hospital for the first time in her life, Dagmola was "not impressed" by the dirty surroundings. The hospital "was built over a stream into which the hospital sewage was emptied. The hospital complex was like a vision of hell: doctors with needles, strange noises, many wounded and ailing people."[19] But most importantly, Kunga Dorje survived.

DODGING THIEVES AND PATROLS

Dagmola never complains. I have not heard a single word of anger or bitterness about the violence and poverty she witnessed. She just calmly recounts her journey through a war-torn Tibet. Dodging thieves and Chinese patrols, crossfire and spies, mumps and pneumonia, her small family (including her mother and aunt) made it back to Lhasa, Tibet's capital. In the four-and–a-half years they were gone, the capital had transformed into a different city. "The changes were shocking," a dismayed Dagmola observed. Chinese construction had replaced many of the traditional houses, Chinese propaganda was blasting out of loudspeakers, and the pressure on the influential Dagchen Rinpoche to work for the Chinese government mounted daily. However, in Sakya, their home monastery, her people did not yet feel the Chinese presence much.

Again, little Kunga Dorje fell ill with pneumonia. When Tibetan medicine failed, a Chinese doctor was called. This was Dagmola's first contact with X-ray machines and antibiotics. The doctor urged a blood transfusion, something Dagmola had never heard of. Yet Dagmola volunteered as the donor—which was considered extremely grave by her family. Since Tibetans regard their body as a sacred palace inhabited by deities, cutting into the body or drawing blood was regarded as exceptionally dangerous, especially in the case of such a noble woman as Dagmola Sakya. Her servants wept when she gave blood twice at the palace in Sakya. Little did they know that one day, working in a blood bank would become Dagmola's full-time profession.

CAUGHT IN THE TURMOIL OF REVOLUTION

Dagmola gave birth to her third boy, Lodrö Dorje, in 1958, and affectionately called him Mati-la. Together with her growing family, Dagmola got caught in the turmoil of the revolution in Lhasa in 1959. On March 10, a near-decade of tension and violence peaked when the Chinese ordered the Dalai Lama to attend a theater show—and to come alone, without attendants or bodyguards. Such invitations had become a common ruse by the Chinese, and many Tibetan lamas had inexplicably disappeared after these "cultural events." The news spread like a contagious virus, and within days, tens of thousands of Tibetans surrounded the Dalai Lama's palace to protect their leader. Dagmola witnessed firsthand the unfortunate showdown that felled the Tibetan government. On March 12, about fifteen thousand Tibetans gathered all day in front of the Dalai Lama's summer palace to protect their leader, protest the Chinese regime, and proclaim Tibet's independence. Dagmola did not participate in person but sent her servant to show her support. On March 13, the Chinese arrested all the major lamas and their families that they could. When they came for Dagchen Rinpoche, a dozen well-armed guerrilla fighters happened to be waiting in front of his room for an audience, and the smaller Chinese search troop, afraid to risk a standoff, retreated in order to come back with a stronger force.

In the ensuing showdown of Chinese military force and Tibetan patriotism, two Chinese artillery shells hit the Dalai Lama's quarters. The Dalai Lama realized he had no choice but to flee for his life. He slipped out of the palace at night, disguised as a soldier, forging his way across Tibet to India. Acutely aware of the danger to their own lives, Dagmola and her family, including Dezhung Rinpoche, left in a rush. Scrambling to buy a few horses, they walked several hours as if on pilgrimage, then took to riding day and night, their three small children tied to their horses. For several weeks they held out hope they could get home to Sakya, yet encountering more and more horror stories of burned-down monasteries and bombed camps, they had no choice but to head for the neighboring kingdom of Bhutan. Hunted by the Chinese army, hearing gunshots close by, they hid from Chinese planes that surveyed the few escape routes from the air and dropped bombs directly into crowds of those fleeing.

Dagmola was still nursing her youngest son, thirteen months old. "Often it meant stepping behind a rock to get out of the wind and cold for a few minutes,"[20] Dagmola recalls. Without adequate sunglasses, they became snow blind. Frostbitten ears and toes got infected. They had to leave behind some of the horses that collapsed in exhaustion. Their group was the last to cross the mountain pass to Bhutan without being confronted by the Chinese—yet they still were not safe. The Bhutanese government refused to let these despondent refugees into the country, fearing that the Chinese army would pursue them into Bhutan. Thousands of refugees camped at the border for weeks, Dagmola's family among them, with nothing to eat but nettles. Hundreds saw no choice but to retrace their steps back into Tibet to escape starvation.

But after a few weeks, the Dalai Lama too had survived his arduous ride across Tibet. Upon reaching India, he personally implored Prime Minister Jawaharlal Nehru to appeal to the Bhutanese king to end the refugee crisis at the border. Finally, the refugees could find peace. Dagmola believed they had reached their final destination.

THE FIRST TIBETANS IN AMERICA

But a chance encounter turned her life in another unexpected direction. In exile in Kalimpong, North India, they met Dr. Turrell Wylie, "a colorful tattooed ex-merchant-mariner"[21] and Tibetan scholar from the

University of Washington in Seattle. He was looking for learned Tibetans to help the Rockefeller Foundation study their language, history, and culture. Extremely impressed with Dezhung Rinpoche's erudition, he invited the whole family to Seattle. This prospect seemed far more appealing than life in one of the desolate Indian refugee camps. Not only did the large family have trouble supporting itself, many Tibetans were dying in the camps due to the heat, contaminated food, epidemics, and appalling hygienic conditions. Dagmola admits that at the time she was not even sure where America was on the map. She thought it was probably a part of Europe. But then, the Americans knew very little about the Tibetans too. The plight of the Tibetans, the escape of the Dalai Lama, and the unimaginable destruction Mao's reforms wreaked in Tibet occupied the front pages of the newspapers for only a short time. In early October 1960, Dagmola and her family were the first Tibetan refugees ever to seek asylum in America.

This was the fourth time the Khampa girl had had to readjust her life and start all over again. Suddenly she found herself on the other side of the planet in the middle of Seattle. All throughout her childhood and youth, she was used to having servants. Though she had a hand in the chores, servants did most of the trading and bartering, cooking, cleaning, and child care. Now she had to manage everything by herself—not an easy feat with several small boys. "Sometimes the men helped dry dishes," says Dagmola, "but most of the time I had to do everything. The men did not even know how to put diapers on right." Dagmola was pregnant again when they arrived in the United States. Her fourth son, Gyalwe Dorje Sakya (Victorious Thunderbolt), was the first Tibetan child born in the USA. She gave birth to her fifth son, Lekpa Dorje Sakya (Virtuous Thunderbolt), in 1962.

The family was a novelty. The pictures of the cute boys in their traditional fur-lined brocade robes were distributed through an international news agency. When they got a Lhasa Apso* from India, this too was a top story for the curious public. "I found the people very, very nice," Dagmola beams. "Though I didn't speak the language, people were so

---

*A Tibetan terrier.

helpful, often I found cookies or toys on the doorsteps for the children. At Christmas, foundations brought Christmas trees and presents for the children, so from then on, we picked up the tradition and now we have Christmas every year."

The late Ellis Gene Smith, then a twenty-five-year-old doctoral candidate from the University of Washington, moved in with the family in their modest Ravenna District home to study the Tibetan culture but soon found he could not keep his scientific detachment. "They don't pry, yet they are concerned," he told the local newspaper at the time. "It is such an unusual combination." Living with the Tibetan family round the clock, who was studying whom soon became blurred. "Before I knew it, I was brushing my teeth in front of this gallery," he referred teasingly to the five dark-eyed little lads who followed his every move, "in order to teach them health habits." In the two years that he lived with them, Dagmola and the boys came to call him their "brother," and Gene Smith enjoyed juggling his roles as scholar, translator, tour guide, babysitter, and trusted friend. His friendship with the Sakyas spurred the former Mormon from Utah to a new fifty-year mission. "I thought this must be a pretty cool religion that produces such awesome people." Since he could find hardly any Tibetan texts to study, he single-handedly set out to collect literature and later founded the invaluable Tibetan Buddhist Resource Center, a unique digital archive that preserves a treasury of Tibetan texts from extinction. "Living in the middle of this family places me in an awkward position at times," he said, for he was there to offer guidance, but in Tibetan society "you do not offer advice unless asked." For instance, when Dagmola's uncle, Dezhung Rinpoche, got on the local bus, he would say 'hello' to every single person on the bus. "I wouldn't tell him not to for the world."[22]

CLASH OF CULTURES

The Rockefeller Foundation had invited the family in order to research the Tibetan way of life. Dagmola and her family assumed they would stay until the conditions in Tibet changed and then go back. Before agreeing to the three-year contract, she even questioned Dr. Wylie:

"What if Tibet becomes free before the three years are over, will we be allowed to return earlier?" The chance she might be stuck on a foreign continent while all her people returned to their homeland made her anxious. But when the research grant ended, the situation in Tibet was still hopeless, and returning to the destitute refugee camps in India was too depressing a prospect. Dagmola was adamant about not wanting to leave. So they stayed as immigrants. Dezhung Rinpoche became the first Tibetan to be hired as a permanent staff member at the University of Washington. The boys enrolled in a Quaker elementary school, earned pocket money by washing cars and mowing lawns, and soon found playing basketball with their new American friends more exciting than studying the traditional texts with their uncle. To call this a clash of cultures would be an understatement.

Dagchen Rinpoche arrived in America wearing the traditional ankle-length white robes of a yogi and long, plaited hair. Americans kept mistaking him for a woman. When he was once taken for his uncle's wife, he quickly cut his hair.[23] On his right hand he carried a tattoo of the swastika, a graphical representation of eternity in the Buddhist culture that the Nazis later distorted. The Americans were so shocked by what they perceived as a Nazi symbol that he had to have the image reworked into the innocent picture of a little bird. He found work at the Washington State Burke Memorial Museum and later at the Museum of Natural History in New York. Traditionally, religious masters don't work ordinary jobs but rather focus on teaching and practicing. So Dagmola hurried to find a job instead. After all, they had to put five sons through college. Because she hardly spoke any English when she first started, cleaning was the only job available. For thirty years, she worked in the same company—the King County Central Blood Bank. People soon realized the earnestness, superior intelligence, and integrity of their "cleaning lady" and trained her to be a laboratory assistant. This was ironic.

TURNING A BLOOD BANK INTO A TEMPLE

Only fifteen years earlier, in Tibet, she had been one of the first Tibetans ever to donate blood. But now, taking blood became her job. "She transmuted the work into dharma like an alchemist," says B. Alan Wallace, the American Tibetan translator, best-selling author, and teacher. "She was constantly saying mantras and blessing all the blood that was sent out." Alan Wallace met Dagmola almost thirty years ago, while he was translating for a Tibetan lama. He was immediately struck by "the purity of her presence, her kindness, her utter humility. It warms my heart just to think of her," Alan marvels. "If Tara were to take birth as a human being, how would she be different from Dagmola?" Along with the Dalai Lama and Gyatrul Rinpoche, he counts her as one of his most important teachers, his "dharma mother." One of the qualities Alan finds so inspiring is "that she's totally engaged: having a full-time job, running the dharma center with her husband, and raising five sons; it is simply spectacular." In his foreword to her autobiography, Alan Wallace writes, "Clearly here was someone who had experienced the depths of Buddhist practice and set a heart-warming example for others seeking an integration of spiritual and worldly life."[24]

Dagmola admits, "It wasn't easy. I was the only one working, taking care of the children and the household." These were the sixties. The Vietnam War poured hundreds of thousands of students onto the streets in antiwar protests. The Rolling Stones could get no satisfaction. The rise of feminism broke down the last legal barriers to equality in the workplace. LSD was sold even in Seattle. Dagmola found herself in a more radically different world than she could ever have imagined. Yet in the seventies, the first "serious" American students came knocking at the door, and finally Dagmola's family was able to open their first dharma center. Albeit the start was rough: they got broken into and robbed twice. Mysteriously, the robbers emptied the inhabitants' rooms but touched none of the precious objects on the shrine.

Dagmola has created a Tibetan oasis in the midst of modern-day America. Their monastery in Seattle—a converted church—is a bright yellow, three-storey building with dark red trim in a quiet, tree-lined residential street, on a corner lot. A white bell-shaped reliquary shrine (Skt. *stupa*) to the right of the entrance serves as a tribute to her uncle Dezhung Rinpoche who passed away in 1987. Thirty-two prayer wheels along the east side of Sakya Monastery carry the prayers of compassion across Seattle through anyone who sets these wheels in motion. Sculptures of deer flank the golden wheel above the entrance—a reminder of the historical Buddha's first turning of the wheel of teachings 2,500 years ago in the Deer Park near Varanasi, India. The huge teaching hall houses a bright golden, triple–life-sized Buddha statue. Bernardo Bertolucci filmed his Hollywood epic *The Little Buddha* in this elaborately painted shrine room. To the left of the monastery entrance, the American flag is raised; to the right, the Tibetan flag with the blue-and-red sunrise flutters on a high pole in the breeze.

"WILL WE EVER SEE IT AGAIN?"

Dagmola has undertaken the arduous journey back to her homeland three times, in 1986, 1996, and 2006. Until her first return in 1986 she had called America her second home. As with almost every native Tibetan, the hope that Tibet would improve and that she could return for good had never left her. But the changes she saw shocked her into a different mind-set. The first time she went by herself, sneaking in under the radar. When she returned for a second time in 1996 with Dagchen Rinpoche, David, his wife, and several other family members, the Chinese only granted them a visa on several conditions: They were not allowed to give teachings, donate presents, or accept gifts. They could not speak with their fellow countrymen unsupervised. "It was heart-wrenching," David says. "Often thousands of Tibetans would line up to see my father, but the Chinese would turn around the car and drive us somewhere else, not even allowing the Tibetans to get a glimpse. They denied us the trip to East Tibet altogether. As my father is getting on in years, he keeps saying, 'Will we ever see it again?'"

Mao Zedong's iron-fisted regime in the sixties turned Tibet into a living hell. Most of Dagmola's friends and family who had stayed behind died at the hands of the Chinese, including her mother and her aunt who perished in a Chinese prison in Lhasa. Dagmola admits that the memory of her mother's and aunt's fate still keeps her up at night. One purpose of Dagmola's visits to Tibet was to find out more about the circumstances of her relatives' deaths, but her requests fell on deaf ears. Her questions remained unanswered until she recently attended teachings by the Dalai

Lama in Pasadena, California. By pure coincidence, she sat next to a Tibetan nun who had happened to be incarcerated alongside Dagmola's mother near Lhasa, but got released and was able to smuggle some food to her mother afterward. Dagmola estimates—along with the Tibetan government-in-exile—that hundreds of thousands of Tibetans got killed through torture, forced labor, malnourishment, and starvation during these years. Many of them simply disappeared, without any trace. "We no longer have a home there. Even if Tibetans got freedom tomorrow, I don't think I would go back," says Dagmola. "Now America is our home."

REVIVING THE LINEAGE

In exile, Dagmola's greatest wish has not been fulfilled: all five of her sons have been recognized as high-ranking incarnations of Sakya masters, yet none wanted to adopt the traditional role. Her first-born, Manju Vajra, officially recognized as the incarnation of the previous head of the Sakya dynasty, insists on being called by the ordinary name David and chose as his surname the more Western-sounding name of his clan, Khon. He moved to Los Angeles, married a bright, high-powered lawyer, Carol Hamilton, and works as a financial executive for Sony Entertainment. In Tibet, the villagers carried him on their shoulders, built him a throne, and were moved to tears when the hand of the little boy touched their heads as a blessing. Back then, he was called "the precious one." Had Mao's minions not leveled almost all of the six thousand monasteries during the so-called Cultural Revolution, several of those monasteries would be his to guide.

The Tibetan community has criticized him harshly for abandoning his traditional role, but David articulates a very different perspective. He is an extremely pleasant, engaging man, fully embodying the Buddhist spirit. However, assuming his spiritual heritage "would have meant tearing the family apart, because I would have had to return to a monastery in India as a small boy to go through the traditional training." David remains unfazed. "After all we'd been through, the thought of splitting up was just unbearable."

Dagmola Sakya teaching together with her
thirteen-year-old grandson, Asanga Sakya Rinpoche.
Photo by Amy Gaskin. © Amy Gaskin

Yet the pressure of history was there. When David decided to marry
his American girlfriend, Dagmola objected. She attended the wedding,
but it took her years to come to terms with his life decisions. Turrell
Wylie, who had started the whole process of bringing the Tibetans to
America, wrote in a local magazine: "Ironically, the project killed part
of what it set out to preserve, for it is doubtful the Tibetans will even be
able to pass on much of their 1300-year-old cultural tradition to their
own children."[25]

This might be too pessimistic, for the tradition gets passed on after
all. Dagmola beams with joy as she talks about her ten grandchildren.
Several are ordained and intensively studying in Himalayan monaster-

ies. For the first time she went on a tour through California teaching side by side with her thirteen-year-old grandson, Asanga Sakya Rinpoche, who has just begun to give empowerments and impressively erudite lectures. "My aspiration for my grandchildren is to maintain the Sakya teachings," says Dagmola. "We are nonsectarian and respect all traditions, but it is important that they carry it on." Dagmola recently returned from visiting Dagchen Rinpoche's designated successor, her seventeen-year-old grandson Avi Krita, in the hills of Bir, North India. There, the charismatic teenager studies Buddhist philosophy at Dzongsar, a Buddhist institute led by the incarnation of Jamyang Khyentse Chökyi Lodrö, the famous master that Dagmola spent a year with in East Tibet. Thus, the lineages and friendships she encountered in Tibet now persevere with the next generation in exile. "It will continue," she says, "brighter and more vibrant than ever before."

Jetsunma Tenzin Palmo during a teaching tour in Europe.
Photo courtesy of Dongyu Gatsal Ling Nunnery

3: JETSUNMA TENZIN PALMO

(DIANE PERRY)

SANDPAPER FOR THE EGO

---

*Why a London librarian started a revolution from
a cave in the Himalayas*[1]

BRISK LIKE a whirlwind, Helena burst into the tiny Tibetan Café next door to the Dalai Lama's monastery in Dharamsala, North India. She threw her backpack onto a chair and couldn't wait to share the big news with her girlfriends. "I found my teacher!" she shouted excitedly, having just returned from a meditation weekend in a monastery on the hills above the mountain town. I couldn't help but eavesdrop on their conversation at the neighboring table while eating spoonfuls of spicy noodle soup during a short break from the Tibetan language classes I was taking in the winter of 1999. Meeting one's teacher is the one encounter every Tibetan Buddhist longs and prays for, as connecting with a realized master is considered essential for progressing on the path. Helena was raving about the kindness and eloquence of her newfound teacher, before she delivered the punch line. "And the best thing," she exclaimed, almost breathless, "it's a woman!"

A woman! The other girls cheered with glee, while I sat back wonderstruck. It was this chance encounter in that rundown noodle shop that sparked my journey for this book. Though I had studied Tibetan Buddhism for a couple of years, up to that point I had never met a female guru. Now I was intrigued by Helena's overflowing enthusiasm.

Being a reporter, my curiosity was piqued. Three days later I chartered a taxi to drive three hours north on the winding roads to the monastery where this teacher reportedly lived. I had wanted to travel to Tashi Jong anyway. It is not only the seat of the renowned Khamtrul Rinpoche* but also of the togdens, legendary yogis who let their hair grow without ever cutting it. Through an arduous training from a young age onwards, the yogis have gained a reputation for having superhuman powers. For instance, they are said to produce enormous heat through their breathing exercises—to such extent that they can dry wet clothes on their naked bodies in the snow, even in the middle of Himalayan winters.

The entire taxi ride I entertained doubts: Would my Tibetan be good enough to communicate with this teacher? Since she had no phone, I could not call ahead. I didn't know her age and envisioned a tiny, weathered, old lady like some of the elderly Tibetans who sit outside of the Dalai Lama's monastery, their hands working their prayer wheels, their creased faces beaming in the presence of their beloved leader.

I asked my way to her door, knocked, and she promptly opened. Two bright blue eyes sized me up with curiosity and warmth. Without even questioning who I was or what I wanted, she said in crisp British English: "Perfect timing. I just made lunch, enough for the two of us. Come on in!" Her slender figure disappeared into her tiny room, a grey enclave of bare concrete. She heaped vegetable rice onto two plastic plates while I tried to absorb my bewilderment. How could I possibly have known I was going to meet the daughter of a London fishmonger in the midst of the Himalayas?

For the first time, I encountered a Western woman who commanded the same presence as Tibetan incarnations. Tenzin Palmo has set an unprecedented example of following in the footsteps of the most dedicated Tibetan yogis, immersing herself so deeply in this tradition that she has earned the unabashed respect of traditional Asian teachers and modern Westerners alike. Only years later did I realize that I had met the most senior Western Tibetan Buddhist nun alive.

*Tashi Jong is currently the seat of the Ninth Khamtrul Rinpoche, Shedrub Nyima, who was born in India in 1980.

Nurturing the Flame

I found her easily accessible, and we talked for hours. She answered each question with humor and poise, piercing wisdom, and no-frills clarity. She shared her heartfelt aspiration: to build a nunnery solely dedicated to offering the nuns optimal opportunities to study, debate, and meditate—a privilege usually reserved for monks. Her teacher, the late Eighth Khamtrul Rinpoche,* made her promise to build such a nunnery, with a daunting ulterior motive: he wanted to revive the lineage of the *togdenmas*, the female yogis who had mastered the secret practices of the legendary Himalayan saints. With the lineage nearly eradicated after the Chinese takeover, only one master remained who still holds the transmission. "If we don't do something soon, it will be too late," Tenzin Palmo warned with a sense of urgency. "The practice has to be passed from person to person, like a flame. Once the flame goes out, that's it, you can't transmit it."[2] Today nothing is left of the togdenmas but rare snapshots. Tenzin Palmo proudly held up a tattered black-and-white photograph that showed a dozen weather-beaten ladies in sheepskin coats. Like their male counterparts, they never cut their hair, and a thick mane of Rastafarian dreadlocks frames their dark faces like oversized turbans.

What a stark contrast to Tenzin Palmo's own looks, her rusty-red robes and her freshly tonsured head! She has what I call "the X-ray gaze," a warm, deeply penetrating gaze that seems to cut through your shield. They are wisdom eyes, the eyes of someone who has ventured beyond our ordinary preoccupations. Tenzin Palmo certainly demonstrates the tenacity and strength worthy of the togdenmas' lineage. She spent twelve years of her life practicing just as one-pointedly as the togdenmas—in a cave in the Himalayas.

---

*The Eighth Khamtrul Rinpoche Dongyü Nyima (1931–1980) fled Tibet in 1958. After initially settling in West Bengal, he moved to Tashi Jong in Himachal Pradesh, North India, in 1969.

TWELVE YEARS IN THE CAVE

You can't even really call it a cave. A bare depression in the rocks, ten feet deep, with a stony overhang. Rough brick walls, covered with a layer of clay and cow dung, have been added to hold back snow and ice. The smoke from the woodstove painted the ceiling black. The tiny room hovers above a precipice on the mountain like an eagle's nest, easy prey to blizzards and avalanches. The earth drops vertically from the ledge into deep space, far down into the slim Lahoul Valley.* In Tibetan, the name for Lahoul means "Land of the Dakinis," another indication for Tenzin Palmo that no location could have been more fitting. On the other side of the valley, the Himalayas hold on to the horizon as if to keep the enormous sky from taking off. The thin air makes even the most seasoned trekker gasp, and the cold drops to minus forty degrees in winter. This is where Tenzin Palmo took up residence on a precipice at 13,200 feet. She was thirty-three years old when she first climbed the steep, overgrown path to the cave and forty-five when she left.

A box served as a table, a ledge in the wall held the books, while the Buddha of Compassion watched over her on a poster to her left. "Very cozy," says Tenzin Palmo about her cave. "I was very happy there and had everything I needed." Happy, maybe. Hard not to believe her when she says it so confidently, with a wide ear-to-ear smile. But cozy? A cave with no electric light, no running water? Not to speak of occasional treats like a hot bath, a chat with a dear friend, or a steamy espresso. And she did not even have a bed! She spent the nights sitting upright in her wooden meditation box, little more than two feet by two feet wide, slightly raised to prevent the moisture from creeping up.

Retreat is not for the lazy. Every morning she got up at three o'clock, practiced for three hours, made herself a cup of tea on her woodstove, ate some barley flour for breakfast, then embarked on the next three-hour meditation session, and so on. Her days were attuned to the clock. Between sessions, there was water to fetch at the nearby spring, snow

---

*It lies between Manali and Ladakh, geographically an Indian border region, but the culture and religion are Tibetan.

JETSUNMA TENZIN PALMO — 73

to melt, wood to chop. She ate only lunch, no dinner, and each day the same dish was on the menu: rice and lentils, sometimes with vegetables. In order not to waste this precious lifetime with unnecessary hours of unconscious sleep, she slept a mere three hours, sitting upright in her box. This is how the most dedicated spiritual virtuosi throughout the centuries have practiced.

SUBMERGED IN THE BLIZZARD

At first Tenzin Palmo used the summers to go to the monastery to receive teachings, stock up on food supplies, visit her teacher, and prepare for the winter when the snow would completely cut her off. But after nine years, her teacher suddenly passed away, prompting her to immerse herself in a long, strict retreat—three years in complete solitude.

One year a huge blizzard raged for seven days and nights. The villagers didn't think this crazy cavewoman could have survived. The snow smothered her door, window, and the whole cave in complete blackness. "This is it," she thought, turning to her final prayers. Then she heard the voice of her teacher. Tenzin Palmo imitates him with eye-rolling ostentation: "Oh, come on, just dig!" Luckily, a seasoned local builder had insisted that the door must open to the inside. She used a saucepan lid and dug a tunnel, filling the cave with the snow. She had to repeat this three times before the blizzard subsided. "The Tibetans have a saying: 'If you're sick, you're sick; if you die, you die.' We're all going to die and where better to die than in retreat?" She speaks matter-of-factly and quotes Harry Potter's wizard-mentor Albus Dumbledore: "To the well-organized mind, death is but the next great adventure." She strongly emphasizes the "well-organized" mind, for "otherwise it could be a great terror rather than a great adventure."

She was the first Western woman ever to dedicate her life in the total seclusion of the Himalayas to organize her mind for the greatest fruition a human life could possibly bloom into: enlightenment. "We are on this earth to realize our own nature and innate potential," she says, utterly pragmatic. "I wasn't trying to break any records. I didn't have a fixed set of years in mind when I went into retreat. I just couldn't think of a better place to be. And I really *like* being on my own." Tenzin Palmo is as talkative and amiable as the girl from Bethnal Green at five-o'clock tea—not really what one expects from a hermit who spent more than a decade hardly talking at all. Isn't the retreat to a lonely cave an escape from the challenges of modern life? "For me the worldly life is escape," she replies with sudden vigor. "When you have a problem, you can turn on the TV, call a friend, or make yourself a nice cup of coffee. In the cave you can only turn to yourself. In winter, you can't even go for a walk."[3] Tenzin Palmo had always thought of herself as not very capable. "I quickly turned to others for help and advice."[4] Alone in the Himalayas, she learned to rely on herself—to repair mud walls, chop wood, and most of all, get an intimate look at her own mind. "In the cave you have to face your raw nature as it is. You just have to sit there and find your way with it!"[5]

In *Reflections on a Mountain Lake*, she writes:

> There was an infinite amount of time without external distractions just to see how the mind functions, how thoughts and emotions arise, how we identify with them, how to disidentify with them and to resolve all the thoughts and emotions back into spaciousness. I was very fortunate to have the opportunity to do this. I look back upon that time as one of the greatest learning periods of my life.[6]

"The Sanctuary of the Genuine Lineage"

Twelve years after our first meeting, I am only too happy to find her sitting in her light-filled attic in Himachal Pradesh in North India. The arched windows give way to a beautiful view over sprawling rice paddies in the valley below, dotted with the first buildings and shrine rooms of her own nunnery, Dongyü Gatsal Ling, "Sanctuary of the Genuine Lineage." She is living her dream. The huge three-storey temple is still bare concrete, soon to be painted. Tenzin Palmo is eager to show me the recent progress. The white snow caps of the Himalayas gleam behind her in the pink sunset as her frail frame carefully negotiates heaps of concrete and rubble. The hammering and banging of the Indian workers drown out some of her words. She points to imaginary shrine rooms to describe where the statue of Manjushri, the Buddha of Wisdom, and his colleagues will live. Her voice builds a lively, flourishing nunnery into the sunset, brimming with smart, devoted nuns engaged in debate and prayer. Already, seventy-five of "her" nuns sit cross-legged on the surrounding rocks like orange and red birds, their shawls spread out like wings, loudly reciting their study texts in high-pitched voices. They are urgently trying to memorize them before the next class, because their study courses are rigorous. "Even Tibetan masters are beginning to realize, if you want real devotion and focus, you have to look to the nuns," Tenzin Palmo says proudly. "I tell my girls, now you are given all the opportunities, you can accomplish whatever you want, just like the lamas!"

Tenzin Palmo barks orders to an Indian worker, stops to inquire in a heartfelt tone about the health of one of her employees, then shoos away a teenage nun who recites her text at the top of her voice within earshot of the nuns' three-year retreat center. "Sweetheart," she approaches the round-cheeked girl, then switches effortlessly into rapid-fire Tibetan to explain that the nuns in retreat might be distracted by her recitation.

Why are no Westerners among the nuns—did maybe none apply? Tenzin Palmo doesn't hesitate: "I don't accept Westerners, only girls with Tibetan origins, because most of my nuns are simple village girls. Western nuns are almost always highly educated, so they just come in, know everything better, and run the show." I chuckle at the irony of hearing this from her, the London librarian turned abbess, but she does not seem to notice the contradiction. "Usually a nunnery would be run by a monk or a lama," she explains. "They wouldn't let the nuns run their own show. That's all right on one level, on the other hand it doesn't help them mature where they are supposed to be growing up instead of behaving like little girls waiting to be told what to do." She is eager to clarify that she does not accept students of her own. She does give refuge vows and teaches her nuns, but she insists repeatedly that she is just an ordinary person and that there is really nothing interesting or special about her. She's dead serious. Of course, most of us who fidget

Jetsunma Tenzin Palmo with her nuns.
Photo courtesy of Dongyu Gatsal Ling Nunnery

uneasily on our soft meditation cushions in our centrally heated apartments for the brief time that we manage to strike the pose would have left her cave with chilblains after the first night.

ELVIS PRESLEY AND STILETTOS

Nothing, not the tiniest detail in Tenzin Palmo's early years hinted at her later accomplishments. When Diane Perry was born in 1943 under the carpet bombing of Hitler's drones, the doctors predicted a short life. She entered this world with an inwardly curved spine. Severe meningitis infections almost robbed the life of the sickly girl before she could even walk. Her father died when she was only two years old, leaving her mother to raise Diane and her older brother, Mervyn, on the meager earnings from the fish shop. "My mother was a spiritualist, and we had séances in our house once a week, with tables flying around the room," Tenzin Palmo recalls. "We often discussed death, not out of fear, but as a subject of interest. This is a very Buddhist thought, as an awareness of death gives great meaning to life." The doctors advised her to choose an entirely unchallenging career—the bland routine of a low-key librarian seemed just about right.

Despite her constant physical pain, photos show a charismatic teen-ager with a blond mane of curls, an avid Elvis Presley fan in petticoats and stilettos, courted by a host of admirers. Inexplicably, the inkling that she was in the wrong place haunted her. She asked her mother to take her to Chinese restaurants so that she could surround herself with Asian faces. She felt a curious fascination with nuns, no matter which denomination. When asked what she wanted to become, Diane used to say assertively, "a nun," without knowing anything at all about what that actually meant. She instinctively felt that everybody was innately perfect—a core Buddhist belief—and "that we are here to discover who we really are."

How do we live up to our perfection? This question tormented her. She studied the scriptures from the world's greatest religions, the Bible, the Koran, and the Upanishads; she asked teachers and priests, even the spirit guides at her mother's séances, but nobody and no book gave her a satisfying answer. "Everybody said things like, 'You have to be good,' but even as a small child, I always knew that this wasn't it. Of course you have to be good. I knew people who were very good and kind but nonetheless not perfect. Being kind was the foundation, but there had to be something more." Diane Perry never felt a very deep connection with Jesus. "I wasn't very theistically inclined. I didn't believe anybody up there was pulling the strings. Only we can save ourselves. You have to discover your own innate sparks of the divine."[7]

Unknowingly, Diane Perry resorted to beliefs she would later recog-nize as pivotal Buddhist views. She stumbled upon her first Buddhist book in a library at eighteen. She still remembers the title: *The Mind Unshaken*, written by a British journalist. She was captivated when she read about the Buddha's teachings, such as the four noble truths* or

---

*The four noble truths are important principles in Buddhism and believed to be the very first teaching of the historic Buddha Shakyamuni. The first noble truth is the truth of suffering, pointing to the suffering of birth, old age, sickness, and death that everybody undergoes. The truth of the origin of suffering includes ignorance and craving, which leads to imprisonment in the cycle of existence. The truth of cessation of suffering reveals the possibility of overcoming ignorance and craving by following the truth of the path.

the eightfold path.* Someone had put on paper the very ideas she had entertained all along! She was only halfway through the book when she turned to her mother and announced: "I'm a Buddhist." Unshaken by the confident declaration, her mother replied calmly, "That's nice, dear." Infected by her daughter's zest, her mother became a Buddhist six months later. Reading about the Buddhist ideal of renunciation, Diane Perry gave away her fashionable clothes and stitched her own version of Buddhist robes, "sort of a yellow Greek tunic, which I wore with black stockings," she says with a laugh. She had not actually met any Buddhist teacher and was conjuring up her own version from the books. She wanted to be like the Buddha, or rather, how she imagined him to be: an austere mendicant draped in yellow cloth. When she finally attended her first gathering at the Buddhist Society in London, she was shocked to find that the other Buddhist women there showed up in makeup and high heels![8]

Tibetan Buddhism in postwar Britain was largely unknown. The few crumbs of knowledge that had been dispersed on the island were dismissed as shamanistic make-believe. The kind of Buddhism available to her at the time was Theravada, the fundamental vehicle.† The simplicity, clarity, and logic of these teachings spoke to her. "A Tibetan Buddhist was the last thing I wanted to be," says Tenzin Palmo. Yet in a general book on Buddhism she came across a description of the four traditions of Tibetan Buddhism: Nyingma, Sakya, Kagyü, and Gelug. A shy inner voice popped up: "You're Kagyü."

The first Tibetan teachers were just finding their way into exile in England, among them the later-famous Chögyam Trungpa Rinpoche. He had been an enormously renowned teacher in Tibet, but with no eager audience for his teachings in exile, he begged Diane Perry to allow

---

*Right view, right intention, right speech, right action, right livelihood, right effort, right mindfulness, and right concentration.
†*Theravada* (Pali) means "ancient teachings." This relatively conservative Buddhist tradition is close to the earliest Buddhism and widely practiced in Southeast Asia. Tibetans believe that it belongs to the fundamental vehicle (Skt. *Hinayana*) that forms the foundation of the path, whereas they consider their own tradition to be part of the great vehicle (Skt. *Mahayana*), which they believe to have a greater vision and skillful means that also yield greater accomplishments.

him to teach her meditation. The instructions hit home. For the first time, she got a taste of what it means "to stop the unrelenting chatter of mind."

Trungpa Rinpoche's unconventional behavior did not put her off. Although still wearing monastic robes, he tried to seduce the nineteen-year-old seeker. When his hand wandered up her skirt, Tenzin Palmo neither got upset nor walked out. She simply dug her stiletto heels firmly into his bare foot. She laughs when she recalls their unusual meditation sessions and confesses that she would have been curious about a sexual relationship with him, if only he hadn't presented himself as a pure, celibate monk.[9]

Diane Perry read everything Buddhist she could get her hands on. She did not fail to notice "that there is never any mention of nuns, only monks. I found this depressing." Then she heard about a Kagyü nunnery in exile, "probably the only Buddhist nunnery in India at the time." Freda Bedi (1911–1977), a now-legendary Englishwoman, had started it along with a school for Tibetan refugee masters. Years earlier, Bedi had married an Indian whom she had met at Oxford University. She was imprisoned by the British along with her three children (and Mahatma Gandhi) because Bedi sided with the Indians in their demand for freedom. After her release, she worked for the Indian government until the Prime Minister, Jawaharlal Nehru, enlisted her help to receive the stream of Tibetan refugees that was pouring over the border. Many Tibetan masters say that when they came across the mountain passes, exhausted, penniless, and with frozen limbs, Freda Bedi was there to greet them with a hot bowl of soup and a bed.

It took until February 1964 for the twenty-year-old Diane Perry to save the ninety pounds for a ship passage to India from her weekly library salary (nine pounds). She left an uncounted number of broken hearts and exchanged a place in her mom's cozy apartment for an icy room in North India. The rats dropped through the broken roof along with the rain. But none of that mattered. What mattered was that the "Young Lamas' Home School" was just around the corner. She felt at home for the first time in her life, surrounded by strangely familiar-looking faces. She met the young Dalai Lama, many charismatic little tulkus—and the man who would turn her life upside down: Khamtrul Rinpoche.

THE BEST BIRTHDAY PRESENT EVER

On her twenty-first birthday, the phone rang. Her friend Freda Bedi answered, then turned to her. "Your best birthday present has just arrived."[10] Khamtrul Rinpoche was at the bus station. Tenzin Palmo had never met him, did not know if he was old or young, fat or thin, for she had never even seen his picture.[11] But she did know her teacher had come. The recognition happens differently for everybody, but for her, it was like a mega-earthquake—even if you have never encountered one, you can't miss the signs. When she was led into his room to greet him, she did not even dare to look up. She just stared at his brown shoes for several minutes, until she mustered the courage to raise her eyes: "It was like seeing somebody I knew very well that I hadn't seen for a long time, a deep moment of recognition. At the same time it was like the very deepest part of my being had suddenly taken an external form."[12]

Wasting no time, she asked him to give her refuge vows, the formal entranceway to becoming a Buddhist. Only days afterwards she requested him to ordain her. "I was looking for perfection. I knew that Tibetan Buddhism offered not only the most stainless description of that state but the clearest path to reach it. When one wants to follow that path, one needs the least distractions possible."[13] Three weeks later, she became a nun—the second Western woman ever to do so after Freda Bedi,* long before most people in the West had even heard of the existence of Tibetan Buddhism.

What looked like a hasty, impulsive step was only too logical, if not inevitable, for Tenzin Palmo. "It was the greatest blessing of my life," she says, and she adds with an amiable twinkle: "As a nun you never need to worry about the right hairdo or which colors are in style." Although she'd had boyfriends and an intense love affair with a young Japanese man before her full ordination, she never wanted to marry and never

*Tibetans know her by her ordination name, Khechok Palmo.

felt the urge to have babies. "Clothes, who cares? Food, who cares? Television, I'm glad not to have to watch. As for sex—I couldn't care less. In this society, sex is constantly thrown in your face but to make it the be-all and end-all of life is pathetic; it puts you on the same level as the monkeys. Many women leading fulfilling lives don't even think about it. I don't need or want a one-on-one personal relationship. That's why I don't get lonely."[14]

THE YOGI IN THE CLOTH PAINTING

Diane Perry became Drubgyü Tenzin Palmo, "the Glorious Holder of the Practice Lineage." After all these years, she suddenly understood why she had always felt in the wrong place in England. A cloth painting in Khamtrul Rinpoche's temple shows a yogi with piercing blue eyes above a curiously long sharp nose like hers.[15] The yogi had been an old acquaintance of the Khamtrul Rinpoches for many lifetimes. The figure bears such an uncanny resemblance to Tenzin Palmo, Khamtrul Rinpoche and his monks recognized her immediately. There is not a speck of doubt in Tenzin Palmo's mind too that she merely picked up the thread where she left off in her last lifetime. The Buddhist belief in reincarnation has long become a firm conviction for her. "Rinpoche said to me, 'In previous lives I was able to keep you close. But in this lifetime you have taken female form, so it is very difficult.'"[16] She believes that she has been a monk and yogi, and Khamtrul Rinpoche's personal attendant in previous incarnations. In the light of this background, her homesickness for Asia as a young girl in London, her determination never to get married, and her longing for the cave all seemed perfectly reasonable.

She moved to Khamtrul Rinpoche's monastery in exile in Dalhousie, North India, became his personal secretary, and taught English to the little monks. Her life appeared to have reached its peak. Yet in reality Tenzin Palmo was about to enter the most forlorn phase of her life. For six years she lived among eighty monks as the only woman, the only nun, the only Westerner—completely isolated. She barely spoke their language, belonging neither to the laypeople nor the monks. "I could not live with them, I could not eat with them, I could not study with them." What is worse, she was not allowed to join the teachings and receive the practices she was longing for. In the Tibetan tradition, where nuns pray daily for rebirth in a glorious male body, Tenzin Palmo did not have equal access. Male Western visitors were waved right in and given the teachings that she hungered for, she recalls, her voice still ringing with the frustration of that time. "I felt totally excluded," she says, "as if there was this huge banquet of Buddhist thought and practice and I'd get little crumbs, but never quite enough to make a meal."

THE VOW TO BECOME A FEMALE BUDDHA

Khamtrul Rinpoche kept her close, but even he couldn't dismiss centuries of patriarchal tradition. While the monks excelled in their study at the monastic university, competed in debate, and showed off elaborate dances, the nuns were banished to a remote nunnery without teachers and libraries, confined to performing simple rituals without knowing their meaning. The monks kindly prayed for Tenzin Palmo to meet the good fortune to be reborn in a male form, so that she could participate in the monastery in her next life. Tenzin Palmo cried herself to sleep every night. She was lonely, frustrated, angry—and bent on showing the chauvinists that women are equally equipped to follow the spiritual path. She made a pledge that continues to inspire women everywhere in the world. "I took the vow to attain enlightenment in a female body—no matter how many lifetimes it may take." This means nothing less than the aspiration to become a female buddha. Whether that is even possible, (male) Buddhist scholars debate to this day, as some hold the female body to be unfit buddha material. But spurred by her frustration, Tenzin Palmo researched the matter and now confidently quotes the Buddha himself. "The Buddha said that women can attain enlightenment! He was much more open-minded than modern-day lamas." Utterly determined, she set off to Ladakh, to her cave in the ice. She knew full well that solitude is the most potent catalyst for attaining realization. Immersing oneself in stillness allows for wisdom to emerge from beneath the layers of busyness and distraction.

Yet she also learned a lesson about caution from her accomplished yogi-friends, the togdens. When someone asks about her realization, she just says, "Nothing," because compared to the Buddha's realization, it is dwarfed.[17] People always want to know what she got out of being in the cave, but she thinks this question "is totally irrelevant. It's not like you're doing a PhD, and at the end you receive a diploma, and all the buddhas and bodhisattvas of the ten directions applaud you." Everything in life, she says, is a journey of discovery and so is being in the cave. "It is not about what you gain but what you lose. The idea that there is somewhere to get to and something to attain is delusion. The more you realize, the more you realize there is nothing to realize." In daily life, she explains, we hide behind our roles and activities, as father or mother, teacher or painter, male or female. "When you are on your own, there are no roles to play, and one can uncover deeper and deeper layers of consciousness, like peeling the layers of an onion. For me, retreat is like breathing; it is what I was born to do." Retreat works like a pressure cooker—the heart softens fast. The meditation instructions she now passes on to her nuns reveal that she does indeed have most profound insight: "The whole point of meditation is to learn how to wake up, to develop greater clarity, to be more aware and absolutely in the moment. It is to be conscious in the moment without all our usual projections, opinions, ideas, and mental chatter going on. In meditation, we try to understand the mind and to become ever more conscious, ever more aware, ever more awake."[18]

MOZART AND TIRAMISU

Nobody can fake the qualities of a true practitioner, no matter how holy they talk. It is an inner radiance and luminosity that give away the qualities of genuine spiritual accomplishment—the uncanny ability not to be rattled by anything, no matter how unforeseen. In Tenzin Palmo's case, the last thing she expected in her cave was a loud bang on the wooden door. An Indian policeman barged in, completely disregarding the traditional custom not to disturb a hermit in retreat. He abruptly handed her a notice, signed by the superintendent. Even world-class

Jetsun Tenzin Palmo drying her possessions in front of her cave.
Photo courtesy of Dongyu Gatsal Ling Nunnery

meditators are subject to visa regulations, and she had been exceeding the limits of her visa for several years. She was charged as an illegal immigrant, ordered to come down the mountain within twenty-four hours, and promptly expelled.

Now, what? Tenzin Palmo met the new turn of fate with surprising aplomb. She neither got upset nor wept about the broken retreat, yet she was not really prepared to leave India, after having lived there for twenty-four years. She had aspired to just spend the rest of her life in retreat. Her mother had long since passed away, therefore she had no reason to return to London. A friend's invitation to come to Italy sounded appealing. So, suddenly the cavewoman found herself in the street cafés of Assisi. After all these years of single-minded seclusion, her Asian asceticism fused with the savoir vivre of the West. Much to her own surprise, she reconnected with her Christian roots, enjoyed sitting in the cave of Saint Francis, and she fell in love with Mozart, cappuccino, and tiramisu. Italy seems just a logical step after India, she jokes.

"The bureaucracy, the postal system, the general nothing-quite-works environment; I immediately felt very much at home."

The first invitations to teach and speak at conferences trickled in, with more and more nuns of various denominations seeking her out for guidance. She was faced with a huge decision: Should she continue a life in solitude, or fill her schedule with speaking engagements? Remembering Khamtrul Rinpoche's wish for her to build a nunnery, she consulted an astrologer. He foretold that retreat would be very harmonious and peaceful, whereas starting a nunnery would bring many problems, conflicts, and difficulties. He then concluded, "Both are good! So you decide." For Tenzin Palmo, the result was obvious: "Back into retreat!" But when she mentioned her predicament to a Catholic priest, he advised, "Of course you start a nunnery. What's the use of always being in a peaceful, pleasant situation? We are like rough pieces of wood, and if we are always stroking ourselves with silk and velvet, that's very nice, but it doesn't make us smooth. To become smooth, we need sandpaper."

And sandpaper it is. With the same untiring energy and vividness that kept her persevering in the cave, she started fundraising. Soon the word got out, and invitations trickled in from all over the globe: Europe, Australia, the United States, Asia. She sometimes finds herself the only female keynote speaker at international Buddhist conferences, and with her uncompromising charm, she points it out. "This is basically a boys' club with the girls doing all the work. The big guys are all guys."

A FEMALE DALAI LAMA

Does she ever long to return to the quietude of her cave? She recently went back for the first time in more than twenty years, on a pilgrimage together with thirty students and donors who were able to afford the $15,000 price tag for the trip. Tenzin Palmo rolls her eyes skyward, sighs with audible exasperation, and murmurs, almost as if presenting an excuse: "It's only because they made me do it!" She insists that the only reason she returned was the prospect of setting up a fund for her beloved nunnery.

Was she not excited about returning to the most important place of her life? "It's a thing of the past." She brushes away any trace of nostalgia. Yet when the pilgrims had all made it up to the cave after a four-hour trek along narrow ledges with big drops down the mountainside,[19] Tenzin Palmo could not help but feel moved. Just as she was sharing her memories of the cave, the head of the village turned up to promise that the cave with its broken roof would be restored to its original condition. A nun, Ani Kalden, has recently moved in to embark on a solitary retreat and emulate Tenzin Palmo's feat. But Tenzin Palmo leaves no doubt she won't return for another retreat there. She points to the small apartment that is being built on the top floor of her new temple. "The nuns think I should do retreat *here*," she says. The attic would be fitting: right in the middle of her nuns and on top of everything, yet removed, hovering above like the mother eagle. "This whole venture here is taking much longer than we anticipated," she says, looking out on the construction site. "Honestly, who knows what is happening in the next moment? I can't think of anything I could do with my life except going back into retreat. But who knows—by that time I could be blind and crippled. If I am mentally and physically capable when all this is over, when the nuns can run the nunnery themselves and have the confidence to take it over, then I would like to go into retreat."

The nunnery is her inspiration now, her raison d'être: giving the nuns all the opportunities she did not have, turning these bright young truth-seekers into true spiritual powerhouses. Tenzin Palmo learned from her lonely years at Khamtrul Rinpoche's monastery that knowledge is key. In her nunnery, the nuns study every day. Not only are they taught by a senior khenpo, but Tenzin Palmo also recruited two senior nuns from a monastery in South India, so that they have role models. "When I ask the nuns if men are more intelligent than women, they say, 'Yes.' 'Oh *no*,' I say, 'they are not more intelligent, you just think so because they get better education. You can do everything they do.'"

While she carefully maneuvers through piles of concrete, sand, and bricks, she moves toward a female statue. Tenzin Palmo lifts the red cloth that covers the statue's eyes. Who is this? Mahaprajapati, the Buddha's foster mother and the first woman he ordained. He denied her request to become a wandering renunciant three times. She and five hundred like-minded women had to shave their heads and walk 350 miles barefoot to show their unwavering determination, before the Buddha finally granted their request—a revolutionary decision at the time. Apart from the Jains, the Buddha's order was the first in Asia to formally allow women in its ranks. One hardly ever sees a statue of Mahaprajapati in a "normal" monastery, but here in the nunnery, femininity abounds: a flaming red Vajrayogini raises a blood-filled skull to her chest, her breasts and vagina bared in a fiery dance. Next to Buddha Shakyamuni, the peaceful green Tara stretches out her palm to grant protection. As in all religions, a certain form of femininity has always been idealized in Buddhism too. But Tenzin Palmo intends to take the colorful images of female deities as blueprints for helping living yoginis emerge: "The Buddha himself was very open-minded, then the community became more hierarchical and patriarchal." To make her point, she recalls her recent trip to Bhutan, now the only country in the world where Tibetan Buddhism is intact as the state religion. "The monasteries of our tradition are completely supported and maintained by the Royal Family; the monks all have very good conditions there," she attests, pauses, and delivers the punch line, "but the nuns get nothing. Their nunneries are often far away in the mountains, which makes it difficult for them to get provisions. They have run-down, remote buildings, not enough to eat and, of course, no education. When I asked them what they wanted most, they did not say food or a temple, they said, 'Knowledge!' And it is the same in Cambodia, India, and in most other Buddhist monasteries around the world. That's why there are no female Dalai Lamas, no impressive dharma queens, and hardly any biographies of exemplary female saints."

THE ORDINATION CONTROVERSY

Everything in Tenzin Palmo's neat, sunny nunnery is geared toward boosting the nuns' knowledge along with their self-confidence. "The mother of all the buddhas, the Perfection of Wisdom, is female," Tenzin Palmo emphasizes. "So don't think women are intellectually inferior.

But the big problem in all the nunneries is lack of self-confidence, lack of self-esteem. The aim is to help the nuns to gain a sense of healthy self-esteem and the feeling that they can really do anything now. They don't need someone to tell them what to do. Before, they weren't given the opportunity, but now they are, and if they make use of all of this, they can definitely in the future become not only accomplished themselves but also teach others." Some of the nuns have studied for twelve or eighteen years and acquired just the same proficiency in philosophy as their male counterparts. "But no matter how learned they are," Tenzin Palmo complains, "they cannot get the title of *khenpo* or *geshe*," the Tibetan equivalents of doctors and professors. They can only be called nuns. Because they cannot take full ordination, they are not allowed to study the full curriculum with the entire monastic codex.

In 1973, Tenzin Palmo's long-term sponsor, the author John Blofeld, offered her a plane ticket to Hong Kong. Dressed in the traditional all-black Chinese robes, she was probably the first Western woman after Freda Bedi to become fully ordained. Three prominent round burn marks just above the hairline still show where the incense cones burned down on her freshly tonsured scalp.

A full-fledged discussion is underway about the position of Buddhist nuns. To this day female monastics in the Tibetan tradition have to obey ninety-eight more precepts than the monks, including the rules that they have to obey the monks, can't give them advice, and even the most senior nun still has to take a lower seat than the greenest rookie monk. Tenzin Palmo seriously doubts that these extra precepts were really taught by the Buddha, and her research leads her to believe that they were added by later patriarchs to reflect the dominant views about females at that time. What started out as the most revolutionary welcome to women at the Buddha's time has turned into a misogynistic saga. "It's just time they get their act together!" Tenzin Palmo says pointedly about the male lamas. "Give the nuns their full ordination!"

But make no mistake, Tenzin Palmo does not side with outraged feminists. "People get so worked up about feminism and women's rights," she says. "We've all been male and female in many lifetimes, like actors taking on different roles. The Buddha's mind is neither inherently female nor male."[20] Righteous indignation is foreign to her, and she walks a fine line of speaking out candidly against the patriarchs while holding her teachers in the highest respect. She introduced her nuns to His Holiness the Dalai Lama in Dharamsala and begged him in person to weigh in on the subject. He greeted her with a big bear hug and tenderly stroked her chin. Tenzin Palmo watched, her eyes welling up, as her nuns filed before him one by one to receive his blessings. Although he is supportive of her mission, he points out that he is not an autocratic leader and cannot simply dictate change. When he suggested an international conference to discuss the matter, she respectfully demanded more action on his part. "With all due respect, Your Holiness, we've been talking for years! How much progress have we made? Honestly, Your Holiness, you're not a female, you cannot imagine the denigration!" "Buddhists always talk about change," she muttered after their meeting, and shrugged her shoulders, "but like anybody else they don't like to change at all."[21]

The Dalai Lama also welcomes a vision of having well-qualified abbesses in the nunneries instead of the male abbots that are the norm today. "Then, if a female lama passes away and she's been a good scholar and practitioner, it is quite possible that the reincarnation will be a female, too. So, I think, that in the twenty-second century, there will be more female reincarnations at female institutions. Then there'll be competition between male lama institutions and female lama institutions." While resounding with his signature deep belly laughter, he adds, "It'll be a positive sort of competition!"

ACKNOWLEDGING HER SPIRITUAL MASTERY

Of course, the men got a couple of centuries' head start. His Holiness the Gyalwa Drukpa (b. 1963), head of the Drukpa Kagyü lineage, finally decided to take an unprecedented step. "He is extremely enthusiastic about nuns and supports women wherever he can," Tenzin Palmo says proudly. "In fact, one time he wrote me the nuns are the reason he's living. He actually lives in his nunnery, not in his monastery." On his birthday, in February 2008, he enthroned Tenzin Palmo in his own nunnery in Kathmandu, Nepal, and gave her—a historic first in his lineage—the highest title the Tibetan Buddhist tradition can accord a female practitioner: *Jetsunma* means "Venerable Master," or, as the Gyalwa Drukpa explained, "*Je* stands for her accomplishments as a yogini, and *tsun* for her accomplishments as a nun. It is for the sake of the female practitioners who have been neglected for a long time, for hundreds of years. Now it is time to have a revolution through Jetsunma's kind example of spiritual mastery."[22]

One hundred and fifty nuns, many with tears in their eyes, filed in procession before her, offering her white silk scarfs, golden mandala plates, and statues. The Gyalwa Drukpa even handed her the traditional red Drukpa Kagyü hat. After a few seconds of amazement and disbelief, Tenzin Palmo broke into laughter, putting the hat on her head, her whole face one big grin. The nunnery might be sandpaper for her, but she is also sandpaper for the monasteries.

Sangye Khandro at Tashi Chöling in Oregon.
Photo by David Gordon. © David Gordon

4: SANGYE KHANDRO

(NANCI GAY GUSTAFSON)

ENLIGHTENMENT IS A FULL-TIME JOB

A candid interview with one of the most prolific
Western Tibetan translators

SANGYE KHANDRO has translated and mastered some of the most profound Buddhist teachings. In her late fifties, she is strikingly beautiful by any definition, but you will likely first notice her vibrant, spacious blue eyes. Despite her long-limbed figure and her cascading blond hair, she comfortably blends in with the Tibetans as she usually dons their traditional, ankle-length dress. Many times I have heard her translate some of the most complex topics from the Tibetan language with a seemingly effortless grace. One of her renowned translator colleagues says she might be the Western woman who has received more teachings and transmissions than anybody else. She lives on the beautiful 100 acres of Tashi Chöling, a retreat and teaching center in the mountains near Ashland, Oregon, that she founded together with her husband and teacher, Gyatrul Rinpoche.* She has translated for the finest Tibetan teachers, including Dudjom Rinpoche, Thinley Norbu Rinpoche, Penor Rinpoche, and Khenpo Namdrol Rinpoche. Despite receiving many invitations, she rarely agrees to teach, preferring a reclusive lifestyle focusing on translations and retreats. Together with her partner, Lama Chönam, she has founded the translation committee

---

*Gyatrul Rinpoche (b. 1924) escaped Tibet in 1959. Since 1972 he has lived in America, where he has established several Buddhist centers.

Light of Berotsana. Among her many published translations is the biography of Mandarava,[1] the Indian consort of Padmasambhava who is credited with establishing Vajrayana Buddhism in Tibet.[2]

MH: How did your journey start?

SK: I had just finished my sophomore year in college in 1972. Quite disillusioned with the education system, I wanted to learn more about the world. Visiting my parents in Hawaii, I ran into this man, Jessie Sartain, who had just returned from meeting the Dalai Lama in Dharamsala, a former British hill station in North India where thousands of Tibetan refugees had settled to be near His Holiness and never left. He told me the most inspiring stories about his experience. Much to my parents' horror, Jessie said, "I will take you there to meet the Dalai Lama. Let's go." We went around the world, the cheap way.

MH: Overland?

SK: Hitchhiking. It took us five months. We ran into the war between India and Pakistan, so we had to go back to Iran, wait a month, and then use the rest of our resources to fly to Delhi. We were dirt poor. We arrived in Dharamsala at the end of November when it was absolutely freezing. We set up our quarters in a little makeshift shack. Although we were suffering on the material plane I was completely overwhelmed and amazed on the spiritual plane.

MH: Were you religious?

SK: I was raised a Mormon and was actually quite religious. That was one of the catapults for my search. As I grew older and started to ask questions, the answers I got were not satisfactory. So I knew this wasn't really my path.

MH: What kind of questions did you have?

SK: For example, I wanted to know why there were no black people at our church. I was given a ridiculously racist answer that really upset me.

MH: Where did you grow up?

SK: I am originally from Oregon. My dad worked for Kodak as a professional photographer and he was often transferred. We lived in Salt Lake City, Chicago, Portland, and Hawaii. We were uprooted a lot as children, which was hard but also fostered a more open mind. I really just had a regular middle-class American upbringing with a very loving, stay-home mom.

MH: Quite amazing that a college girl from Oregon would travel all the way to India just because someone had told her some stories.

SK: There was a force in me, and my whole life changed. Who I was before was almost like a past lifetime. It became difficult later on to bridge the gap, especially with relatives.

AGAINST ALL ODDS

MH: One of the most inspiring aspects of the lives of the teachers I have been interviewing is that all followed their intuition against all odds. I meet so many people who are dissatisfied and looking for deeper meaning, but they don't have the courage to venture out and leave their comfort zone.

SK: When you're younger, there is a certain ability to be rather fearless. Flying off to India, by myself, with no money, would I do that now? I don't know. Something woke up within me, and the time was ripe for that.

MH: In Dharamsala, did you know immediately that you wanted to learn the language and become a translator?

SK: No, that came a few years later. Initially it was for selfish reasons, so that I could talk to my teachers directly, read my practice in Tibetan, and learn the chanting.

MH: How did you support yourself?

SK: I borrowed money from my parents. I also sold a sugarcane field in Hawaii that I owned. I would barely get by. We lived on Indian sweets, chai, and chapattis—a really bad diet. I was a vegetarian. I got sick many times, twice with hepatitis; the second time I almost died. But I have no regrets.

MH: How did your parents react?

SK: In the beginning, they thought it was a fad that would pass. As time went on, they had all these concerns that parents have, like "Isn't she going to get married and lead a normal life?" Yet they saw me improve as a human being, and they knew I was happy. Later, I could use translation as a profession in speaking with them, so it appeared to them I was doing something meaningful. My brother who is two years older always respected what I was doing.

MH: Was he ever curious?

SK: He never asked me too many questions about the philosophy, nor did my parents. This was always curious to me, because here is your child, completely consumed in something, but they never asked me about what I really believe in. I think they were afraid to know.

MH: Like finding out that as a Buddhist you do not really believe in God?

SK: Exactly. Both my parents have passed away, but when my mom got Parkinson's disease, I helped her a lot with visualization. Instead of using Buddhist icons, I told her to focus on Jesus Christ, which worked very nicely. She was open to that. I felt good that I was able to help her. Later, I was also able to be there for my dad when he died.

MH: So they were able to appreciate your training after all.

SK: Well, they didn't have much choice. [laughing] I was gone for long periods of time, and they were always worried about me. Now I feel really bad about the heartache I caused them; however, at the time nothing was going to stop me.

EXPANDING HEART AND MIND

MH: What was Dharamsala like in those days?

SK: Very poor. People were getting sick all the time. The food stalls had two or three dishes that all tasted the same. It was freezing cold. No heaters, the walls were just boards with no insulation. The Tibetan people lived under very funky conditions; however, it was beautiful too, because the Tibetans, quite fresh from Tibet, were very much holding their culture. At the Tibetan New Year, it was fantastic to see the cultural events and dances. The Dalai Lama was always available, you could go and sit in the temple in front of him on the throne; I just loved that.

MH: Was there anything in particular that clicked for you?

SK: Near the Dalai Lama's monastery, the Library of Tibetan Works and Archives had just opened, where Westerners could study the lan-

guage and philosophy with Tibetan lamas. Geshe Ngawang Dhargyey*
taught *The Way of the Bodhisattva*³ and it was amazing to learn about
bodhichitta, the aspiration to become enlightened for the sake of all
sentient beings, and to be taught by someone who lived and experienced
this. I felt that sense of commitment from almost all the Tibetans. They
impressed me so much. I was real shy and somewhat in the shadow of
my companion who was a wheeler-dealer kind of guy, a triple Leo. At
the end of the first six months, I took refuge and *bodhisattva* vows† with
Geshe Dhargyey. We were launched on the path, and it has been that
way for me ever since. In those days, no one seemed to have any bias
about different sects or gender. Our minds and hearts were opening in
ways that we had never known.

MH: No bias? Did you have access to all the teachings?

SK: In a way, I was given every opportunity. No one was putting
women down. For instance, I could walk right into the monks' quarters
in the Dalai Lama's monastery to see my tutor. But sometimes the monks
would suddenly be called to the temple, and they would all jump up and
run off. I would be left on my own, thinking, Where are all the women?
At the time, there was no nunnery around. It was a man's world, and
that part of feeling a bit excluded did make me feel sad. But it didn't
discourage me either.

THE MISTAKEN NOTION OF PATRIARCHAL VAJRAYANA

MH: In the introduction to your translation of Mandarava's life story,
you write, "The notion that Vajrayana is male-oriented is mistaken."

SK: I know that for a fact. That notion is just a cultural issue and
has nothing to do with Vajrayana as a Buddhist vehicle, only with the
context it is in. In Vajrayana, the feminine principle is clearly respected.
Whenever there is a dakini empowerment, the texts talk about *prajna*‡
as primary, the feminine principle as the birthplace or womb of all the

*Geshe Ngawang Dhargyey (1921–1995) was asked in 1971 by His Holiness the Dalai
Lama to start a teaching program for Westerners at the newly constructed Library.
†The vow to attain liberation for the sake of all sentient beings.
‡*Prajna* (Skt.; Tib. *sherab*) means "wisdom," "intelligence," or "highest knowledge."

buddhas, so anyone who knows anything about Vajrayana understands that there is no bias concerning gender. It bothers me that some Western teachers have caused others to believe that Tibetan Buddhism is patriarchal, which I think is misleading. I disagree. I have strong feelings about that.

MH: How do you distinguish the "real" teachings from the Tibetan culture when the explanations are mostly given by teachers who are part of that culture?

SK: The more you study the teachings, the more you know that answer. Maybe the teacher is teaching with cultural bias, but still, you have to find out what the true teachings are. That's why we have to check on our teachers before we fully accept them. In Tibet, of course, it is a complex issue; the women themselves are at fault too. They surrender to their roles and refuse to step out of it. Obviously, the reason that so many people get the impression that Tibetan Buddhism is patriarchal is because it looks like a lot of men and very few women are stepping up.

MH: If girls don't get any training, how could they step up?

SK: In East Tibet where my partner Lama Chönam is from, there have been some very powerful dakinis, revered by all. Yet many women would never *dare* to step up. Female Tibetan friends tell me that we're supposed to sit in the back, put ourselves in a lower, reduced position when in the shrine room. You go to the end of the line; you cook, clean, and serve—all these cultural things that Tibetan women do really well. I don't think you need to take such a humble stand. I have even been told you should not enter a shrine room when on your moon cycle.

MH: Really? I came across that in Thailand and Burma, but I was never told that by Tibetans.

SK: I have a few friends who are horrified that we don't think that way. Right now we are in the middle of a series of empowerments by the Venerable Yangthang Rinpoche* who is surrounded by young female shrine assistants serving him with the rituals. These Western girls are

*Yangthang Rinpoche, born in Sikkim in 1923, was later imprisoned by the Chinese Communists for twenty-two years after attempting to escape from Tibet. He was released after Mao Zedong's death. When he found his monastery in Tibet in ruins, he returned to Sikkim in North India and is now teaching internationally.

fantastic. Yangthang Rinpoche has become comfortable with them, and now he's just enjoying the wonderful energy. He's laughing and joking with them; it is really a historic event. The translators are both female too. Nothing against the men, but it is nice for everyone to see what a good job women can do as well. This rinpoche is eighty-eight years old, but I guarantee you, in Tibet *never* in his life did he have a female shrine assistant, standing that close to him, holding up the substances. Impossible. For Tibetans who come in to get the empowerment and see that, it is shocking!

MH: And empowering, right?

SK: One would hope so, but maybe not due to the mindset.

NEVER GIVING UP

MH: You translated the biography of one of the most important female figures in Tibetan Buddhism, Mandarava, the Indian consort of Padmasambhava who was a prime agent in establishing Buddhism in Tibet. She was a princess who walked away from the kingdom in order to follow the path. What impresses you about her?

SK: Mandarava was willing and able to renounce that which is most difficult to renounce, namely attachment to the so-called pleasures of worldly life. I love how she never gave up, overcame tremendous hardship, and became a wisdom dakini. She and Padmasambhava traveled to a cave in Nepal, a present power spot, where they practiced together and became immortal wisdom holders. Therefore she is said to have achieved longevity accomplishments and is often invoked in long-life empowerments.

MH: How is she a role model for practitioners today?

SK: If someone applies the same fortitude and qualities that Mandarava had, they will succeed in accomplishing the path. Dharma is timeless and transcends conventional circumstances. Ultimately, she defies gender distinctions.

MH: In hindsight, was there anything foretelling that connection before you actually became a Buddhist?

SK: Yes, I was always searching, looking for something deeper. Life seemed superficial and unsatisfying. I wanted to know the purpose of life, and what happens after people die. What I was being taught in Christianity didn't ring true. I didn't know what I wanted to be, but I never had a yearning for getting married, being an ordinary wife just raising the kids and getting by. People often ask me, don't you miss having kids? I do love children, but I never felt the longing to have one myself. Ironically, now, at fifty-nine, I do have a child and he is delightful!

MH: How come?

SK: I am living with Lama Chönam, who has a very special eleven-year-old boy, Sangye Tendar. Tendar was brought up in Thinley Norbu Rinpoche's* Buddhist boarding school, and now he is living with us. So, we're parenting. [*laughs*]

MH: Why is that funny to you?

SK: Just at this stage in life, it is so totally unexpected. You never know what's coming your way, right? I have been with Gyatrul Rinpoche all this time as well and am one of Rinpoche's principal students and caregivers. At eighty-seven years old, Rinpoche is more dependent on his students. He is our main focus, and we stay close as a family unit.

MH: How did you meet Gyatrul Rinpoche?

SK: At the beginning, whenever my Indian visa ran out, I would return to Hawaii to scrape up more money so as to return to India. Jessie and I wanted to bring the dharma to Hawaii, so we secured land, fixed up a temple, and brought Nechung Rinpoche† over to Hawaii from Delhi.

THE HAUNTED TEMPLE

MH: Quite amazing, since you had only been a dharma student for two years at this stage.

SK: Yes, I was just one hundred percent immersed from the time I started and basically did *nothing* else. Magically, we found this aban-

---

*Thinley Norbu Rinpoche (ca. 1931–2011) is the son of Dudjom Rinpoche, who was Sangye Khandro's root teacher.
†Nechung Rinpoche (1918–1982), the head of Nechung Monastery, fled Tibet in 1962.

Sangye Khandro with Lama Chönam and his son Sangye Tendar.
Photo courtesy of Sangye Khandro

doned Japanese temple by South Point, but the locals thought the place was spooked and wouldn't go near it. So the sugar plantation leased the temple to us for one dollar a year. We worked hard to fix it up and then invited rinpoches to come. The temple is still flourishing.

MH: Who did you invite?

SK: Kalu Rinpoche came first. He gave empowerments and a sealed letter and named this a Kagyü center. When Nechung Rinpoche came, he felt that the temple was haunted as he heard knocking noises at night, and he wanted out of there. We were left with no choice but to rent a center in Honolulu and start all over again. Nechung Rinpoche begged Gyatrul Rinpoche to come help us as none of us could speak fluent Tibetan at that time, so we had a very hard time communicating. Gyatrul Rinpoche did speak some English since he had been sent to Canada in 1972 by the Dalai Lama with the first group of Tibetans who settled there.

"TAKE CARE OF HIM FOR THE REST OF YOUR LIFE!"

MH: Was your connection instantaneous?

SK: No, this slowly evolved. I was intrigued, because he was so funny, personal, and informal. I had never met such an open and loose rinpoche. Meeting him was really serendipitous, because it was the beginning of a lifetime with him. I had never seen anybody that skinny, wearing a red vest and all these clothes—in Hawaii! A few months later, when the Sixteenth Karmapa visited, Gyatrul Rinpoche fell seriously ill with a perforated ulcer. The Karmapa turned to me, saying, "Take him to the hospital. Now! Help him!" This didn't happen just once. When the Karmapa left, he said, "Take care of him for the rest of your life." And so our relationship developed. Then Rinpoche started inviting other teachers, and they needed translators. I was the only one to try this in the late seventies. I ended up translating almost by default. I can remember being horrified at first, because I was always very shy about speaking in public.

MH: How did you experience living with your teacher round the clock?

SK: It's not easy to be really close. If you have the choice, it's better to be at a distance. That's why the Karmapa famously said, "My disciples who are in close proximity with me will probably go to the lower realms. But those who are at a distance have a greater chance for liberation." If you're always with the guru, you start seeing the guru with ordinary mind, because we are ordinary. But regardless of that pitfall, one can use it as an opportunity to break through and have a pure view in difficult circumstances. It's a practice. It's all just your mind anyway. We're the ones thinking with pure-impure thoughts, so we can adjust this. You just have to be mindful enough to catch yourself.

MH: How interesting that you use the words "If you have the choice"! Didn't you have a choice?

SK: No, I didn't. I was always right there, front and center. I have had an amazing opportunity that I really wouldn't exchange for anything. I can always learn from Rinpoche and his example, serve him, and he also gives a lot to me, we practice together and benefit beings. There are always difficult situations, but really this isn't that bad.

MH: What was difficult?

SK: There was jealousy. I probably made a lot of mistakes too. Perhaps I was arrogant; maybe I could have been kinder or more humble. A lot of people want to be close to the teacher without getting the opportunity, and sometimes those of us who are close to the teacher forget that. I have come to be more sensitive to this.

MH: Did you feel entitled?

SK: There is some of that, yes. Initially I was working really hard all the time and actually I was treated very poorly. I was taking care of Rinpoche, cooking for him, and translating his teachings. I was giving all of my time and energy, but I was still required to pay rent. So it was not like I was being put on a pedestal. As years went on, I earned my position as Rinpoche's companion, main student, and translator, so I was taken care of, but the whole thing is new for people; it has been a work in progress. We were pioneers.

MH: How did you do it?

SK: I just did not want to do anything else. I did not even think about it.

MH: Were you and Gyatrul Rinpoche actually married?

SK: We still are. Our relationship is a hard one to understand. Rinpoche and I are spiritual companions. He is of course my teacher, and I am his student, but we've never really had an ordinary married relationship.

MH: Whatever that is.

SK: [laughs] I do have a relationship with Lama Chönam now as well, and we live together with Rinpoche most of the time as one big happy family. Rinpoche is really happy that I'm with Chönam and has grown to love him. The whole situation is harmonious and healthy. Rinpoche is a lot older than me, and he knew, inevitably, that things would become like that.

A LIFE-SAVING KARMIC SETUP

MH: When did you meet Lama Chönam?

SK: In 1992. He was a monk who left Golok in East Tibet with a few other monks in order to meet the Dalai Lama in India. He was planning on returning back home to his family in East Tibet when Tarthang

Rinpoche* coaxed him into coming to America. He still had no intention to stay but then fell very ill with tuberculosis. This was somewhat of a karmic setup that actually saved his life, because if he had returned to Tibet he would definitely have died.

MH: You seem to have a gift for saving lamas' lives.

SK: [laughs] Chönam had contracted drug-resistant tuberculosis and was quarantined. I took care of him, because he did not speak English and no one else could communicate with him. I helped him get to a hospital. The National Jewish Hospital in Denver, well known for its tuberculosis ward, admitted him for free for six months. The mayor of Medford, Oregon, chartered a plane, and we flew into Denver, with masks on. It was an unforgettable plane flight.

MH: Did you have a connection with him from the beginning?

SK: No, he was a monk, and I was with Gyatrul Rinpoche and very involved in my life. We definitely had a connection, a strong sense of mutual respect and positive energy. Our encounter caused many folks to gossip and spread rumors such as, "Did you hear that Sangye Khandro left Gyatrul Rinpoche for a monk from Golok?" Actually at that time that was not the situation at all, and I was just helping Chönam. It was just one of these juicy dharma gossip stories that everybody latched on to, and that's what eventually caused him to offer his robes back. He was horrified by all of that. Everyone who knew him from before said that he was a perfect monk. He took his vows very seriously. Well, you really find out who your friends are in such situations. But I don't hold on to that. This was an upheaval that got things moving when they were stagnant.

MH: Lama Chönam told me that he wrote a letter to Gyatrul Rinpoche and the community, apologized, and offered to make amends. Did Gyatrul Rinpoche take a while to accept that you were in a new relationship?

*Tarthang Tulku Rinpoche (b. 1934) is a Tibetan teacher in the Nyingma tradition who fled Tibet after 1959 and has lived in America since 1969. He is the founder of Dharma Publishing and the Tibetan Aid Project.

sk: There was an adjustment period. But Gyatrul Rinpoche and I always communicated, and we waited until the time was right for all three of us to live together.

mh: In the West we have a certain model of what a marriage is and how things are supposed to be. Do Tibetans take marriage less seriously?

sk: They are freer; they often don't even get married. The situation is much more open, especially for masters. The bottom line is, Chönam and I were meant to be together, so that we can do our translation work. Our connection has been amazing for that. Gyatrul Rinpoche sees very clearly how important that is. This also shows Rinpoche's lack of ego and his enlightened state of mind. So in the end, once people get over their ordinary phenomena, they can gain a sense of appreciation and respect.

No tempering, no watering down

mh: When did you actually become Sangye Khandro? When did Nanci Gustafson disappear?

sk: Sangye Khandro is my refuge name Geshe Dhargyey gave me, right at the beginning of my path in Dharamsala. *Sangye* means "buddha,"* and *khandro*, or *dakini*, means "space traveler," or "female buddha." Sangye Khandro is one of the five dakinis of the five directions. I feel really blessed by the name.

mh: And you took it right away as your main name?

sk: No, but I was with Tibetans all the time, and they could not remember Nanci, so they started calling me Sangye Khandro and it stuck.

mh: Your caller-ID still says Nanci Gustafson.

sk: [*laughs*] Legally, that's who I am, but Sangye is the name I respond to. My parents used to ask, "What's that weird name they call you?"

---

*Sangye (Tib.; Skt. *buddha*) literally means "purified" and "blossomed," indicating that a buddha has purified all obscurations and perfected all enlightened qualities. Traditionally, there are five buddha "families," or clans, each of which embodies aspects of enlightenment. The buddha family Sangye Khandro is referring to here represents the wisdom of all-encompassing space and the transformation of ignorance.

MH: Did they keep calling you Nanci?

SK: Of course.

MH: Is there anything you enjoy doing outside of the dharma?

SK: Nothing. It's been that way ever since I met the dharma. Before, I enjoyed music, like playing the piano and singing, or riding horses. Now I'm so uninformed about current events that it can be embarrassing. I sometimes have a hard time just striking up a normal conversation with people who are not in the dharma, because I don't really even know what they're talking about.

MH: You don't read the paper, you don't watch the news?

SK: I do watch the news on TV from time to time, but I have never looked at Twitter. We are completely absorbed in our world, translating, traveling, practicing. Sometimes I think, Sangye, you really should be better informed, so that you can relate to people better. But then I remind myself about priorities and think, hang on, my teachers are my best examples, and they did not spend their precious human life being informed about these things but rather chose to focus on dharma. I feel I don't know nearly enough about dharma, so I talked myself out of reading ordinary books and articles. There are so many things that will just take your life away from you if you get involved in them. I see email in that way too. It is so time consuming.

MH: Do you find sponsorship in order to translate books that have a dedicated but small group of followers?

SK: That's a little shaky. We take a very minimal salary and live very carefully. This is not a profession where money comes easily.

MH: Do you always translate with Lama Chönam's help?

SK: I believe strongly that right now we Westerners are not capable of translating Tibetan without the help of qualified Tibetan teachers. We're still not quite to the point where we Westerners can take the ball and run with it. Just like we are not at a point where we can give empowerments, transmissions, and pointing-out instructions and be lineage holders in the same way Tibetan masters are.

MH: What's still missing?

SK: Excellence in every aspect of Tibetan. For example a Westerner must know dharma thoroughly and also actualize the practice in extensive retreat, so that they become a qualified *vajra* master in their own right. They could then give an empowerment with the Tibetan text in front of them while translating simultaneously. Eventually, from that point, if their translation skills are keen, accurate, and imbued with the wisdom blessings, then the English language could be used exclusively. I am hopeful that we Westerners will get to this point over time with hard work and dedication just like the Tibetans did. But it won't happen in my lifetime.

MH: Are you sure?

SK: How many Westerners do I know who are qualified in that way? Think about it.

MH: Chagdud Khadro comes to mind.

SK: That's true, she is specializing in an area that she was authorized to transmit by her teacher, and so this is authentic and full of blessings. It is limited, though. Compare that with the qualifications to transmit every aspect of the lineage that Tibetan masters possess. For example, if Gyatrul Rinpoche, Dzongsar Khyentse Rinpoche, or Dzigar Kongtrul Rinpoche, to name a few, need to give any number of empowerments or teachings they are completely qualified to do so. They are fully trained as lineage holders in every way.

MH: But they all started getting transmissions when they were two years old! Westerners begin in their twenties at the earliest.

SK: I believe this will occur in the West as well; it is just a ways off. But if we don't take learning Tibetan seriously, it can become problematic. That is the key right there.

MH: Many Western students do their practices entirely in English, as instructed by their teachers.

SK: I am not saying everybody has to learn Tibetan. But the teachers and lineage holders really need to, otherwise the transmissions will be incomplete. Because then they are qualified to draw from the wisdom knowledge of the lineage tradition as they bring this into the new environment and will not just rely on their own ideas. There are a lot of good Western teachers; I am not putting them down in any way. But for the path that actually brings fully enlightened buddhahood and accomplishments as well as the rainbow body* we need to draw from Buddha's own speech, authentically, with no watering down, no tempering, no adjusting. I have strong feelings about that.

MH: I can't imagine Westerners would start their kids with rigorous tulku training at age two and hand them over to a monastery.

SK: That may be true. Thinley Norbu Rinpoche's school is unique because it brings the traditional values to the forefront. Rinpoche has been training children of his students, and those students clearly understood that they had to give up their boys and girls and not even see them for long periods of time if they expected this to work. It has worked really, really well. But Rinpoche has said, the biggest obstacle has been the parents, because occasionally parents want to visit and take the kids out for holidays when that is not part of the curriculum.

BUDDHA, THE PATRIARCHAL BOSS?

MH: Such a different concept and culture is hard to accept. We are in the process of a transition from Tibetan Buddhism placed in a hierarchical, patriarchal culture to the liberal, coed Western culture, and many think that several aspects of Buddhism need to reform. In a widely regarded letter you spoke out against the need for reforming Tibetan Buddhism.

SK: Several years ago some Western teachers criticized Buddha Shakyamuni as a 2,500-year-old patriarchal boss. I responded, Don't you think it is illogical to reject Asian teachers, after learning from them, because they are from a foreign culture, and then call this new form of Buddhism "American" because it is in this culture? Is it really possible for the blessings of the dharma to grow old like an ordinary material substance or perishable food?

MH: There is a clash of cultures, and sooner or later Westerners tend to be challenged by one or the other aspect, whether it is the teachings

---

*"Rainbow body" (Tib. *jalü*) is a practitioner's accomplishment of dissolving their physical body into mere light at the end of their life.

on reincarnation, the pantheon of deities, or demand for complete surrender. Did you ever experience any difficulties on the path?

sk: No, not really. I just pushed ahead, and I haven't really run into
any barriers—aside from my own neurotic mind, and the obstacles it
poses. The dharma is so incredibly complex and profound; very few
people are able to understand the depth of the Buddhist path. That is
why there are fewer Buddhists in this world. One has to really *think* and
use one's intelligence to figure out the true nature of phenomena. It is
much easier to accept some theory about a god or to just be atheistic,
disbelieving in past and future lives or the law of cause and result. As
Buddhist, if you know this is your path, you continue to be educated the
deeper it goes. The more I study the more amazed I am how vast it is. We
are not even scratching the surface. I am convinced that this is a treasure
trove of wisdom knowledge that we have just begun to discover.

mh: Was it ever challenging for you to go deeper and deeper?

sk: Of course, but that's a good thing. It's challenging to do the
preliminary practices with a hundred thousand prostrations, and so
on. It is a big deal the first time you do it, like going on a diet to lose
two hundred pounds or so. Yet if you're progressing in this way, then
you're also making progress in going to different levels with your own
mind. Still, there are so many layers of obscurations and habit that we
need to peel off, it becomes more and more challenging to peel off the
crusted layers that are stuck on underneath. At this point in life too, as
my time becomes shorter, I think, wait a minute, if the goal is enlightenment in one lifetime, I need to get more serious. Giving it all up and
going into retreat to realize my mind's nature—which is what I should
do if I am really serious—would be the ultimate challenge. If you're
serious about choosing liberation over remaining in samsara,* then the
challenge becomes more frightening, almost inconceivable. I never think
Buddhism is easy at all. It is much easier to just choose one of the other
religions or spend your time being distracted by outer appearances.

---

*Samsara (Skt.) literally means "wandering" and refers to the Buddhist belief in a con-
tinuous cycle of birth, life, death, and rebirth.

Sangye Khandro in Tashi Chöling, Oregon. Photo courtesy of Sangye Khandro

THE MISSING LINK

MH: I guess if you're really serious, any one of them is challenging, and all have a rigorous path.

SK: If you're practicing under an authentic Vajrayana master, then they will certainly be demanding and push you to really produce. These days we don't have enough realized masters around to inspire us. They are the missing link. People aren't inspired, because they are not being pushed by that kind of a teacher. So they are dabbling in dharma, which becomes just more of an outer, surface-level experience. It's certainly better than nothing, but it does not necessarily bring liberation.

MH: If you want to take the opportunity that Vajrayana promises, enlightenment in one lifetime, is it a full-time job?

SK: Definitely. You can say, in Dzogchen* the view means being aware of the mind's nature in all instances, you don't have to go off and medi-

---

*Dzogchen (Tib.), lit. "Great Perfection," or "Great Completeness," refers to the primordially pure state of mind and the body of teachings and practices designed to realize this state, most commonly found within the Nyingma tradition.

tate. That may be true, but until one gains a firm grounding, honestly, anyone who's even just practiced a little bit knows how easy it is to fall back into ordinary habits. To have the right dharma environment available to people is a big wish of mine, to create more retreat centers, educational programs, and practice possibilities. It is sorely lacking. We have a lot of teachers who come through and sow seeds, but there is no following through.

MH: Scott Globus, the president of Gyatrul Rinpoche's center in Alameda, says he's asked you many times to teach, yet you always say, "Why me? We have all these great masters here to teach." Why don't you have any interest in teaching?

SK: I do occasionally teach, but I don't call myself Lama Sangye, put on robes, and shave my head. It seems more skillful to appear in ordinary clothes, because people relate easier. As long as my masters are still alive, they are the true teachers. The sorry day will come when they are no longer with us. Then, I suppose, I will have to step up. But right now, I can serve them. And as a translator, you *are* in fact teaching. You have a tremendous amount of authority. First you have to understand what is being said. And then you have to reiterate it according to your understanding, not just repeating ordinary words as though you're translating a factual issue for the United Nations. Dharma understanding involves wisdom awareness and an understanding that comes through training for many years. It is a wonderful position, because I have the great fortune of bringing the dharma into the language of the listeners.

A LANDMARK DEAL

MH: What does a translator need to transmit the teachings in the best possible way?

SK: There are two points, the golden standard: one is accuracy in terms of content. The second is to translate as if you were actually that teacher speaking. You really represent them, sound like them, deliver the talk with their personality and style. You become that teacher and are no longer yourself, if possible. Also, a good translator must do retreat, since this ability to understand and connect in a selfless way comes through practice. No matter how hard you study, you won't really know the teachings until the meaning is internalized. I need to do more retreat.

MH: You have translated some of the most profound, restricted texts, such as the most important meditation manual of the Great Perfection, *Yeshe Lama*, and several commentaries on the *Tantra of the Secret Essence (Guhyagarbhatantra)*.

SK: They are restricted because they are quintessential innermost Vajrayana. So one needs the authorization of an authentic master before one can study them. I have always been interested in highest Tantra and Dzogchen. I have skipped over the Sutrayana studies for the most part as well as the outer Tantras and really honed in on the inner Tantras. I did this under the guidance of my teachers as this was a bit non-conventional. I requested Khenpo Namdrol Rinpoche* if he would teach me the *Tantra of the Secret Essence*. Much to my delight he invited me to India where he was teaching this to the ninth-year students. It was a landmark deal because this was the first time for women to sit coed with the monks in the monastic university in Mysore, India, in 1996. Prior to that only the monks had studied this.

MH: Were the nuns allowed too?

SK: No, there were no nuns. These days there is a nunnery down the road, and they have their own study program, but monks and nuns do not mingle programs. That would not be a good idea.

MH: But Western women were allowed in?

SK: Khenpo Namdrol was so open-minded to include five women in our small group. He believes that Westerners are very intelligent, sincere, and willing to practice.

DRYING WET CLOTHES ON THE BODY

MH: Were you also the first Western woman to receive the *tsa lung*† teachings at Penor Rinpoche's‡ monastery?

---

*Khenpo Namdrol Tsering was born in Kham, East Tibet, in 1953 and fled Tibet in 1959. He mostly teaches at the late Penor Rinpoche's monastery in Bylakuppe, South India, and at his retreat center in Pharping, Nepal.
†*Tsa lung* (Tib.) literally means "channels and wind." Here it refers to advanced yogic exercises, which consist of breath work, meditation, visualization, and dynamic movements.
‡Kyabjé Drubwang Pema Norbu Rinpoche (1932–2009) was the head of the Nyingma School. He fled Tibet in 1959 and established Namdroling Monastery in South India.

sk: Yes, in the nineties. Before that only monastics got them. I asked if I could join the course. Penor Rinpoche was also very open-minded. It is kind of shocking that he allowed that to happen.

mh: Were you a trailblazer for other women?

sk: He did start to make those teachings available at his upstate New York retreat center. But no, women did not start to receive teachings at the monastery; I might have been the only one. I mainly practiced alone, though. I would receive the empowerment and transmission for each stage, then go back to my room and do four practice sessions a day by myself. At the end, there were two days of tests, where we all had to demonstrate that we had mastered the exercises, for instance that we generated enough heat to dry wet clothes on our bodies, and so on. Later he authorized me to teach this.

mh: Have you traveled in Tibet?

sk: Several times, but the most memorable was the first pilgrimage to East Tibet in 1987 with Penor Rinpoche, Gyatrul Rinpoche, and a large party of monks. I was the first woman to actually stay *inside* Penor Rinpoche's monastery in central Kham. Even to find facilities was very challenging. This was the first time Tibet opened up since Mao's death, and the Chinese were relaxing their grip to a certain degree and releasing many masters from prison. The pain and trauma were palpable. The Tibetans were still wearing their traditional clothing, and they were very poor and desperate. Few foreigners had been there yet. Chinese spies shadowed us wherever we went, and at some point they forced us to end our trip early. Except for the ruins where the monasteries used to be, Tibet was also incredibly beautiful, with wildflowers and wild animals in abundance. Nowadays things are different. The Chinese have pretty much gone through every acre, hunted down the wild animals, and driven the nomads from the land.

The string on the toe

mh: You have worked with so many great masters over the years. Does it take a special connection with the teacher to translate well?

sk: You have to have a karmic bond in order to translate for a teacher. There are groups who will invite masters to teach, and then they will start frantically calling around for a translator at the last minute without having considered from the beginning that the translation is an integral part of the transmission. That's really not the way. The translator needs to be a student of that teacher, know the subject, and be qualified. Otherwise no matter how good the teacher is, it can come out flat.

MH: Sometimes it is tempting for translators to take a shortcut when the teachings seem repetitive, or to make it more entertaining. Did you ever feel the urge to alter what the teacher says?

SK: I did that with Kusum Lingpa,* many times. When he first came to the States fresh out of Tibet, he was like a crazy, wild man with no social skills. Upon meeting somebody he would push, "How much money does he have? Ask him!" He did not want the money for himself, as he did not even wear a watch; all the money he acquired was solely to take back to Tibet and feed the practitioners. So the motivation was clearly pure, but it was just a little abrupt.

MH: Another teacher who is quite unconventional is Thinley Norbu Rinpoche. How did he push you?

SK: Thinley Norbu Rinpoche was a master of the English language, so he did not normally use translators, or if he did, he would usually toss them out after about ten minutes. [*chuckles*] The first time I was invited to translate for Rinpoche many were wondering how long I would last. I was nervous. The first night went really well. The next night, Rinpoche sent his attendant to tie a string around my toe, with Rinpoche holding the other end. Each time Rinpoche needed to correct me: yank! I would know that it was time to stop talking. It was hilarious. Then Rinpoche would whisper to me, and of course, his suggestions were absolutely brilliant. I had the time of my life. The string came off my toe after about a week. Then Rinpoche began teaching for longer and longer periods, even for thirty or forty minutes. When it was my turn to translate, sometimes Rinpoche would get up and go to the forest. On occasion you could hear him clapping from the forest when I was done. I have learned so much from Rinpoche that words cannot even

---

*Orgyen Kusum Lingpa (1934–2009) was a Nyingma master from Golog, in Amdo, East Tibet.

express this. Any ability to translate Dzogchen I might have is due to his kindness one hundred percent.

MH: That story is very sweet. Did lamas ever crush you?

SK: No. I like criticism. I am willing to drop my ego if I can learn from that.

A WISDOM DAKINI IN NEW YORK

MH: Do you have any women teachers?

SK: I have the greatest devotion for Dudjom Rinpoche's* consort, Sangyum Kusho Rigdzin Wangmo, who is one of my root teachers. She was Dudjom Rinpoche's source of everything, giving Rinpoche the energy he needed to benefit sentient beings. As a wisdom dakini, she extended his life. As an aristocrat, she is very proper and formal, completely unique. She always looks immaculate, very beautiful and feminine, wearing finest jewels and silks. She has been in retreat for many years, upstairs in a brownstone in the middle of New York City, in this one room with one window. She *never* goes out. Any ordinary person such as me would go crazy. Enlightened beings don't have a self like we do, so they can be a lot more at ease.

MH: Is she your role model?

SK: If there is any woman on the planet who I admire most and want to be like, it's her.

---

*Dudjom Rinpoche (1904–1987) was the head of the Nyingma school in exile and especially renowned as a great treasure revealer. He is also known for preserving many of the historic texts that would otherwise have been destroyed.

Venerable Pema Chödrön.
Photo by Liza Matthews. © Liza Matthews

5: PEMA CHÖDRÖN

(DEIRDRE BLOMFIELD-BROWN)

RELAXING INTO GROUNDLESSNESS

*The lessons the most beloved Western Buddhist teacher
learned when her own life fell apart*[1]

WHEN PEMA steps onto the stage, she admits she is "pretty amazed at this turnout, even dumbfounded." On a sunny October day in the San Francisco Bay Area, three thousand people gather in the Craneway Pavilion on the waterfront. Through the massive windows, Pema sees the silhouette of the city jut out from the endless blue. Another two thousand have not been able to book a seat and are listening online at home. In 1936, when Pema Chödrön was born, Ford assembled its legendary V8 in this acre-size car factory. Now the enormous hall is barely big enough to contain the high-powered energy of a very different icon: Pema Chödrön, who will be teaching on how to become fearless. Twitching her maroon robes, she looks frail, yet it only takes her minutes to captivate the audience with her presence. Pema's soft, slightly hoarse voice fills the space to the very top joists of the soaring ceilings. An artist presents her with a collage in which Pema's face is superimposed onto Rosie the Riveter's, the famous feminist idol of World War II. Rosie replaced male workers in the factories, showed off her muscles, and boosted the propaganda slogan "We Can Do It!" A fitting, eye-twinkling comparison for a woman who has superseded the traditional male teachers as the most beloved Buddhist teacher in America today.

This teaching is a historic event, for the organizers point out that it might be Pema's "final" retreat in the Bay Area. With the very characteristic benign humor of the kindergarten teacher that she once was, she immediately pulls some teeth. Busting some hagglers who complained that they had expected a much more intimate setting, she frames the event "in a very large global context of wanting to wake up." With the motivation of bodhichitta, we do not only want ourselves to be happy, but we will not be happy unless everybody else is. Now you could hear a pin drop.

Her hands paint quotation marks around "spiritual" in the air when she addresses the "spiritual" seekers: "It can be somewhat selfish in that it is all about taking care of oneself and not about how this affects others. What makes us feel comfortable and secure is actually at the expense of other people." Within minutes she heads straight into groundlessness, one of her favorite subjects to explore. The first sentence in her most successful book, *When Things Fall Apart*, reads: "Embarking on the spiritual journey is like getting into a very small boat and setting out on the ocean to search for unknown lands." Where other teachers might promise their students that meditation will make them feel better, more peaceful, and more grounded, Pema breaks the bad news (or good news, if you're fond of the truth) right at the beginning: There is no solid ground to be found, at least not in Buddhism, certainly not in her teachings, nor anywhere else. "The ground is always shaking. The groundlessness is eternal. So here we are," she says, smiling, quoting the title of the event, "to smile at fear."[2]

A FIRST-AID KIT FOR LIFE

Facing what scares us is Pema Chödrön's signature topic. A glance at her book and audio titles provides a first-aid kit for handling life: *When Things Fall Apart*, we have *No Time to Lose* so that we *Start Where We Are, Don't Bite the Hook*, and go to the *Places That Scare You* for *Taking the Leap: Freeing Ourselves from Old Habits and Fears*, becoming *Comfortable with Uncertainty*, and *Practicing Peace in Times of War*. These slogans encapsulate Pema's heart advice. Where everybody else tells us to run away, to distract ourselves, to seek comfort, or even to retaliate, Pema Chödrön always nudges us to stay in the present moment where it hurts—raw, naked, and uncomfortable.

Because she urges us to do so gently, with kindness and humor, she makes it obvious that this is the only sensible thing to do—that this is, in fact, the only possibility if we want to wake up. In the Craneway Pavilion in Richmond, she lays it out:

> The first step is to develop an unconditional friendship with yourself. Unconditional friendship means staying open when you want to shut down, when it is just too painful, too embarrassing, too unpleasant, too hateful what you see in yourself. The whole mark of training in cultivating bravery is so you could go anywhere on the earth and be of help to people because you wouldn't shut down on them. The first step is looking at yourself with a feeling of gentleness and kindness. It takes a lot of guts, as Trungpa Rinpoche says, because it means staying present when you begin to fear what you see.

Pema Chödrön's success is surely also grounded in the fact that she herself is such a great example of how to live this. In Richmond, Pema describes a truly genuine person who is not afraid of honest self-examination:

> When you feel someone is a genuine person it means they are not hiding anything, they are not putting up masks. Genuineness means that you can trust the person because they are not conning themselves, and they won't con you. They have seen it all about themselves. It does not mean that they are not still embarrassed or uncomfortable about what they see, but they don't run away. The truth doesn't cause them to avoid feeling what they feel; it doesn't cause them to put up masks or to armor themselves. The genuine person does not have an iron heart but a vulnerable, tender heart.

This is a precise description of Pema herself. She is extremely easy to be with; everything is simple and straightforward around her, with no posturing necessary.

Pema animatedly mimics a dialogue she had with her alter ego, the self that doesn't want to stay present, and at the end she sums up ego's attitudes in one word, albeit spelled out: "B-u-l-l"—the entire audience breaks into laughter, and Pema slowly finishes the word, "s-h-i-t." Extremely refreshing to hear that a senior nun has no hesitation to call a spade a spade.

THE BIG EQUALIZER

The first time I met Pema Chödrön, about ten years ago, she was not sitting on a stage or wearing robes. In an old pair of work pants and a worn maroon pullover, she was lounging on the wooden bench in front of the tool shed at Samten Ling, her current teacher's retreat center. This is where she spends the bulk of her time now: by herself, in one of her retreat cabins either in Nova Scotia or Colorado. She teaches no more than two or three public programs per year, with opportunities to meet her in person becoming exceedingly rare. In fact, she has worked hard to be left alone for most of the time and just spent another year entirely in retreat despite the urgent wish of millions to connect with her.

In Samten Ling, Dzigar Kongtrul Rinpoche's* retreat center in the Rocky Mountains, she is treated like any regular Joe, and she clearly enjoys the luxury of being ordinary, with no demands made on her time, no role to play. About a dozen small cabins are dotted across a vast mountainside, perched high above the small village of Crestone, overlooking the Sangre de Cristo (lit. "Blood of Christ") Mountains. Retreatants spend their time alone in their own cabins, in silence, beyond earshot of the others, but once a day all come together for an hour of T'ai Chi exercises and work on the land. Fifty acres of wild land require maintenance, usually physically taxing work like chopping wood, carrying provisions up the steep hill, or working the shovels,

*See chapter 6.

picks, and jackhammer to repair holes the last rain dug into the rough road. Frankly, none of these tasks fits an elderly nun.

When she did her first two hundred-day retreats at Samten Ling many years ago, Kongtrul Rinpoche indeed let her keep to herself. But afterwards he asked her to join the daily work periods. "What, me?" she confessed thinking, but, of course, she soon saw the wisdom in it. This was what Kongtrul Rinpoche wanted: he set up the work period not only to render the retreatants self-sufficient but also "to rub shoulders with each other" in between meditation sessions and to jolt them out of the comfort of their own cocoon. Kongtrul Rinpoche does not allow his students to misunderstand retreat as an opportunity to withdraw into self-absorption. How better to test one's practice of loving-kindness and compassion than by working together in a group? After all, digging and shoveling can be as much a spiritual practice as sitting on a cushion—or not.

THE PAIN OF BEING IGNORED

So, the organizer would give out the jobs of the day, scrambling to find a small task for Pema. She might be asked to label tapes, roast barley flour, or collect pine nuts in the wild. Pema would always sit in the round on the wooden benches with everyone else, occasionally breaking the silence with a joke, and quietly take her job assignment. I never saw a second of hesitation. Here she was, an internationally recognized teacher, yet she did not consider herself above any small task. When I first arrived, I quietly gasped at the scenario. I once even made a remark to the manager: You have this fabulous best-selling author roasting barley flour for two hours—couldn't she do something that utilizes her unique writing and teaching abilities instead?

"For all these years Rinpoche always stressed that there is no way that I could have so much fame without it puffing me up," Pema confesses. She used to reply, "No, Rinpoche, honestly, I don't think that's true!" Yet it haunted her that he just would not let go of this one point. When he finally introduced her to the work period, "It was WOW! When I go to work period, I am absolutely nobody. In fact there are a number of people there who actually don't like me and it is just really painful!" She adds, "It was an enormous equalizer for me. It showed me that I did have arrogance and some sense of 'Don't you know who I am?' It was a really good experience. I can honestly say that by the end of the retreat I had worn out whatever that was. I had to go through the pain of being ignored."[3]

Once there was nothing physically unchallenging to be done, so the work manager assigned her to dust the rocks around the spring with a broom. We all got a good laugh out of this one, including Pema, for in the middle of arid mountains, dusting rocks is obviously a pretty futile endeavor. However, she simply picked up the broom and went off to the spring. She later confessed that she held her breath for a second, but in retreat everybody is treated the same. The TV host and the carpenter, the best-selling author and the supermarket cashier, all are equal, because that's what we fundamentally are, equal, and that's how Kongtrul Rinpoche set it up. He often warns against "entitlement attitude" and "one-upmanship." That he is not impressed with any worldly credentials might be one of the many qualities that attract Pema to him as a teacher. Traditional teachings advise that a dharma student should be like a comfortable belt, sitting easily with everybody. Pema does exactly that. Despite all her many accomplishments, she has no detectable arrogance. She calls herself "a student-teacher, because it's very threatening to actually think of being a teacher. Of course, there are people who consider me that and so I have to take responsibility. But you get pride in being a teacher and a kind of false humility can set in."[4] When she is asked if she lives by her own teachings and succeeds in being serene and kind 24/7, she breaks into laughter, confessing that her "kids could blow my cover anytime."

Still, I have yet to meet somebody who has a negative story to tell about Pema. She often teaches about curiosity as the key ingredient of her spiritual life, and she does indeed appear to look out on life constantly wondering, open-minded, with an almost childlike curiosity. Despite being usually the most experienced, she is always the one to ask the most questions. When I was going through a difficult time and approached her for advice, I felt no judgment, only kindness and care.

She never forgets to thank anybody who does her the smallest favor. When I carried a few propane tanks to her retreat cabin, she gave me a color painting of a joyful nun as a gift, with one of her favorite lines from the Buddhist teachings: "Always keep only a joyful mind!" It still hangs above my desk, because it reminds me of her: Even when weighed down with back pain or other sorrows, she lives up to that slogan, keeping a joyful spirit.

A PREDICTION BEYOND THE PALE OF POSSIBILITY

Of course, Pema was not always the Pema Chödrön we know now. Pema's life can roughly be divided into two segments of almost equal length: Her life before the day her second husband told her he was having an affair, and the forty years after. Before that infamous autumn day in New Mexico when her husband came home early from work, Pema's life was utterly conventional.

Pema was born Deirdre Blomfield-Brown in New York City in 1936, and her Catholic family moved to New Jersey when she was three months old. She grew up as the youngest on a farm in the countryside with an older brother and sister. She remembers her childhood as pleasant and peaceful. She lived in the family's traditional old farmhouse until she attended the famous Miss Porter's School in Farmington, Connecticut. That elite, stiff-upper-lip, girls-only prep school prides itself on imparting to its students a healthy sense of self-confidence and the importance of service to mankind. Jackie Onassis and Gloria Vanderbilt are among its graduates. Pema, who was a boarder at the school, remembers that the teachers there challenged her intellectually "to go deeper."[5]

She married a young lawyer just before her twenty-first birthday and soon had a daughter, Arlyn, and a son, Edward. The family moved to California, where Deirdre graduated with a bachelor's degree in English literature and a master's in elementary education from the University of California at Berkeley. As an elementary school teacher, her extraordinary teaching skills stood out from day one. "Pema was such a natural teacher," remembers her friend Basia Turzanski, who knew her before she became Pema. "She was so vibrant, openhearted, down-to-earth. This was her calling in life." But within a few years, Deirdre's marriage fell apart. Without much of a gap, she married a writer, and the couple moved to New Mexico, where Deirdre continued to teach as they raised her children from her first marriage.

Deirdre Blomfield never felt a longing to become a nun. She tells of one occurrence that, in hindsight, foretold her future. One day in New Mexico she was walking through a flower field with bare feet, her long blond hair flying in the wind. She still remembers the color of her dress—pale lavender. A young rabbi saw her in the distance, silhouetted against the New Mexican sun. He approached her and stunned her with a prediction that she thought was entirely beyond the pale of possibility: "I just had a vision of you as a nun." Pema was flabbergasted. "We were hippies, and there was no idea further from my mind than this." Growing up Catholic, becoming a nun was "the *last thing* I ever dreamt of," she says, and is quick to add, emphasizing every word, "Not that I had a negative experience with nuns, but I *never- dreamt- of- being- a- nun.*"[6]

FEAR, RAGE, AND CONFUSION

But then came the day she describes at the beginning of her international best-seller *When Things Fall Apart*, the day when *her* world fell apart. In her midthirties, standing in front of their adobe house sipping a cup of tea, she heard the car drive up, and the door bang shut. Then her husband walked around the corner and without warning told her that he was having an affair, and he wanted a divorce. Her mind shattered; time stopped. "I remember the sky and how huge it was. I remember the sound of the river and the steam rising up from my tea. There was no time, no thought, there was nothing—just the light and a profound, limitless stillness."[7] Then anger stormed in. "I picked up a stone and threw it at him,"[8] she says, while breaking into laughter in remembering her outrage. Getting over the hurt took her years of hard work. Struggling to find some ground, she went on a spiritual spree. She lived in a Hindu ashram for a while, did weekend intensives in Scientology, booked Sufi workshops. None of this lasted very long, and nothing helped. "The pain was so great. The rug had been pulled out so completely."⁹ Reality as she had known it "just wasn't holding up any more."

Toward the end of that horrible first year, someone left a magazine open. An article with the headline "Working with Negativity" caught her attention, "because I was feeling fear, rage, and tremendous confusion about my rage and my hatred and a kind of a deep, profound, unshakable groundlessness. And nothing could fill it. People would take me to the movies. They'd take me to nice dinners. They'd do all these things. And nothing could get the pieces back together."¹⁰ At this point in her life, Deirdre had no idea about Buddhism or about the article's author, Chögyam Trungpa Rinpoche, but she still remembers the first line of this article: "There is nothing wrong with negativity." That spoke directly to her. "From day one, I thought there's something very profound in what is happening here. Because I see that a lot of us are just running around in circles pretending that there's ground where there actually isn't any ground. And that somehow, if we could learn to not be afraid of groundlessness, not be afraid of insecurity and uncertainty, it would be calling on an inner strength that would allow us to be open and free and loving and compassionate in any situation. But as long as we keep trying to scramble to get ground under our feet and avoid this uneasy feeling of groundlessness and insecurity and uncertainty and ambiguity and paradox, any of that, then the wars will continue."¹¹

CONFRONTING THE REAL CULPRIT

Pema's terror over the implosion of her marriage, the devastation she felt, sparked her exploration of groundlessness, eventually giving way to a life-long journey of self-reflection. She distinguishes between pain, which is somewhat inevitable, and suffering, which she defines as the mental and emotional anguish we layer on top. "Let's call pain the unavoidable, and let's call suffering what could lessen and dissolve in our lives. You could say that it isn't the things that happen to us in our lives that cause us to suffer. It's how we relate to the things that happen to us that causes us to suffer."¹² There might have been no way of avoiding heartbreak after losing her husband, but she realized in the following years that the much bigger problem was her underlying dependency, her self-centered hopes and fears.

When asked how she got involved in Buddhism, she half-jokingly blames her anger on her cheating husband. "The truth is that he saved my life. When that marriage fell apart, I tried hard—very, very hard—to go back to some kind of comfort, some kind of security, some kind of familiar resting place. Fortunately for me, I could not pull it off. Instinctively I knew that annihilation of my old dependent, clinging self was the only way to go."[13]

Once she identified her own clinging as the real culprit, she came across the right teacher to uproot it. Within days after she had read that magazine article, a friend invited her to a Sufi camp in the French Alps. On the spur of the moment she agreed, leaving her children in the care of their father for a month. In the French Alps she encountered for the first time a Tibetan Buddhist teacher, Chimé Rinpoche (1914–1999). She immediately felt a "strong recognition" along with a sense of familiarity.

Chimé Rinpoche encouraged her to connect with the article's author, Chögyam Trungpa Rinpoche, who would eventually become her main teacher. Trungpa was one of the pivotal figures in establishing Tibetan Buddhism in America. She first met Chögyam Trungpa on a winter's day in Taos, New Mexico, in 1972. She had her elementary-school class read his autobiography, Born in Tibet, and when he coincidentally gave a lecture nearby, she took three carloads of children to see him. One of the kids asked about fear. Trungpa Rinpoche told them how he had once visited a monastery with a ferocious guard dog. Just when they were inside the courtyard, the raging dog broke loose of its chain. Everybody froze, except for Trungpa Rinpoche. He started running as fast as he could—straight at the dog. The dog was caught so off guard that it turned around and ran the other direction, tail between its legs. This is one of the lessons Pema learned from her teacher, and she quotes him in Richmond: "The basis of fearlessness is really knowing fear." What attracted her to him was not initially a feeling of warmth like she had felt with Chimé Rinpoche. "But in Trungpa Rinpoche's presence I felt very exposed and able to see the things that weren't quite finished and were still problematic in my life. When I formally requested to be his student later, it was mainly because of the fact that he put me on the spot so much, and everything about him stirred things up."[14]

Pema describes Chögyam Trungpa as a highly provocative, uncomfortable teacher. The famously brilliant "bad boy" of Tibetan Buddhism in the West shattered many notions of how an enlightened teacher should behave. In *Cutting Through Spiritual Materialism*, he states that the job of the spiritual friend is to insult the student, and, Pema says, "that's the kind of guy he was. If things got too smooth, he'd create chaos."[15] Pema saw the wisdom in his actions. "I didn't like being churned up and provoked, but it was what I needed. It showed me how I was stuck in habitual patterns."[16]

Within two years she did the last thing she had ever dreamed of. His Holiness the Sixteenth Gyalwa Karmapa ordained her in 1974 while she was studying with Chimé Rinpoche in England and gave her the name Pema Chödrön (Lotus Lamp of the Teachings). She herself admits that "it's very, very strange. In my life, when I've had certain thoughts, I say this is a forward thought, and I have to follow it. It just happens every so often. And, for some reason, taking the vows represented a forward thought."[17] Yet her children were still young teenagers at the time. When asked if she feels guilt over her decision, her face crumples: "Yes. Yes. Yes. When I look back, it was premature. It would have been better to have waited until the children were older."[18] She sighs. "I think the timing could have been better, but in terms of having done it, there's no other decision for me in life. I always feel people are very fortunate, when you've found something in your life that gives it deep meaning and that doesn't run out."[19] And eventually, her family came around to supporting her in her unusual path.

Not a one-shot game

Upon returning to the United States after her ordination, Pema moved into the Dharmadhatu Center in San Francisco. For a while she still kept wearing her ordinary clothes during the day, when she taught at a private school, then put the robes on to teach Buddhism at the center in the evening. When the Karmapa met her again during a visit to the

United States, he made an unprecedented move. He looked straight at her during a group audience and said, "You should take full ordination."[20] The Karmapa offered to give her the vows himself. However, this proved to be impossible, as his lineage authorization did not allow him to bestow full ordination on a woman. Instead, the Karmapa gave her the phone number of a Chinese teacher in the Bronx who would eventually direct her to a temple where she could receive full ordination.

Just a few years after Tenzin Palmo, in 1981, she too traveled to Hong Kong. She was probably the first American woman to become fully ordained. Like many other teachers in this book, when asked about the speed with which she radically transformed her life, she resorts to a deeper calling, a reconnection "with some kind of past karmic stream, and you just step into it, and then you know because it starts going forward."[21] She quotes her teacher Trungpa Rinpoche: "It's not a one-shot game, there are many reruns." Her rapid entering into monastic life cannot be easily understood from this life alone. While being raised Catholic, she thought of nuns as somewhat repressed.[22] In her decision to become a nun herself, she discovered "a passion for life, an appetite for realization and you just decide you want to go for it."[23] At this stage in her life, she felt a sense of completion with her domestic life, but she also confesses that just before getting ordained every conceivable sexual and mental desire arose to haunt her. Habitual craving put up one last strong fight—but the dharma won. Having had two marriages and two children, she felt little interest in starting yet another relationship. She was utterly determined to put all her energy into "connecting with the truth," as she puts it. "It also has something to do with not limiting yourself to one person or situation, but actually sharing yourself with everyone."[24]

Nowhere to hide

Pema Chödrön now lives at Gampo Abbey in Nova Scotia, the monastery of Chögyam Trungpa's Shambhala International, a three-storey wooden building perched on a dramatic two-hundred-foot cliff high above the Gulf of Saint Lawrence. Two hundred acres of land on this isolated tip of the Cape Breton coast have been transformed into a sanctuary for spiritual exploration. She describes it as "a vast place where the sea and the sky melt into each other. The horizon extends infinitely, and in this vast space float seagulls and ravens. The setting is like a huge mirror that exaggerates the sense of there being nowhere to hide. Also, since it is a monastery, there are very few means of escape—no lying, no stealing, no alcohol, no sex, no exit."[25] Pema Chödrön is the principal teacher at the abbey, and her successful books have kept it going for decades. She has established the Pema Chödrön Foundation,[26] which holds all the royalties from her books and audio teachings to create a fund to support this commitment to the monastic path.

Basia Turzanski worked closely with Pema in the early years, shoulder to shoulder at the desks in the office of Trungpa Rinpoche's organization. She recalls vividly how scared Pema initially was to fundraise for Gampo Abbey. Pema talked about her insecurities but then concluded, "Whatever I am afraid of, I go toward." Basia says, "This woke me up! From the beginning, this has been her principle on the path, this is how she developed herself." At first, Pema was the only ordained person in the community, but Basia recalls that it never created any separation. "She was pretty much on her own but very accessible. She is a very strong person." When I once asked Pema if it was difficult to become ordained in the midst of this free-spirited, hippie culture in the seventies, she just calmly shook her head and said, "It was the right thing for me to do, and Trungpa Rinpoche was very supportive."

EXPOSING OURSELVES OVER AND OVER TO ANNIHILATION

Trungpa Rinpoche himself had been taken from his family as a small boy and raised in the monastery of his predecessor once he was recognized as an incarnation. Even when Rinpoche was forced to flee to India after the Chinese invaded Tibet, he kept his robes. However, a car crash in England in 1969 left him permanently crippled. The accident marked a turning point. He took it as a message that he had to completely "abandon all props," such as the robes, to eliminate any separation from his students. He gave back his vows, started wearing the same clothes as his Western students, and began drinking alcohol and teaching in radical ways. Once when Trungpa Rinpoche used the example of sexual activity to prove his point in a teaching, Pema raised her hand and asked, "What about me? It seems like I cannot really follow those teachings."[27] She was surprised when he advised her that she would come to understand the real meaning if she kept her vows purely. Despite his own free-spirited life style, Rinpoche encouraged her to be very strict with her precepts, to be a role model for all the other monastics who were to follow in her footsteps. Later, he told his first nun: "You know, they are all going to be looking at you, they are going to watch the way you walk, the way you talk, and the way you conduct yourself, and so you better do it right."[28] She recalls having a conversation with him about setting up the monastery—ironically, while he was lying in bed, presumably naked under the blanket. Pema understood this to mean that she should keep her vows very purely, while at the same time "being extremely flexible and open in my mind."[29] Trungpa Rinpoche "emphasized again and again that we should not use the monastic rules as a way to close ourselves off from the world—the whole point was to see them as a way to further open our hearts and minds towards the whole world."[30]

Shambhala established a unique tradition within Tibetan Buddhism: Gampo Abbey allows temporary ordination, to give laypeople a chance to experience monastic life before either deciding to take it up for good or to go back to their lives. "It is a popular notion that people choose to live in a monastery to escape or hide from the world," Pema says. "In reality, the intensity and simplicity of abbey life demand that we become more intimately involved with life, a life not driven by personal concerns and habitual patterns. The intensity of community life, lived compassionately in accordance with the precepts, demands that we wake up. At first, life at the abbey seems idyllic. But when you stay, then all the places in yourself that you don't want to surrender, become highlighted. Life at the abbey is very earthy and very full."[31] She experienced this herself when Trungpa Rinpoche sent her there as its director, in 1984, just after the place had been bought as an old farmhouse still smelling of cows and chickens. The abbey was the first Tibetan Buddhist monastery in Canada for Western men and women, and Pema Chödrön was its first director, a true pioneer of exploring how to merge the Asian monastic culture with Western minds.

"Being there was an invitation to test my love of a good challenge," she writes in When Things Fall Apart, "because in the first years it was like being boiled alive." What happened to her when she got to the abbey was that "all the ways I shield myself, all the ways I delude myself, all the ways I maintain my well-polished self-image—all of it fell apart. No matter how hard I tried, I couldn't manipulate the situation. My style was driving everyone else crazy, and I couldn't find anywhere to hide. I had always thought of myself as a flexible, obliging person who was well liked by almost everyone. I had so much invested in that image of myself, and it just wasn't holding together anymore. All my unfinished business was exposed vividly and accurately in living Technicolor, not only to myself, but to everyone else as well."[32] Others were outspoken with their feedback. She pinned up a sign on her wall, which read: "Only to the extent that we expose ourselves over and over to annihilation can that which is indestructible be found in us." That's the key message she's been learning and teaching ever since: it is "all about letting go of everything."[33]

In this spirit she also explains the bodhisattva vow in refreshingly nontraditional terms:

> The bodhisattva vow has something to do with going cold turkey, naked, without any clothes on into whatever situation presents itself to you, and seeing how you hate certain people, how people trigger you in every single way, how you want to hold on, how you want to get in bed and put the covers over your head. Seeing all of that just increases your compassion for the human situation. We're all up against not finding ourselves perfect, and still wanting to be open and be there for others.[34]

With the gentleness of a very kind dentist who knows that there is no use pretending the remedy is not going to hurt, Pema sums up the practice in her book *The Places That Scare You*:

> In essence the practice is always the same: instead of falling prey to a chain reaction of revenge or self-hatred, we gradually learn to catch the emotional reaction and drop the story lines. Then we feel the bodily sensation completely. One way of doing this is to breathe into our heart. By acknowledging the emotion, dropping whatever story we are telling ourselves about it, and feeling the energy of the moment, we cultivate compassion for ourselves. Then we could take this a step further. We recognize that there are millions who are feeling the way we are and . . . widen the circle of compassion.[35]

BECOMING HOMELESS

Pema's teacher taught her exactly that. Her devotion to Trungpa Rinpoche developed slowly, over ten or fifteen years. About four years before his death, her hesitation evaporated, and she found her devotion "unshakable." She comforts newer students who are struggling with mixed feelings toward their teachers. "If devotion sets in right away, it could be from a sense that now you have a new mommy or daddy and there's this cozy feeling to it. But by becoming Buddhists, we don't get a new family. Becoming a Buddhist is about becoming homeless."[36]

By the time Chögyam Trungpa passed away in 1987, he had earned the respect of many of his peers as a highly realized master, but his exceedingly unconventional spirit often bewildered students. Several teachers in this book, including Tenzin Palmo and Joan Halifax, recall how he tried to seduce them. In her autobiography, Trungpa Rinpoche's British wife, Diana Mukpo, describes her husband's relationship with quite a number of girlfriends, his freewheeling parties, and the elaborate protocol that ruled life at home. "Trungpa Rinpoche was always trying to teach us to relax into the insecurity, into the groundlessness. I am grateful to him, no matter what," Pema Chödrön said in an interview with Helen Tworkov a few years after his death. "He upset me a lot. I couldn't con him, and that was uncomfortable. But it was exactly what I needed."[37]

SEX AND THE TEACHER

When Helen Tworkov pressed Pema Chödrön about Trungpa Rinpoche's relationships, Pema said, "Rinpoche loved women. He was very passionate and had a lot of relationships with women. In retrospect, I would have said to other women students that that might be a part of it if you get involved with him. You should read all his books, go to all his talks, and actually see if you can get close to him. And you should do that knowing that you might get an invitation to sleep with him, so don't be naïve about that, and don't think you have to do it or don't have to do it. But you have to decide for yourself who you think this guy is."[38] As a woman, she says that she does not "like that many male teachers misuse their positions and come on to women students. But I'm tempted to say that when a teacher is very realized it *is* actually different than when they're not. But who is to decide? . . . My personal teacher did not keep ethical norms and my devotion to him is unshakable. So I'm left with a big koan."[39]

Ultimately Trungpa Rinpoche died of alcoholism. But it was after his death that his community faced their biggest challenge. He had installed a successor who turned out to be both highly promiscuous and HIV-positive, but kept his illness secret and thus infected other students over a period of several years. The ensuing shock shattered the Shambhala community.

After the chaos broke loose, Pema resorted to her core practice: staying with the groundlessness. "The concern here is obviously one of not wanting to see students get hurt."[40] But Pema goes on to say that she would not want to see a list of "bad" teachers or "good" ones, a neat division of saints and sinners. "For so many of us that's our heritage, to make things one hundred percent right or one hundred percent wrong. It has been a big relief to me to slowly relax into the courage of living in the ambiguity. . . . You can't make it right, you can't make it wrong. I've never met anybody who was completely right or completely wrong."[41] Pema holds the view that what she sees in others is a reflection of herself. "I only know about myself. When I hear people judging very harshly, I feel I'm hearing as much about their hang-ups as I am about the issues. I am hearing about the places in themselves that they can't relate to."[42] This, she says, is not to be confused with seeing wrong being done "and we just say, Stop it! No buttons have been pushed."[43] So when women come to her with feelings of anger and betrayal, and complaints about male teachers, she never says, "There's no harm being done, this is just your trip." Instead, she asks, "Do you really want things to heal? Or do you just want to make someone wrong? Revenge and blaming others never heal anything."[44]

She prefers to keep the guru question open: "I know I love him. But I don't know who he was."[45] In reference to the Zen tradition, Pema calls it the "don't-know mind." "My undying devotion to Trungpa Rinpoche comes from his teaching me in every way he could that you can never make things right or wrong."[46]

SUCCESS AND STRUGGLE

It was Chögyam Trungpa who insisted that Pema should write down the teachings, but her own teaching career only blossomed after her teacher's passing. Her main books—*The Wisdom of No Escape*, *Start Where You Are*, and *When Things Fall Apart*—all became best-sellers in the midnineties. Her wisdom resonated so deeply with people from all walks of life that suddenly thousands of students wanted to attend her retreats; letters and invitations had to be delivered in laundry baskets. Just as her reputation was soaring, her body could not keep up. Pema Chödrön had been battling with a compromised immune system for years until her body stalled and called for an abrupt halt. She was diagnosed with chronic fatigue and chemical sensitivity. There is no miracle cure for chronic fatigue, no pill to pop to make you feel better and go out onstage to deliver that wise teaching that people are waiting for. While the real root causes remain largely unknown, the deep exhaustion might flare up unexpectedly and at times render her unable to move at

Pema the Riveter: An eye-twinkling comparison with the feminist icon
of a different era. Collage by Noa P. Kaplan. © Noa P. Kaplan

all. Pema took it with her characteristic willingness to learn from any
experience: "There must be a reason for it to happen," she once told
me. "It always happens to overachievers." And, she added with a wink,
"At least it flattens the ego!"

For more than a decade, Pema had to unexpectedly cancel assign-
ments, follow a very limited, strict diet, and hurriedly leave hotel rooms
that had been lovingly set up for her when chemical residues overpowered her immune system. Many, many times, there was nothing to do
but simply lie in a room by herself, bearing the pain and the frustration.

Most of all, she had to apply her own teachings from *When Things Fall Apart*. "This very moment is the perfect teacher," is one of the sentences she writes there.[47] "Every moment is an opportunity to either open up or shut down, to waken up or to try to run." When I once asked her how to deal with such a debilitating condition, she said she tried to apply the advice Trungpa Rinpoche had given her. "Lean into it. Stay present. Stay curious. Go through it paying meticulous attention as if you wanted to describe it in great detail to someone who's never heard of it."

One of the most pithy teachings in Tibetan Buddhism is called "Turning Happiness and Suffering into Enlightenment." It refers to taking any and every circumstance, whether good or bad, beautiful or ugly, as an opportunity for waking up. Pema did exactly that. She also figured out that the fatigue would bust her whenever she didn't stay true to herself. "I'm a people-pleaser," she says, "and as soon as I try to live up to other people's expectations, it instantly hits me."

One line from the Tibetan master Jigme Lingpa (1729–1798) reads, "Seeing the sicknesses as your teachers, pray to them." The fundamental question in Buddhism is not whether there is or isn't suffering. "It is how we work with suffering so that it leads to awakening the heart and going beyond the habitual views and actions that perpetuate suffering. How do we actually use suffering so that it transforms our being and that of those with whom we come in contact? How can we stop running from pain and reacting against it in ways that destroy us as well as others?"[48] This is the message Pema has been communicating, but people "have to hear it a lot, and with great heart, and from people who really care."[49]

When her health forced Pema to simplify her life, she took the opportunity to go into retreat. She accomplished a traditional three-year retreat at Gampo Abbey. Despite becoming quite ill toward the end, she gained "an appetite for retreat." She even went into complete silence for a year, without speaking at all. When Bill Moyers asked her what happens in that silent space, she quipped, "Well, the first thing that happens is that you climb the walls." She is quick to clarify, "This is personal with me. It doesn't happen to everyone. But the detox is so intense. It's like sensory deprivation. Gradually, what begins to happen is that you sink so deeply into what life has been distracting you from. That's the purpose of the retreat, no distractions."[50] Pema quickly learned "that distractions are not just phone calls and emails and outer phenomena. Our own mind, longings, cravings, and our fantasies are also major distractions. As time goes on, you're feeding it less because you are not talking. You begin to sink deeper into the undistracted state. And then you begin to realize that life is always pulling you away from being fully present."[51]

Knowing that she shares this experience with many, Pema openly talks about the abyss she fell into when she did her first longer retreat. Every time she sat down for a session, depression would bury her. She would try to distract herself, go for a walk, even read a magazine—but as soon as she sat back down on her meditation cushion, old companion Mister Depression joined her. Her own experience of illness, depression, and loss became fuel for deepening her practice further. "When there is suffering and pain," she once advised me, "rather than saying there's something wrong, we want to take this as an opportunity to purify our karma instead of creating more negative karma." At every moment, but especially when things get uncomfortable, "we could choose to do the habitual thing or we could choose not to sow those same old seeds again. At that very point, we can notice our opportunity to practice, rather than being preoccupied with feeling that we just messed up again."[52]

Being fully present "is basically a wide-awake state where your sense perceptions are wide open, in the tradition I follow. If you could imagine seeing and hearing, tasting and smelling and so forth, without any filter between you and your experience, it's as if suddenly all of your sense perceptions have been like narrow little slits and now they're wide open like they have no outer dimension."[53] She remembers that before she met the dharma, there was "the steady undercurrent of unhappiness. Not any big crises—just a steady undercurrent of unhappiness, never being able to contact the quality of the place I was at." In contrast, she now experiences an "ongoing steady feeling of happiness or contentment, a well-being which is really unshakable."[54]

THE REAL VALUE OF A TEACHER

And yet, after all her years of practicing, teaching, and writing best-sellers, she has found the need to become primarily a student again. After studying with Trungpa Rinpoche, and then with his son and dharma heir, Sakyong Mipham Rinpoche, she also entered into a new and challenging relationship with Dzigar Kongtrul Rinpoche. As she puts it, "He's been messing with me ever since."

In 1995 she was invited to a Buddhist teachers' conference in San Francisco[55] and arrived a day early to rest. "I spent all day really sick and sleeping." When she decided to venture out for a stroll and opened the door, Kongtrul Rinpoche walked out of his room across the hallway at exactly the same instant. They recognized each other, so she asked whether he would like to have a cup of tea in her room. She does not really remember what they talked about, but she recalls "very clearly that I started feeling better and the sickness just went away." The longing to find someone to answer her questions had been constantly with her since Trungpa Rinpoche's passing. "I was so inspired by what he was talking about that I began to feel stronger physically than I had for some time. I felt a powerful connection, and when I had an interview with him later, it reminded me very strongly of how I felt when I used to talk with Chögyam Trungpa Rinpoche, my root teacher."[56]

About a year later, when they met again, Pema asked to receive a certain set of higher teachings. Kongtrul Rinpoche refused. "That was a bit of a shock," Pema says, and so she asked him to explain why. He cited several obstacles he felt she needed to take care of first. "Later, when I had dealt with those and told him I felt confident that I could genuinely study these teachings with him, he agreed." Eventually, she started her first hundred-day retreat at Samten Ling in 2000. "At that time, I realized I hadn't met anyone since Trungpa Rinpoche who could sense where I was stuck. I was very good at conning everyone and talking about not getting hooked, but Kongtrul Rinpoche somehow had this great ability to hook me. I knew we must have a really old karmic connection. I felt so grateful to have met him, so I asked if he would take me as his student, and he accepted."[57]

Why is it so important to have a teacher, even with all her experience? "When you're with a teacher, their wisdom resonates with your wisdom. It transcends the two personalities," Pema explains. "Being with them connects you with your Buddha nature. The most important requirements for a teacher are to know you well, see where you're holding on, and be able to create circumstances that highlight your grasping. Situations emerge that allow you to see where you're stuck. Because it's happening with your dharma teacher, you don't run away when you're insulted or uncomfortable, and that's the real value. You hang in there and they help you through it."[58]

YES! YES! YES!

Usually we think of the teacher as the wise elder, but in this case the roles are reversed. Her teacher is nearly thirty years her junior. When Kongtrul Rinpoche teaches, often Pema's hand shoots up first to indicate she has a bunch of questions. "It isn't that the teacher messes with you exactly. It's simply that being in their presence heightens your sense of where you're stuck. We call it devotion because when that happens you don't run away. You get to the point where you feel there's nothing you could do that would cause the teacher to give up on you."[59]

At the time of their first encounter, she was still running Gampo Abbey, had an all-consuming schedule as a teacher and author, and her life was very full. Her heart's desire had been to find more time to practice, but her other commitments pushed themselves to the foreground. When Kongtrul Rinpoche suggested that she go into retreat for a hundred days every year, "I thought: Yes. YES! All along it has been these little nudges of something that I actually wouldn't have done myself, but as soon as he nudged me it was always a YES!" Eventually she found the determination to cut down on her responsibilities. "All these little nudges have been like somebody giving me the most precious gift. I've thought, 'Couldn't I have just done this myself?' But somehow I never would have. Without him, I wouldn't be doing it. It is good to have someone who keeps you in check," she says. Dzigar Kongtrul Rinpoche "really put me through a lot of changes. I was in awe of his ability to nail me exactly where I was stuck—it was uncanny. I trust completely that his motivation is to help me awaken."[60]

Pema strikes me as a very free and unconventional spirit. She seems extremely comfortable in her skin and her robes. Once she used the common bathroom at a dharma center. Finding the bathroom door locked and unaware that a nun was inside, Kongtrul Rinpoche's handsome young attendant started to undress right there in the hallway, rushing to put on a suit as the dharma talk was just about to begin. As Pema stepped out, the attendant in his underwear froze with embarrassment. Pema didn't miss a beat. Glancing at the half-naked young man in his boxer shorts, she whistled at him loudly. With an amused grin on her face, she calmly stepped around him, into the shrine room.

Elizabeth Mattis-Namgyel in Crestone, Colorado.
Photo by Sasha Meyerowitz. © Sasha Meyerowitz

6: Elizabeth Mattis-Namgyel

A WONDER WOMAN HERMIT

A Marxist's daughter explores everything in life as an open question, including her lama-husband[1]

AT DUSK a sudden, energetic knock at the front door startles me from daydreaming. I am not expecting any visitors. Several more determined knocks make me jump to my feet. As I peek out the kitchen window of my mountain cabin, I glimpse the scruffy black back of the late visitor—a huge, skinny mama bear prowling for food. She could probably shove her way through the flimsy wooden door. Years ago a well-meaning visitor fed the bears with salmon for his entertainment. Little did this fellow care that bears faithfully return to the same spot to harvest delicacies—long after he retreated back to the city. I grab some pans and bang them together with so much ear-deafening bravado that Scruffy runs for the woods. Elizabeth warned me she was living in one of the most remote areas of the United States.

Crestone, a hamlet with ninety-two inhabitants, is a major religious junction in the middle of nowhere. If one were to blank out the rusty Ford pickup trucks, the ramshackle clusters of old miners' huts, and the tiny gas station, this rugged tundra might well be the highlands of Tibet. Surrounded by the Sangre de Cristo and the Rocky Mountain ranges, whose fourteen-thousand-foot peaks almost always keep their snow hats even in the middle of summer, Crestone is nestled in the world's largest alpine valley. For millennia the Navajo and Hopi have been worshipping the sharp white peak that scratches the sky at the end of the dale as one of their holiest mountains. Shamans revere the valley as sacred ground, considering it auspicious that the red earth bubbles with hot, steamy water underneath. Ocean and desert, hot and cold—these layers of opposites may kindle sparks of realization. It must be more than just coincidence that several prominent Tibetan Buddhist teachers, as well as a dozen spiritual champions of other traditions, built their temples in this unlikely cul-de-sac of the universe. The small village of ranchers and its surroundings boast at least seven Tibetan Buddhist centers plus a Zen center, a Hindu ashram, a coed Carmelite monastery, and a colorful rainbow of miscellaneous tarot readers, healers, and soothsayers. Throw a stone in any direction, the locals joke, and chances are you'll hit a psychic. Where once miners rushed to unearth unprofitable ore, the locals now search to scoop out spiritual treasures. "People either go crazy," admits Elizabeth, "because the energy here stirs up the mind, or they use the force of the land to transform it for spiritual practice. It is not a gentle but an uncompromising kind of nature, which forces a certain discipline on you."

Practicing with Girl Power!

Leaving the spiritual bonanza below, a treacherously steep dirt track straight up the mountain ascends to Samten Ling, Kongtrul Rinpoche's spectacular retreat land where Pema Chödrön has her retreat cabin. Vertical crags give way to dramatic drops and a sky that could not be vaster. The sun burns at more than ten thousand feet; the path to Elizabeth's retreat cabin is so steep, I stop repeatedly to catch my breath under the pretense of immersing myself in the unending views. Elizabeth sprints ahead, unfazed—after all, she's done this hike hundreds of times!

Elizabeth spent seven years in retreat here in her tiny one-room wooden cabin, which is powered only by solar panels and is without running water. The view is five star: the harsh beauty of the desert plains stretches below her meditation cushion. The heartbeat of stillness is impossible to overhear. No cars chug; planes rarely cross the view, only ravens and eagles. From her cabin window, she can distinguish the brown balcony of the two-storey family house she has shared with

Dzigar Kongtrul Rinpoche for many years, a mere one-hour walk away at the foothill.

What do you think a modern hermit looks like? I bet you wouldn't expect this energetic, eloquent, and athletic elfin figure in a pink Wonder Woman* T-shirt with a bold "Girl Power!" stroke. The muscly super-heroine clenches her fist on Elizabeth's chest, while Elizabeth rummages for tea in her pint-sized palace. A diamond twinkles in her left nostril; big golden earring hoops add a touch of elegance. If you see her on one of her international teaching tours, she might wear an elegant black suit and a white collar shirt, no make-up, the shoulder-length brown hair put up in a casual ponytail. She could easily be mistaken for a successful businesswoman, if she weren't lecturing about meditation posture and compassion for all beings.

FREEDOM FROM EGO'S PREFERENCES

Her hazel eyes sparkle with delight as she points to the single bed—also her meditation seat—in front of her simple, wooden shrine-shelf. "Retreat forces us to learn how to sanely relate to all our experience," she explains with a broad smile. Outside of Tibet, a better place to explore mind could hardly be imagined. The sky falls through the huge windows into the light-filled cabin; framed behind her, a dancing fiery-red Vajrayogini bears witness to the millions of mantras and countless hours of visualization practices she has accomplished in this room. Elizabeth's husband, Dzigar Kongtrul Rinpoche, and her son, Dungse Jampal Norbu, gaze from family photos on the window sill. "I find it humorous that people think retreat is an escape from responsibilities and a withdrawal into oneself," she says. "In retreat, all you have been suppressing comes to the surface. You put yourself in a position of being unable to ignore that. My experience in retreat has shown me that through practice I can actually learn to enjoy my experience, even when the mind is a bit rough, dull, or wild. It has taught me that I don't have

---

*Wonder Woman is a popular comic superheroine. William Moulton Marston created her in 1941 as a new archetype of a strong, unconventional woman who succeeded with fist power, wits, and love.

to struggle so much, that I don't have to feel so intimidated by the activity of thoughts and emotions. This gives an incredible peace of mind."

She clearly embodies and breathes Kongtrul Rinpoche's teachings of living the dharma not only on the cushion but in every moment. "Knowing fear and fearlessness," she says of what she learned from her long retreat. "There's a lot of fear in our wants and not wants. I began to take a keen interest in things that I normally try to avoid. Seeing the nature of things releases us from all the grasping we normally have. So the fruit of the practice is freedom: freedom from fear, freedom from ego's preferences. It provides you with a very big way of being. Even if the insight is momentary, you don't forget that possibility."

Elizabeth appears to effortlessly juggle her commitments as a retreatant, dharma student, wife, and mother. Of course, being married to a Tibetan master and not having to work a nine-to-five job help, but still, her dedication is impressive. Elizabeth does not hesitate to dispense straightforward advice to the many women who long to strike a better balance between family, work, and self-realization: "You need the intention, good scheduling, and you have to be creative. If you don't find the time to practice, one of the three is missing."

BEYOND BLINDISM AND DOUBTISM

I've known Elizabeth for more than fifteen years. I first met her on trips to Europe where she accompanied her husband on teaching tours; later she was guiding me as a savvy, compassionate retreat master at Samten Ling. I have seen her evolve from student to editor, author, and teacher in her own right. She often raises challenging questions in her husband's teachings; discussion groups with her are always lively. But I was surprised when I heard her first international teaching in France, because she chose a most challenging topic, devotion to one's guru. She plunged straight into the conundrum.

She confesses that she has long struggled with this core idea of Vajrayana practice: seeing the teacher as the Buddha. In Tibetan Buddhism, the path of each student is grounded in limitless devotion and trust for his or her teacher. The teacher is no longer seen as an ordinary, human being but as completely perfect, the Awakened One in human flesh. A wonderful teacher, the late Penor Rinpoche, gave Elizabeth the advice "never to see the teacher as ordinary." Elizabeth was "deeply moved by this advice . . . yet I wondered, how do you see anything as perfect when the mind has so many preferences? What do you do with that?" One of the most important traditional practice manuals that Elizabeth follows, *The Words of My Perfect Teacher*, instructs:[2]

> You should have so much confidence in him that you perceive him as a real Buddha. . . . Be like a perfect horse, always acting according to the teacher's wishes in every situation, skillfully avoiding anything that would displease him, and never getting angry or resentful even when he reprimands us severely. Like a bridge, there should be nothing that we cannot bear, however pleasant or unpleasant the tasks he asks us to do. Like a smith's anvil, we should obey his every command. . . . However incomprehensibly the teacher may behave, always maintain pure perception.

If you're married to one, how does this go together with discussing who does the dirty dishes after dinner? She reveals her conflicts, loneliness, and frustration, along with her deep gratitude. "It is like an unspoken rule that we don't talk about our doubts or unresolved questions, and I question that." In the ancient texts, disciples jump off cliffs, stick splinters of wood under their fingernails, and build huge monuments that they have to tear down and reerect, all at the command of their teachers.[3] "It's impressive and touching," Elizabeth says. But what do these examples suggest for our own path? "Do they mean we should put our discerning intelligence aside and simply do whatever is asked? What does it truly mean to be a student?"

THE JUICY PUZZLE OF FAITH

She didn't know, and obviously no one was going to tell her. Elizabeth had to "unscramble this juicy puzzle: What is the Middle Way understanding of faith? Can we have faith while utilizing our own discretion?" And is there a way beyond, as her teacher puts it, "blindism and doubtism?" For years it would nag at her when other students were raving about how they truly saw Kongtrul Rinpoche as a buddha in human form. Not that she didn't think he was wonderful, but she secretly felt her perception wasn't entirely pure. "And then we wonder, 'What happened to my devotion?' What really happens is that we start to wonder about ourselves. 'Why can't I be like the disciples we read about in the texts?' This really big dilemma comes from having a very, very small view of who the teacher is." The teacher-student relationship only works if it is grounded in trust and by letting go of common concepts. "When we think of the teacher as a perfect buddha in this ordinary way we just have a very limited and contrived idea of what that is. What happens is when our teacher does something that we don't understand, we can't maintain this grand and static view, and perfect starts to fall apart. Then we start to fake our devotion a little, pump it up."

In her first book, *The Power of an Open Question*, Elizabeth devotes a whole chapter to the challenge of "the perfect teacher." I happened to be there when she showed Kongtrul Rinpoche this very chapter for the first time.

HOOK AND RING

The occasions have become rare when the whole family is together. On this sunny afternoon after one of Kongtrul Rinpoche's teachings, sitting outside on the small patio in front of his silver airstream trailer in the forest above Boulder, she opens up her laptop and reads aloud to her husband and her son. "When I think about my teacher, Dzigar Kongtrul Rinpoche," Elizabeth starts out, "I feel deep appreciation, love and loneliness, sadness and warmth, all at the same time. But if you were to ask me who or what my teacher truly is, I couldn't tell you. I've spent a lot of time trying to understand him. But every time I think, 'I've got him now—I know who he is,' I run into problems. The teacher, like all things, is beyond definition or objectification."[4] Elizabeth decided to take her relation with the teacher as her koan, a paradoxical question to unravel on her spiritual quest. Inevitably, the question provokes a startling, lifelong search for every Buddhist student: What does it mean to have a teacher? How far are you willing to go, how unconditional is your trust?

Elizabeth has found an answer: "It may sound as if the topic here is the teacher, but our investigation of the teacher really just throws us back on ourselves."[5] In dealing with the teacher we essentially face the same dilemma we have with our own mind. "Because on one hand we want to be a good practitioner, that's very noble, but what do we do with all our humanness, our passion, aggression, and ignorance? How do we reconcile 'me' with enlightenment? Please understand that I'm not saying that the teacher is not extraordinary, but I just don't think we can know the teacher through our ordinary ways of seeing."

She uses the traditional analogy of hook and ring to describe the relationship between teacher and student. "I think we can hear this and think, 'Oh great, if I just hang out with the teacher, he'll hook me like a fish and just pull me out of my misery.' But it doesn't work like that." To her, the image of hook and ring means interdependence. "It's very safe to put the teacher on a pedestal and have a fantasy. Because you don't have to self-reflect, you don't have to change, you don't have to give up your ego. The teacher is the hook, but if we don't become the ring, there is nothing for the teacher to hook." She concludes her chapter with this insight:[6]

> When we meet the perfect teacher we see everything as perfect. This is because we see the world beyond our habitual objectification of it—we see the infinite and boundaryless nature of things. This is the fruit that comes from this special relationship . . . there is nothing else like it. But until we realize the true meaning of perfect, the teacher will just be waiting, and waiting, and waiting . . .

Kongtrul Rinpoche quietly nods after she has finished, and, after a pause that seems endless, grants his seal of approval with only a few words: "Good. This is really good."

FULLY HUMAN, BRAVE, AND HONEST

Unexpectedly, Elizabeth sabotages the reading session and turns the family picnic into a pistachio war, grabbing fistfuls of nuts from the snack bowl and aiming them into her son's mouth. Soon all three of them are throwing, giggling, and ducking. "We have our ordinary moments. As a family we have so much fun together," she says later. After all these years, she admits, it is Rinpoche's humanness that touches her the most: his honesty, bravery, and his profound dissatisfaction with the self and all its wants and not-wants, "for to be fully human and totally present in every activity is a great accomplishment."

She clearly loves her own freedom and independence. Kongtrul Rinpoche would often tease her, lovingly. "She likes to stir things up," he would say, when Elizabeth posed one of her probing questions. I find her example highly inspiring. I have sometimes watched Asian wives carry an extremely devout, submissive demeanor around their husbands, never questioning any of the spouse's manners and decisions. As a young, unmarried Westerner I was not only perplexed by that; it put me off. To see a self-confident Western woman strike that crucial balance between probing and trusting seems invigorating, even crucial, for translating the age-old Asian concept of devotion in the West—not only for the wife of a Tibetan teacher but for any spiritual seeker.

FOLLOWING A PEACOCK TO NEPAL

Elizabeth found her calling in the midst of the most unlikely circumstances. As if propelled by an irresistible voice, she swerved outside the rut her own culture prescribed for her. Spending seven years in solitude around bears and mountain lions might have been a staple in the remote Himalayas, but it is such an unusual endeavor in modern-day America, especially for a mom, it begs the question: How did she get here?

Her mother, Naomi Mattis, remembers that Elizabeth and her classmates had to pick a developing country for a field trip in their second college year. The night before they had to submit their suggestions, Elizabeth dreamed vividly of a peacock in Nepal—a tiny, conflict-ridden

Elizabeth Mattis-Namgyel in her retreat cabin in Colorado.
Photo by Michaela Haas. © Michaela Haas

Asian country she knew little about. When she woke up, she announced
a firm decision: "Mom, I'm going to Nepal." Never mind the small detail
that her school had no connection with Nepal whatsoever. The director
suggested China, Mexico, or Africa, but Elizabeth remained undeterred.

"She threatened she would leave the school if they did not let her go to Nepal," her mom recalls, her green eyes shooting wild looks mimicking Elizabeth's rage. "She was that serious!" Elizabeth even had to appear before the entire all-male school board to present her arguments. "I think she spent the whole second college year just hatching out that plan and did hardly anything else," Naomi says, now laughing. Of course, Elizabeth got her way.

A STAB IN THE FACE

Maybe her spiritual hunger had to do with an attack in San Francisco when she was twenty-one years old: a stranger stabbed her in the face, for no reason, out of nowhere. The knife went straight through her right cheek. Luckily a plastic surgeon happened to be on duty in the emergency room to which the ambulance rushed her. Today only a faint scar gives away the assault. But it heightened in Elizabeth the burning sense of needing protection and guidance.

"I came from a very atheist environment," she recalls, now smiling at the radically different path she took. "My socialist grandparents immigrated from Russia; my dad, a radical socialist type, wrote for the underground communist newspaper in California." After her dad became a top music business executive at a record company, an unending flow of famous rock stars and artists poured through her parents' living room in Santa Monica. Amid the anarchistic debates at home, Elizabeth was eaten up by a yearning question: "What should I do with my life? I wanted to do something meaningful, but I didn't know what that was." Her mother, an impressively warm and vivacious psychotherapist, was already studying Buddhism with Tibetans. Naomi was also caring for dying patients. From their deathbeds she often brought home an urgent sense of impermanence, an imperative awareness of the preciousness of every moment. Yet Elizabeth had to find her own path.

Finally in Nepal, she wandered off on her own into a national park, simply guided by her intuition. At a riverbank, she met a local farmer's wife and accepted her invitation to dinner at her family home. She ended up staying three months in the jungle with this family, without electricity or running water, sharing their harsh and simple, yet earthy and very natural, life. After she came home, all she wanted was to return. Naomi recalls her saying: "Mom, you'll never really know me until you come to Nepal." To which Naomi responded, "Wow, that's quite a statement; graduate first, and then let's go."

Relaxing into unfabricated awareness

On this second trip, together with her mother, Elizabeth started to cautiously explore the Buddhist community in Boudhanath, the Tibetan quarter of Kathmandu nestled around a giant dome, where thousands of Tibetans struggled to rebuild their monasteries and humble huts in exile. Several of the finest teachers at the time, such as Dilgo Khyentse Rinpoche and Tulku Urgyen Rinpoche, opened their doors to the first Westerners and tourists who took interest in their teachings. "But somehow nobody got through to me where I was at the time," she says. "It is only in retrospect that I understood the depth of their advice." At a meditation retreat with Tulku Urgyen in a small nunnery high above the Kathmandu Valley, a young man in a leather jacket and the traditional Indian white wraparound sarong approached her and talked about meditation. Usually she would shy away when Asian men sought contact, but this seemed different. They talked for a while and Elizabeth remembers thinking: "I wish I could meet a teacher like that. His eyes were so clear. He got through to me; his words resonated with me deeply."

Soon she found out who he was: the highly respected Dzigar Kongtrul Rinpoche, believed to be the incarnation of Jamgon Kongtrul the Great, one of the wisest and most influential nonsectarian* masters of the nineteenth century. The young man had just given back his monk's vows earlier that year. Admittedly, he felt a little lost himself, seeking space in the hermitage to recover from the ensuing fallout of handing back his robes, sorting through his confusion about where to go from

*The nonsectarian movement (Tib. *rimé*) aims to hold all major traditions of Tibetan Buddhism in equal esteem.

here. The first instruction he gave her was simple yet perplexing: "Don't create." Practice, he taught, meant leaving the mind in its natural state, without manipulating thoughts and sensations—not creating endless castles of thoughts and fantasies.

This advice was very provocative for Elizabeth, as in her artist family, the most creative people were held in the highest esteem. Yet his instruction rang true. Bringing the mind home, leaving awareness unfabricated, is the simplest yet most profound meditation instruction, which continues to inspire and guide her to this day. Instantly, she and Kongtrul Rinpoche became inseparable. "This was it for her," says Naomi who, in the pre–cell phone era, disbelievingly watched her future son-in-law faithfully show up each morning at the steps of their guesthouse. "I became his first student and his wife almost at once," Elizabeth recalls. She was twenty-three, he twenty-one, when they met and married. Elizabeth added his family name to her own and became "Namgyel," the Tibetan word for "all-victorious." In the few pictures that her mother took of the pair at the time, they look skinny and fresh-eyed like teenagers. "At that age, you don't know who you are," Elizabeth confesses. "I didn't know what it meant to be married either. I had to figure it all out."

The newlyweds moved into a small room tucked into a corner at the great Boudhanath Stupa, the enormous white hemispherical dome that houses some of the most sacred Buddhist relics. Whoever sees the stupa, or so the locals believe, will be blessed with the seven qualities of divine bliss: noble birth, beauty, fortune, virtue, intelligence, power, and wealth. Because Elizabeth lived eye to eye with the Buddha, divine bliss must have been a homerun: since the Buddha's eyes are painted on the central column larger than life, he was practically staring into her kitchen.

"YOU HAVE TO KNOW YOUR OWN MIND!"

In Nepal, the profane and the sacred are effortlessly intertwined with the countless bodies of pilgrims and beggars that shove and push around the relics, almost any time, day and night. The stupa is a public bathroom where Nepalese girls drop their saris to the waist and let their sisters scrub their backs. Beggars with broken limbs reveal their open ulcers to solicit a few more rupees. Devotees light butter lamps to pray for the welfare of their loved ones.

Amid the bustle, Elizabeth was eagerly trying to fit in, memorize Tibetan honorifics, and mimic the traditional customs—so earnestly that Kongtrul Rinpoche's mother, Mayum Tsewang Palden, took her aside and kindly advised, "Dear, you don't have to try to be a Tibetan. You don't have to be an American. Just know your own mind." These words pointed Elizabeth in the direction of true practice, "beyond the foreign cultural forms I was wrestling with." Kongtrul Rinpoche's mother was an extremely accomplished practitioner. "She was not an ordinary woman but a true yogini," Elizabeth explains. She went into retreat when she was thirteen years old and had to be cajoled into leaving her hermitage ten years later to marry the great master Chokling Rinpoche. Together they had five children, four of whom are renowned masters. Though they are among the most accomplished and kindest practitioners, one senses an unusually strong force underneath their boundless kindness. This might be unsettling or intimidating. "You have to hold your ground," Elizabeth admits. "I was this naïve young girl from California walking into this strange new world. It took some time for me to find my way with it."

A SUPER BIRTHDAY PRESENT: A SON

Elizabeth began teaching English at a school in Kathmandu, but soon she was expecting a child. Heavily pregnant, Elizabeth traveled to Thailand with Kongtrul Rinpoche and her mother, in order to give birth at an upscale hospital in Bangkok. As if to show how strong-willed his wife can be, Kongtrul Rinpoche animatedly tells the story how, on the spur of the moment, Elizabeth decided to give birth on Kongtrul Rinpoche's twenty-third birthday, October 23, 1988. Wouldn't that make a super birthday present? Kongtrul Rinpoche remembers thinking, "This was pretty much impossible." Indeed the baby wouldn't come. After more than five hours of off and on labor, the doctor on duty impatiently left to go home. Fifteen minutes before midnight, Elizabeth asked what time it was. Kongtrul Rinpoche told her, and he remembers vividly, "She got really mad! She got up and walked around the room, and within ten minutes the baby came out!" It just seemed "a good present," she now says a little shyly, "and he seemed to appreciate it."

They named their son Jampal Norbu, "the Precious Soft-Voiced One." The first part is also the Tibetan name of the Buddha of Wisdom, Manjushri. When Dilgo Khyentse Rinpoche blessed the baby, he predicted that Jampal would be Kongtrul Rinpoche's successor and lineage holder. Jampal, now twenty-three years old, is an unassuming, lanky gentleman with a perplexing sense of humor. He currently studies with his father at Kongtrul Rinpoche's family seat in the Tibetan settlement of Bir, North India, preparing for his future role as the dharma heir. Instead of handing him over to a monastery for training, as parents of tulkus usually do, Kongtrul Rinpoche kept him close.

Kongtrul Rinpoche acknowledges that he came to the West due to Elizabeth. With Jampal still a baby, they got on a plane to Boulder, Colorado. Kongtrul Rinpoche was offered the World Wisdom Chair at Naropa, the Buddhist university founded by Chögyam Trungpa Rinpoche. Elizabeth went on a rigid schedule. During the day she would pursue her master's degree at Naropa, studying Buddhism with her husband who was slowly building a small but devoted community of Western students. Often getting up at three in the morning, while Jampal was still asleep, she would start doing her prostrations to complete the hundred thousand prostrations, refuge and bodhichitta prayers, cleansing, offering, and guru yoga* practices that Kongtrul Rinpoche's tradition prescribes as preliminaries.

But then, almost overnight, Kongtrul Rinpoche decided to move to Crestone. With a lama-husband, there doesn't always seem to be a satisfying answer to every why. So Elizabeth packed up and went from a hectic city and university life to a godforsaken one-horse town. Sure enough, this was only the first step toward extreme seclusion.

---

*Yoga (Skt.) literally means "unifying." Guru yoga is the practice of merging one's mind with the mind of the teacher.

FEARLESS MEDITATIVE CONCENTRATION IN THE VAST EXPANSE

A multimillionaire businessman and United Nations undersecretary, Maurice Strong, and his visionary partner, Hanne, had turned Crestone into a spiritual haven by offering various strips of land to Buddhist masters and other teachers. Kongtrul Rinpoche fell in love with the most remote, the steepest and wildest part of the pine- and juniper-covered mountain that is now his retreat center, Longchen Jigme Samten Ling (roughly translated from the Tibetan as "Sanctuary of Fearless Meditative Concentration in the Vast Expanse"). As soon as he had built the first wooden cabins, he conducted a traditional three-year retreat for a handful of his closest students. But for Elizabeth, three years turned into seven. "It was my way of avoiding teaching," Elizabeth jokes. Every year Kongtrul Rinpoche asked if she would rather come out of retreat and start teaching, and every year she chose to stay another year.

Elizabeth clearly enjoys that part of her life. What exactly then is the beauty of retreat? "When you're living in the world you sometimes can escape or manipulate experience, there are different ways to distract yourself. We are always trying to get what we want, or not get what we don't want, or struggling with getting what we want and finding out it's not what we wanted after all," she says. "In retreat, you can only struggle with experiences for so long. Ultimately, practice is about enjoying your experience, your own mind. That's the beauty of it."

CHILD'S PLAY IN RETREAT

Jampal was only nine years old when she went into seclusion. How did she do a retreat while raising her son at the same time? Jampal assures me his mother wouldn't have left if he hadn't agreed to it. After all, he'd grown up seeing his parents meditate many hours each day, and he naturally associated meditation with something nurturing. When asked if he needed his mom, he says with a smile, "I'm quite independent. And I liked that I always knew where she was." Still, Elizabeth was fortunate to have close friends living in her house who took care of her son and her household. Since her house is only a few miles away from her retreat cabin, she would go home at night to spend time with her son, read bedtime stories to him, and sleep in the house. In the morning, she would wake him up, have tea together, and a friend would take him to school. At other times she stayed up at the retreat cabin, with an extra bed for Jampal to visit. It sounds like mere child's play when she describes the arrangement, but it is really rather unusual. Whether in the East or West, parents usually have to leave their children to do longer retreats, and therefore most of them won't. To this day, Kongtrul Rinpoche has adopted quite an accommodating approach, not only for his own family. His students accomplish the practices—traditionally done over three years in strict seclusion—in increments of one hundred days or even just a month at a time. When they feel the need, their children can come to visit. The cabins are spread so far apart, no laughter or playing would disturb another retreatant, and the practitioners themselves find that the openness enriches both their practice and their family lives.

Some very traditional Tibetans might not call that a strict retreat then, but Elizabeth offers her own insight into what retreat is: "When am I practicing and when am I not?" This, she says, has emerged as the key question for her. One could spend twenty-four hours on the cushion without a moment of true practice, and conversely one could practice while pursuing seemingly ordinary activities. When is the mind spinning off? When are we pushing away experience? How do we experience the difference between engaging the practice and not? How does this liberate the mind? These are the questions Elizabeth likes to explore on and off the cushion: "This is finding the true inner boundary."

The outer boundaries of her first three years of retreat were strict— she did not even speak for a year and a half. "I was really tight about it, I didn't even want to talk to other retreatants," she admits. "It was good, but there was some neurosis in it." One day, after pulling her out of her hermitage, Kongtrul Rinpoche drove her to a nearby hot spring—a nude hot spring, no clothing allowed. Whereas in traditional retreat, it is very important to create a protected space where the retreatants are not seen by others, this was the exact opposite—total exposure. They ran into an acquaintance who enquired incredulously why Elizabeth wasn't in her cabin. "I was kicking and screaming inside," Elizabeth remembers, "But it was very helpful to let go of the tightness." This is partly what Tibetan Buddhism is about: not holding too tightly to any concept, even concepts that are supposed to be "right."

THE CHALLENGE OF SEEING THE HUSBAND AS A BUDDHA

Elizabeth stresses how fortunate she feels to have this close, intimate bond with her teacher. Yet she does not gloss over the challenges of such an unusual relationship, since any Vajrayana master could safely be labeled unconventional. "Being married so young and finding myself both a student and wife at once had its challenges," Elizabeth exclaims with matter-of-fact honesty. "There is not a sangyum club or a website one can go to and ask for advice. Sangyums never talk about these things amongst each other."

There were only two teachers' wives she ever talked with about her mixed feelings. Once a sangyum whom she had never met before saw her with Kongtrul Rinpoche. "She took me by the arm, really strongly, pulled me into a private room and said: 'If you don't serve others you're going to suffer terribly, and if you serve others you can be happy.' It's like everybody knows there is some challenge to this kind of relationship, but no one discusses it."

At a Buddhist gathering, Elizabeth met another Westerner who had tied the knot with a very unconventional Tibetan master: Diana Mukpo had married Trungpa Rinpoche in 1970, when she was only sixteen years old. In her autobiography,[7] she openly discusses the challenges she struggled with: Chögyam Trungpa's alcoholism; the lack of privacy in a family house that also served as a dharma center and constantly housed many students. Diana also speaks frankly about how she came to accept her husband having numerous girlfriends. As she put it, "Rinpoche was much too big a personality to trap into a monogamous relationship."[8] Upon meeting Elizabeth, without any preamble, Diana Mukpo sprung a rhetorical question on her: "It's hard, isn't it?" Elizabeth instinctively thought this could only refer to marriage with a Tibetan master, felt tears welling up, and could only nod her head. "But," Diana Mukpo continued, "you wouldn't change it for anything in the world, even for a moment, would you?"

Elizabeth is quick to add that she feels extremely blessed, not least "because Kongtrul Rinpoche is very open and very progressive as a person." She can speak authoritatively about her struggles now, because she painstakingly worked through her queries. "These teachers are like a force of nature. Sometimes it's hard to understand why they act and speak in a certain way. If you try to figure it out rationally or according to what the ego wants, you are not going to get anywhere. It really requires you to have a bigger way of seeing things, which means a desire to give up ego." Many times her teacher's words and actions have challenged her. "I could come up with all kinds of justification why something was unfair. But then who would challenge the limits of my conceptual mind? If we understand the teacher-student relationship correctly, we will take everything onto the path. Sometimes I haven't been able to see the benefit for a long time, but eventually I do, it never fails, and my appreciation and love for him continue to grow."

FREEDOM ON THE ROCKS

Though she is not in strict retreat anymore, she often visits the retreat land, if only to guide retreatants who now follow the same path in the simple, wooden cabins that dot the vast land. On other days, she stays home, writes a new blog post in her cozy kitchen, studies, or teaches via the internet. Her feisty orange cat, Don Julio, jumps on her keyboard and strikes a few letters, before she gently brushes him off. One night, the headlights of her car caught the tiny kitten in the middle of the road, shivering. She took him home. A good deed. But now Don Julio turns out to be a skilled mouse and bird hunter and kills many animals. "Is it still a good deed to save a killer?" she asks half-jokingly.

She has found her calling in translating the ancient wisdom of Buddhism into modern-day American. Even her father, the staunch Marxist, grew to appreciate her teachings. Her parents, Naomi and Marvin Mattis, live just down the road from her. Marvin admits, "I started off by removing myself from myself by becoming political. I gave myself to

Elizabeth Mattis-Namgyel seeking balance in Colorado.
Photo by Buddy Frank. © Buddy Frank

Stalin—can you imagine that? When I saw people giving themselves to the guru, I was horrified." Now, more than two decades later, he raves that his "life has opened up as if I was a seventeen-year-old virgin." He attributes his spiritual revival to his daughter's husband but also to her own transformation and teachings. "Elizabeth communicates to me directly," he says, "and she does not paint golden lotuses."

Elizabeth laughs out loud but then lowers her gaze, slightly embarrassed when her parents heap praise on her. Elizabeth is always cordial and willing to break into a hearty laugh but also noncommittal. She only sheds some layers of reservedness when she ventures outdoors, into the wilderness of the mountains around Crestone. For many years, she would watch people conquer the near-vertical rock needles that a giant has stuck into Colorado's desert plains. "I wondered how this was even possible," she says, and sure enough, she had to try it out for herself. Watching her put on the harness and explore the cliffs means venturing into another dharma lesson. Hanging on the wall, stuck between a slippery ledge and an overhang, there too she discovers the dharma and an analogy to life itself. "The experience of being suspended on a rock and not seeing any possibilities for moving up and down is an exaggerated experience of facing the unknown," says Elizabeth. Within this exhilarating, scary, vibrant moment, when she can't find a foothold, "our mind may fall into an open stillness, the same open stillness we encounter in any situation where we lose our familiar reference points."[9] And this, after all, is what the dharma is about: staying present and open, relaxing even into probing situations, and suddenly "all kinds of new patterns and shapes begin to emerge from the rock. We see places to balance we didn't see before."

Later that afternoon, she visits the horse stables, as she does almost every day. This might be the only hobby she has carried over from her teenage years in Santa Monica. She instantly lights up when she calls her mare from the paddock. Of course, she picks the one horse that nobody else could ride: Braeburn, a feisty white female, the strong-willed leader of the herd. I watch Elizabeth gently whisper to her mare, groom, and saddle her. But as soon as she mounts, Braeburn starts to prance on the dirt track. Elizabeth tries to canter, and Braeburn falls into full-speed gallop, racing across the yellow-dotted fields. Against the dazzling backdrop of the Rockies, their racing looks dangerously beautiful. I worry if Elizabeth is in control of her steed. When she turns around and trots back, she admits she got a little nervous too, but she has a big smile across her face. "I feel free," she whispers into the wind, almost sighs, "I just feel so free!"

Chagdud Khadro at Khadro Ling in Brazil.
Photo by Ronai Rocha. © Ronai Rocha

7: CHAGDUD KHADRO

(JANE DEDMAN)

LIKE IRON FILINGS DRAWN TO A MAGNET

---

*A former journalist from Texas opens up on her spiky
marriage with a renowned Tibetan master*

TO A KEEN EYE, all other teachers in this book are immediately iden-
tifiable as Buddhists, whether through their robes or Tibetan clothing, or a protective amulet around their neck. This refined, fair-haired
lady with the pageboy cut wears no dharma jewelry or rings at all when
we meet in Los Angeles, just a pearl necklace over her casual business
outfit—a grey skirt and white cardigan. Chagdud Khadro has unusually
bright blue eyes and a kind gaze that can turn uncomfortably probing.
She speaks very softly and almost hypnotically slowly, whereas I nearly
have to shout my questions so that she can understand them. *Chagdud
Khadro* is the title her late husband, Chagdud Rinpoche (1930–2002),*
gave to Jane Dedman after several years of marriage. Chagdud Rinpoche
and Khadro were married for twenty-three years, until his passing in
2002. Now in her sixties, Chagdud Khadro spends most of her time
near Três Coroas on the East Coast in Brazil, in a Buddhist center that
bears her name—Chagdud Khadro Ling. She is especially renowned
for her teachings on *phowa*, the traditional Tibetan transference of
consciousness at the time of dying. When I ask her students about her,
they all stress her impeccable work ethic and humility. Bel Pedrosa, one

---

*Chagdud Rinpoche was the sixteenth recognized Chagdud incarnation. Chagdud liter-
ally means "iron knot" and is said to derive from the first Chagdud incarnation who
folded an iron sword into a knot with his bare hands.

of her Brazilian students, vividly recalls how she visited Chagdud Ling for the first time many years ago, signed up for cleaning the outhouses, and found herself scrubbing them side by side with Chagdud Khadro. Despite being Chagdud Rinpoche's wife, Bel goes on to say, "she does anything, is always the first to jump in when something needs to be done that nobody wants to do, nothing is beneath her." Dzongsar Khyentse Rinpoche, whom Chagdud Rinpoche asked to help guide his centers, calls her "a perfect example of a lama's wife. She puts all the others to shame, even the Tibetans." The signature sentence Chagdud Khadro keeps repeating during our three-hour interview is: "I am really very ordinary." However, her extraordinary life tells a different story.[1]

MH: How does a girl from Texas end up as a spiritual leader in Brazil?

CK: I did not meet the dharma until I was thirty-one. I had quite an ordinary childhood. I grew up in a big, rip-roaring refinery town, Port Arthur, Texas, the home of Janis Joplin. At night the sky was a lovely green color because of the oil refineries. But I loved it there. Both my parents were creative, intelligent people. My father was an engineer and eventually became the head of construction and maintenance of Texaco's supertankers; my mother had social skills that brought a lot of life to his corporate advancement, and she invested the family money quite wisely. When I was fifteen, my father's work took him to New York City and we moved to a Connecticut suburb. After high school I went to college in Virginia and majored in English, and after that I joined the Peace Corps and went to Sierra Leone, West Africa. I taught English—I loved teaching reading—in a village elementary school, and after school I took care of horrific tropical skin infections. In 1970 I returned to the US, after traveling through West and East Africa, Turkey, and Europe. I then moved to New York, where I worked as a researcher, fact checker, and freelance writer for various magazines.

MH: What made you then leave your dynamic New York life?

CK: One day, I was making a cake and the oven exploded. I had second- and third-degree burns on my face. My whole life changed in that moment—in appearance I went from being a reasonably attractive woman to somebody nobody wanted to sit next to in the subway.

That was a big teaching in impermanence. Inwardly and outwardly, I was shocked, unmoored. I had always been very interested in women travelers, and about the same time as the burn, I started reading about fascinating women who had traveled through Africa and Asia. Eventually I wrote an article about Alexandra David-Neel, who in 1924 was the first Western woman to reach Lhasa, the Tibetan capital. That article paid two thousand dollars, and with that money I bought a round-the-world ticket. I traveled alone, first to Afghanistan; I had gathered a few magazine contracts to write about my trip.

MH: Did you think it was just a trip and you would return to New York?

CK: I thought I would return, but I also had an intuition that I might not. Before leaving New York, I bought fifty thousand dollars' worth of life insurance. I wanted to repay my parents for my education, and I told my friends, if I die have a big party. In Afghanistan, I took a bus trip to Bamyan* with a group of French tourists, one of whom was murdered the day after we arrived. This was sensational, front-page news and could have been a major story for me, yet I did not write about it. Instead it haunted me, as another sign of how easily circumstances change, how easy it is to die. When I finally reached India, some weeks later, I was enormously relieved not to be a woman traveling alone in Muslim countries, and I gravitated to the Buddhist holy places—to Ladakh, to Dharamsala, and finally to Tso Pema,† where I met accomplished masters and yogis and where I formally became a Buddhist. In Tso Pema, there was an incident where I almost died because of a heater that gave off carbon monoxide. To me, this was another lesson in impermanence.

---

*The Bamyan Valley, northwest of the Afghan capital, Kabul, lies on the historic Silk Road and was home to two monumental Buddha statues from the sixth century until they were destroyed by the Taliban in 2001.
†Lit. "Lotus Lake." A small town in northern India where the pioneer of Tibetan Buddhism, Padmasambhava, is said to have practiced and performed miracles in the eighth century.

WADING INTO AN OCEAN OF COMPASSION

MH: How did you meet Chagdud Rinpoche?

CK: When my Indian visa expired, I left for Nepal. In Boudhanath, I attended empowerments given by Kyabjé Dilgo Khyentse Rinpoche. Chagdud Rinpoche led the procession of the high lamas as they left the monastery. As soon as I saw him, I was riveted. I asked someone, "Who is that?" I made a big effort to meet him. I offered him a white scarf and a jar of honey at our first audience, and about two weeks later I proposed marriage. The outer conversation was about Rinpoche's coming to the United States, but inwardly, I had developed a very deep wish to be with him. I said, "Why don't you marry me?"

MH: I can't believe you said this!

CK: Rinpoche looked at me sternly. When he eventually accepted, he likewise said, "This will not be a passport marriage."

MH: When you first saw him, do you remember what you felt at that moment?

CK: It was not conceptual. It was just as they say in the teaching, iron filings moving irresistibly toward a magnet. In Bodhgaya, just before traveling to Nepal, I had made an aspiration prayer before the Tara image on the wall of the temple. I prayed that I would realize the highest compassion and the highest love between a man and a woman. Four days later I met Chagdud Rinpoche who provided an avenue for both aspects of that prayer.

MH: Did he speak English at the time?

CK: Very little; he developed his own English. He had a tremendous vocabulary and spoke fluently, but he always used Tibetan syntax. His students loved his way of speaking, but Rinpoche regretted not having proper English.

MH: How would you describe him to someone who never met him?

CK: One friend described meeting him as wading into an ocean of compassion. He was a warm and wonderful listener. He had a magnificent presence. His room was full of art projects and texts, and usually one or more small dogs. He liked to sing, to sew, to paint and sculpt, and he was surrounded by constant activity. We felt rich around him, abundant, because he held a limitless wealth of teachings and wise advice. He had confidence in Western practitioners, and he did not hold back any level of the teachings. He wanted to be called the "motivation lama." His main teachings were on pure intention, and he constantly reminded us to check our motivation for actions of body, speech, or mind.

MH: In his autobiography,[2] he mentions that when he first spotted you in the audience, he saw you surrounded by a red radiance, a powerful and compelling light. Do you have a feeling that you've met before in other lifetimes, and this was just a rekindling?

CK: He later joked that he should have known the red light was a sign of anger. Whether it was a rekindling of past connection or simply all my good karma ripening in this lifetime, things happened very fast and very powerfully after we met, and the relationship endured.

Honeymoon and kitchen sink

MH: How was the beginning of your relationship with him?

CK: The beginning in Nepal was a teacher-student "honeymoon" for about six months. Rinpoche was very peaceful and seldom criticized me, even though I am sure I was often unskillful in serving him. In the mornings he would usually do ceremonies for various people who had requested them, and in the evenings he would teach until late at night. His energy seemed inexhaustible, but I was often exhausted. After that initial honeymoon period, Rinpoche became much more challenging. As my teacher, he was committed to my cutting through negative habits and finding liberation in my mind.

MH: How did he work with you?

CK: It was a really spiky teacher-student relationship. It was difficult, because I had an angry personality and harsh speech. In the world of New York journalists that I had left, tough, cynical speech seemed to win respect. With Rinpoche it did not, and if I became angry, he would blaze with pure wrath. Compassionate but overwhelming; thought-stopping. So, I learned to talk less and more carefully. Later I clearly saw how my words and tone of voice hurt others, and I developed a purer motivation for my communication. All this took a long time, however, and we also had miscommunication because of English/Tibetan language and cultural differences. Still, the storms passed, and his wrathful clarity was like lightning. Afterward the air was clean, with no residue of resentment. Despite this difficult process of transformation, I never thought of breaking off the relationship. I revered his wisdom, and I could not imagine being anything but bored without him.

MH: Was Rinpoche unpredictable?

CK: He was predictable in having pure motivation and totally reliable in his deep compassion, but sometimes surprising in his methods. I was unpredictable in my understanding of his motivation.

MH: Were you inseparable from the first meeting onward?

CK: I left Nepal about four months before Rinpoche and went to Japan, which I found fascinating. Then I got a message from Rinpoche: "Go to Los Angeles and wait for me at the airport"—no date, flight number, or anything—so I did. When I arrived, which was late at night, I called the few phone numbers I had after being in Asia for more than two years. Finally I reached a friend who told me, "Rinpoche is coming tomorrow night. Just wait in the airport." We immediately went to San Francisco where we stayed with an American friend of his whom he had met in India. That first year was challenging because of uncertainty and not having much money, but it was wonderful to have a lot of time with Rinpoche. Later, when Rinpoche gathered his heart students in Oregon, things became easier.

MH: Why did he want to come to America?

CK: Just after escaping from Tibet in 1960, he had a dream in which he heard the word America. He asked other Tibetans, "Where is this America?" They told him, "Far away, across the ocean, and the people there have strange blue eyes." Then in India and later in Nepal, he began to meet people from the United States, including me. He had a sense that his activities would take him to the US, and indeed, once he arrived in 1979, things flourished quickly.

A WEDDING FEAST IN A GAMBLING CASINO

MH: So did you finally get a traditional Tibetan marriage?

CK: Not exactly. We were married in South Lake Tahoe, in a chapel with a heart-shaped entrance, adjacent to a gambling casino. Afterward Rinpoche went to the blackjack table and played until he had won enough money for a wedding feast—strangers joined us. Then he went back and played again until he won exactly what he had spent. He never gambled again as far as I know. Although the ceremony was unconventional, even humorous, the inner connection was stabilized. It was not a passport marriage; it endured. Rinpoche died on the day of our twenty-third anniversary, on November 17, 2002.

MH: Did your parents come to the wedding?

CK: No, and at first they did not approve. But later Rinpoche traveled to the East Coast without me, and my parents hosted him in their home, and they respected him. My mother particularly had great affection for him and he for her. I think she had her own spiritual path, rather different from the Presbyterian upbringing of her childhood. She certainly was very intuitive. My father never gravitated toward the Buddhist path, but he was proud of what Rinpoche accomplished. After Rinpoche's death, when he learned that I was now the spiritual director of the South American centers, he said with his thick Southern accent, "Well, Jane, I didn't know you were that caliber of lama." [*laughs*] He was proud of me for maintaining Rinpoche's activity.

MH: What about your siblings, did they show any interest?

CK: I have one sister, Ann, who has attended some of my teaching events and those of other lamas. She actually has better meditation than I do. She is a chef in New York City. If you ever see a chef in action, you see one-pointed concentration.

MH: With that family background, how could you dive into the dharma that quickly, from Texas into a world rich with empowerments and reincarnations?

CK: The teachings fascinated me and made total sense, especially the four thoughts, especially contemplation of impermanence.* Meditation

*As Chagdud Rinpoche writes in his autobiography, "For almost everyone the path of Tibetan Buddhism begins with four contemplations: the preciousness of human birth; impermanence and death; the karmic law of cause and effect; the pervasiveness of suffering for all beings trapped in realms of existence conditioned by delusion, attachment and aversion." *Lord of the Dance*, p. 39.

was a challenge, as I had no meditative background. It remains an ongoing process; I did not begin as a natural meditator.

MH: What makes you think so?

CK: Rinpoche was a great Dzogchen master, but I was the densest of his students. I had strong faith, but it took me a long time to even begin to fathom his teachings on how the mind works, how it is. I would listen to teachings and think about them, but without deep meditation, my direct experience was limited. My path has been step-by-step, not great leaps.

MH: Do you feel that his blessings speak through you?

CK: I hope so. Sometimes when I sit down and pray to the lineage, it feels like a cord is plugged into electricity. The teaching starts to flow. This does not mean that I can transmit the teachings perfectly—I have limitations, and I only teach what Rinpoche specifically authorized me to teach, which does not include Dzogchen—but I deeply wish that those who hear me are benefited.

THE SPHERE OF ENLIGHTENED ACTIVITIES

MH: When did the transition happen from Jane Dedman to Chagdud Khadro?

CK: After I married Rinpoche, I received no new name, because all his names were titles. I was kind of grumpy about still being Jane Dedman, so after a few years, he gave me the family name, Tromge. This was a huge honor, because his family is very special. Then he ordained me as a lama in 1997, and during the ordination he explicitly said that I would succeed him as the spiritual director of the Chagdud Gonpa* centers in South America. We discussed which lama name would I take, and he said, "Well, traditionally you would be called Chagdud Khadro." Again, I felt honored. The name change signaled a weightier responsibility.

MH: What does it mean to be the *khandro*?

CK: The dakini principle refers to the sphere of enlightened activi-

Gonpa is the Tibetan word for monastery. The original Chagdud Gonpa, founded in 1131, is one of the very few monasteries in eastern Tibet that survived destruction after the Chinese invasion.

Chagdud Rinpoche and Chagdud Khadro.
Courtesy of Chagdud Gonpa Brazil Photo Archive

ties. What it means to me is to be the hands and the voice of the lama's mind, with the aspiration to be the mind of the mind. Since Rinpoche is not here anymore, my hope is to bring his voice more clearly into focus again through writing.

MH: Traditionally, students think of you as the same as Rinpoche.

CK: Perhaps it is useful for them to feel and practice with that perception, but if I were to think that way myself, I would be in very big trouble, very deluded. Self-identity as a khandro is fatal; the whole idea is to be beyond that self-identity.

MH: How did you reconcile being a student with being the wife at the same time then?

CK: I tried not to presume on my role as a wife and to maintain my role as his close student. Tibetans have a very deep sense of family, and Rinpoche's family was the entire community. He had a Tibetan wife, Karma Drolma, who is the mother of his two children. The collapse of their marriage was really painful for him, but later, she found a different and integral role in his family. She is a very great practitioner, and I don't think Rinpoche would have lived such a long life without her.

Each person had his or her own special relationship with Rinpoche. To have been close to him in any capacity was good fortune. My role as his wife allowed me to be with him in a lot of special moments. I had my own niche in his life, and other people had theirs as well, and one just could not bump them out of it because one wanted more. He was orchestrating the time and the relationships.

MH: Was there some jealousy?

CK: Oh, yes, sometimes I was jealous, terribly jealous. For instance, when people could speak Tibetan, they had a special avenue with Rinpoche. I had no facility with languages whatsoever, and I am hard of hearing, so that was a big source of jealousy for me.

MH: I also meant in terms of sharing the lama.

CK: He made it clear that his life was with his students, and that I would be serving all of them. Sometimes they would receive teachings, and I would be falling asleep, dead on my feet after long days. There were no illusions about that; he was not withholding that piece of information.

VAST INSIGHT AND PURE PERSPECTIVE

MH: Diana Mukpo, Chögyam Trungpa Rinpoche's wife, writes that she really never saw her husband as ordinary, because he was so extraordinary. How did you perceive Chagdud Rinpoche?

CK: I never did see him as ordinary. But I would fight with him anyway. [laughs]

MH: How do you reconcile fighting with your husband while seeing him as your teacher?

CK: Sometimes he was right on the mark about the incident that inspired his wrath, and sometimes it was not that exact incident but a build up, and a small mistake would detonate a big explosion. I learned to listen on a lot of levels rather than stoutly defending myself. But sometimes I reacted!

It all sounds very turbulent, but honestly, I don't know if any other lama would have had the patience to deal with me, especially at the beginning. It is not always the case that a lama marries the best person—perhaps some marry the worst who most needs their guidance. I did not assume that I was the most wonderful wife possible, believe me!

MH: Yet you helped him fulfill his vision and work.

CK: What he really wanted me to do was to write down and edit his teachings. I was more comfortable in a subordinate position, just taking care of him, cooking, cleaning, organizing things, but he would push me to write. He thought I had a potential to benefit beings through writing, but it was like trying to get a horse to jump through a fiery hoop because of my writer's block.

Once I was working on the Tara commentary,[3] and I asked him yet another question—a delaying tactic. Saying furiously, "You are never going to complete this!" he tore the manuscript in half. Everybody present was aghast. I went to a bedroom, flung myself down, both crying and laughing at the comic aspects of this drama. When I regained my composure, I rejoined him again, and he handed me the manuscript, each page taped back together! We both laughed then.

Another time I was working on a *ngondro* commentary,[4] a compilation of his teachings. Even so, he insisted that my name should be on the book, offering me all the credit. Rinpoche invested me as a teacher very early on, and his confidence in my potential was much greater than my own.

MH: One of the practices he authorized you to teach is phowa, the transference of consciousness at the time of dying. How did your connection with teaching phowa come about?

CK: Rinpoche first taught me phowa in Nepal in 1978, and I got good signs, not because I had good meditation but because of his power of practice. So, I felt an affinity for that practice, and I was riveted by his teachings on dying and the stages after death, which I compiled into a manual.[5] Later I had a dream in which I was teaching phowa, which I told to Rinpoche. When an opportunity arose, phowa was the first teaching I gave—only one person attended, the lady at whose house the event was held. That was in Austin, Texas! My mom drove me there.

MH: You taught phowa to your mother too?

CK: My mother listened to my teachings but did not practice. I was fortunate to do phowa for her when she died in 2005.

MH: Are there other empowerments or teachings that you give?

CK: I offer in-depth teachings in the Vajrayana preliminaries (*ngondro*) and for several deity practices, for which I give empowerments. The Vajrayana path is very clear and structured, and opens the door to vast insight and pure perspective.

MH: Chagdud Rinpoche was one of the first Tibetan teachers who authorized Western women as teachers.

CK: The first teacher he authorized was Inge Sandvoss, now known as Lama Yeshe Zangmo, after she had completed a very diligent three-year retreat. Later he ordained six more women. One of the differences in Tibet and the West is that except for nuns who were abbots of their nunneries, there were not many women in the hierarchy, orchestrating the teachings and practice of large communities. Rather, there were great female yoginis who practiced as retreatants or as householders. Now centers—and not only Chagdud Gonpa centers—are often run by women. There are female scholars and translators as well as the continuation of the lama tradition of individual yoginis in the West. I believe a beneficial cross-pollination has occurred between Asia and the West, and that we will now see more scholars among Tibetan nuns—with proper training, there is no reason for them not to become khenpos, for example. And Western women ordained as nuns are finding more support here.

A WILD AND UNPREDICTABLE DAKINI

MH: Have you been to Tibet?

CK: I went to Tibet with Rinpoche and his son Jigme Tromge Rinpoche for the first time in 1987, shortly after it opened. The trip was difficult, emotional for both of us, but I began collecting the stories that later were woven into Rinpoche's autobiography.

MH: In Tibet, did you meet Rinpoche's mother and sister?

CK: Rinpoche was born into an extraordinary family. His mother, Dawa Drolma, was widely regarded as a dakini, a healer, and a *delog*,*

Delogs (Tib.), literally "returned from passing," are believed to have died and then returned to their human body to report their visions.

someone who had traveled to the dead and come back. She died giving birth to a baby boy when Rinpoche was eleven years old. He later said that her death brought him direct experience of impermanence and the illusory quality of existence, and it profoundly deepened his spiritual practice.

The baby boy did not live long, but Rinpoche's sister, Trinley Wangmo, is still alive, a wild and unpredictable dakini. She is rather strange looking: I took a series of photographs of her during that trip, clicking the shutter a few seconds apart, and in that short time her face was peaceful, wrathful, charming, horrifying—an unstoppable play of emotions, not at all like the dakinis painted in Tibetan art. And she disconcerted the monks at several monasteries by abruptly moving her residence and making impossible requests. It would not have been worth the disruption and distraction if she had not also demonstrated the powers of meditative accomplishment such as clairvoyance and supernatural actions.

MH: In his autobiography, Chagdud Rinpoche describes how she defied the Communist invaders.[6]

CK: They tried to execute her at least three times. In one event that was witnessed by several hundred people, guards stripped her down to the waist and drew a target on her chest. The executioner pressed the trigger two times, but the gun did not fire. He shot in the air, successfully. He aimed at her a third time, and again the gun did not fire. Frustrated, he threw the weapon on the ground, and the guards handcuffed her. Suddenly, in front of the whole crowd, the handcuffs shattered into small pieces. They threw her in prison for one night and the next morning sent her away, saying, "Get out of here, you crazy woman!"

In a previous lifetime, she was an old woman who lived under a bridge, seemingly without food but well fed. She had a dog that likewise had no food but appeared well fed. Then the area was struck by famine. The villagers decided she was a demoness and the source of their misfortune. They seized her, threw her in the swift, icy river, and then watched with amazement as she floated upstream, against the current. They knew they had made a serious mistake, fished her out, and treated her with respect from then on. In this lifetime, the Communists did the same thing, and again, she floated upstream. They likewise fished her out and avoided her thereafter.

MH: Was marrying into such an obviously unconventional family terrifying for you?

CK: I never doubted Rinpoche's compassion. The second time we went to Tibet, we went on horseback. I don't have much affinity for horses, and Tibetans have mean little ponies with triangular saddles. They gave me the last one. The horse ran away with me, along a very steep ravine, before one of the Tibetans got it under control. At that time, I had a doubt. I thought his sister might have given me this mean little horse so that I would die. I didn't think that she liked me. But it wasn't so, they were just not paying attention.

Sixteen lifetimes of enlightenment

MH: You spend most of your time in Brazil now. How did that come about?

CK: I'm still wondering myself, how did this all happen? In the early 1990s Rinpoche began teaching in Brazil quite often, and in 1994 I traveled with him, and we bought the land that is now Khadro Ling. It was almost raw land, with two small houses, a feeble electrical line, and water from a little spring that sometimes dried up. With the help of a generous student, the first construction began in 1995, and seven years later when Chagdud Rinpoche died, he had built a fine infrastructure and a large, traditional Tibetan temple.

MH: I understand that he gave it to you since he named it Khadro Ling, and you live there?

CK: Rinpoche named Khadro Ling the "Place of Dakinis" not because of me, but because dakinis represent enlightened activity. He did not give it to me. It was not like a house or an estate that could be given but a field of merit to which many people could contribute. An ongoing collaborative effort involving other lamas, practitioners, artists, volunteers, and even paid employees has allowed the Chagdud Gonpas in South America to continue and to thrive. Rinpoche had sixteen lifetimes of recognized enlightenment. There are so many lifetimes of aspiration and realization, no one of us holds all of this.

MH: Are you developing your own sphere of activity?

CK: In terms of the dharma, I only aspire to provide wise custodianship of the Chagdud Gonpa centers, to continue my training, and to help the students as they come to me. Sometimes I have other wishes, like to take an extended automobile trip in the United States, and to listen to and write people's stories, or to take a garden tour in Europe, but I doubt that I will do those things. I am sixty-five now, I teach about impermanence and death all the time, and it is hard to make anything but dharma a priority. Except, I really may try to become fluent in Portuguese or Spanish, just so I have that satisfaction of accomplishing something that I could not do when I was younger.

MH: You were in retreat when Rinpoche passed away. Did his death come unexpectedly?

CK: Rinpoche had a heart condition and diabetes, and we were always concerned for his health. Just before his death, he had been in retreat and only came out to give phowa teachings to about three hundred people. At the beginning he said, "We have two days together." The students corrected him: "No, we have three days together." But he died after two. There were preparations to get him to his cardiologist, but he resisted going and died before they could take him. He remained seated in meditation posture for five-and-a-half days after his last breath, with no deterioration of his body.

MH: Do you feel he is still with you?

CK: [*hesitantly*] Yes, I do. It is not as if I have visions and dreams, although other people do. I just try to align myself with his intention, checking my motivation for ego-bound biases. I think about what Rinpoche would do in a similar situation, and sometimes students remember stories about what he actually did do. And I pray, to him, to my living lamas, and to the lineage masters. When blessings come through, they are like fresh air on a hot day. But I live with a lot of uncertainty.

Venerable Karma Lekshe Tsomo at the author's home in Malibu.
Photo by Gayle Landes. © Gayle Landes

8: Karma Lekshe Tsomo
(patricia zenn)
surfing to realization

How a Malibu beach girl became mother to the
"Daughters of the Buddha"[1]

GETTING TO LADAKH is the easy part. In hindsight, the twelve hours of intense heat and acute thirst in the rickety bus from Dharamsala to the airport in Chandigarh seem like deluxe travel—the bus only breaks down twice. Now the airport clerk balks at Karma Lekshe Tsomo's luggage. The bags are already ninety-five pounds overweight, due to six hundred feet of maroon and yellow cloth a friend has sent for the nuns from Bangkok. Charmed by her patient, unperturbed friendliness, the clerk relents: "We are lenient with tourists." On the magnificent flight from Chandigarh to Leh, the old capital of the former kingdom of Ladakh, the snowy peaks of the Himalayas glitter in the sun almost eye to eye with the tiny plane. "It is like floating through Shangri-La," Lekshe says, gazing in awe, until the emerald valley of Leh with its bustling bazaar emerges below and the plane lands.

But getting to Zangskar from Leh is a whole different story. Buddhist women live in many remote corners of the earth, yet there is hardly a place as remote as the Zangskar Valley, located in the desert of North India along the western reaches of the Himalayas. Centuries ago, these moonscapes were part of Tibet. They are a long way from Malibu, California, where Lekshe grew up. Yet she is determined to again visit the school for young nuns that she established there more than twenty years ago.

LIKE ANOTHER PLANET

"Ladakh is like being on another planet," Lekshe says with unveiled enthusiasm. "The altitude, the rarified air, and the barren, extraterrestrial terrains create an unearthly atmosphere." The village women in their distinctive animal-skin dresses with huge turquoises woven in their long braids, beckon with welcoming voices. "*Jullay!*" they peal, issuing the standard Ladakhi greeting, "Where are you from?" "I come from America," she replies. "Are you a lama?" they inquire incredulously, pointing to her maroon woolen robes. "I am a *jomo*," she tells them in fluent Tibetan, using a local respectful term for a nun that literally means "revered woman." After living and traveling in Asia for more than twenty years, this wisp of a woman easily blends in. With her evenly shaved head and her five feet three in maroon robes she does not stand out in the market bustle, but word about a curious white-skinned visitor is spreading fast. Crowds gather around her with keen bemusement the next day, along the main bazaar street of Leh. Why is the foreign nun buying thirty pairs of identical red socks? Quality ascertained and fair value bargained for, the seller solemnly deposits the purchase in an ancient, crumbling plastic bag that will surely not survive a truck ride or a trek up a mountain. She rolls her eyes and breaks into laughter all at once.

Lekshe speaks Asian languages such as Tibetan and Japanese like the locals. Her clear, grey eyes in her soft face have taken on an almost Asian expression, a blend of equanimity, super-sharp intelligence, and do-not-take-yourself-so-seriously poise. She is not easily rattled, not by a bus that has just left an hour ahead of schedule, not by inquisitive villagers who circle her in throngs, not by the inevitable disasters that come with traveling through the most remote parts of the world. She seems to have picked up the best traits of the countries she has lived in—the easygoing laissez-faire of the Malibu surfers, the vivid joyfulness of the Hawaiians, the discipline and simplicity of the Japanese, the humbleness of the Thais, and the ability to happily endure the complete chaos of the Indians.

When I first met her in her modest home near San Diego, her hilarious deadpan humor won me over instantly, and I almost couldn't imagine what would get her to lose her temper. She seems as calm and clear as the Malibu coast on a picture-perfect day in spring. In a way, the California girl has come full circle: now she lives in California again, in a sun-filled one-bedroom cottage in Pacific Beach near San Diego, where she teaches Buddhist philosophy at the University of San Diego. But whenever she can, she goes to see "her" nuns. Fifteen study centers dotted all over the Himalayas would not exist without her untiring efforts.

FIGHTING AN UPHILL BATTLE

About twenty-five years ago, Lekshe single-handedly started a movement to give nuns access to education. At the time this idea was, at best, treated as a waste of time, or even discouraged by the established monasteries. "They're telling the nuns, 'Oh, you're so humble, you're not interested in gaining prestige and power like these Westerners,'" Lekshe says with a calm voice but a quizzical look. "Well, I just wonder why they are not telling the monks that. If women are perpetually disadvantaged, this is what you end up with. Surveys show that the nuns' health is by far the worst of any group. Their educational standards are by far the worst too. There is a lot of work to be done, and awareness raising, especially among women."

Now, in the midst of the Himalayas, the task of getting provisions to the small, remote nunneries means fighting an uphill battle, literally. The Zangskar Valley opens to motor vehicles for only three months a year, even in the best of times, but recent snowfall and avalanches have just closed the only available road, though it is already July. Supplies of food, kerosene, and other essential commodities are rare and expensive. Aware of their bargaining power, the only available truck drivers demand ludicrous amounts for the journey. For a one-day road trip, they want to charge a sum that roughly equals three years of wages for a Ladakhi.

"Highway robbery," Lekshe Tsomo puffs and starts rummaging through her bags. Aware that she and her nun friend may need to trek for several days in the snow over fourteen- to seventeen-thousand-feet passes carrying everything on their backs, she takes along only the necessities: warm clothes, sleeping bag, American granola, powdered milk, medical supplies for the nuns, and a camera to record their lives. The footpath, long and treacherous, will take more than ordinary determination to traverse. But hoping to bring educational opportunities to a new generation of Zangskari women, she is ready to spare no effort to achieve her goal.

Of course, many people have noticed that Asian women are disadvantaged, but it speaks volumes that Lekshe did not leave it at taking notice. She set out to develop a network of supporters, even at the cost of her own life and health. Along with her late teacher Freda Bedi and her friend Tenzin Palmo, she is among the earliest and fiercest advocates for the education of Tibetan nuns. Her own experiences as one of the pioneer Western nuns shaped her determination.

The accidental Zen heritage

Lekshe carries the seed of Buddhism in her family genes. "My path was pretty clear, because my family name was Zenn." A misspelling at immigration when her family came to the United States three generations earlier, the name should have read "Zinn," the German word for tin, or "Senn," for shepherd. Her classmates in Malibu teased, "Zen? Are you a Buddhist or what?" At eleven years old, she went to the library asking for a book about Zen to find out what this taunt was all about. The librarian handed her *The Way of Zen* by Alan Watts[*] and *Zen Buddhism* by D. T. Suzuki.[†] "I read them from cover to cover and said, 'That's it!' The minute I opened these books, it all rang true. It was that straightforward." Who could have known that the teasing of sixth-graders would cause a revolution some decades later?

---

[*]Alan Watts (1915–1973) was a British writer who became a counterculture celebrity and best-selling interpreter of Eastern thought for a Western audience in the late sixties and early seventies.

[†]Daisetz Teitaro Suzuki (1870–1966) was a Japanese lay practitioner and preeminent author of many books on Mahayana Buddhism, especially Zen, that had an enormous impact in Europe and America.

Her mom, a Southern Baptist, was horrified when Patricia announced her new faith. "In her belief system, there was only one true path, while everybody else was going to hell," Lekshe says. Her father's religion? "Capitalism," Lekshe shoots back. He was an aeronautical engineer at Douglas Aircraft, a fabulous storyteller, but a strict, domineering man. In his daughter's words, "Anyone who wasn't making a bunch of money was just wasting his life." Without the slightest understanding of his daughter's spirituality, he disowned her several times. Lekshe did not see her father for many years. "He disappeared," she says, shrugging her shoulders. "He only started talking to me again when I got a PhD. We were just the typical dysfunctional American family." Her younger brother, Philip, now a fisherman on the Hawaiian island of Molokai, got swept away by drug addiction but developed some interest in Buddhism. "It's his birthright too, in a way, because of the name," Lekshe says, "but he never got into it completely." When her mother remarried several times, Patricia withdrew and lost herself in books. "I was quite reclusive, and my mother was really worried about me. I had a strong inclination toward contemplative life ever since I was a child. If I had grown up next to a monastery, I would have become a nun a long time ago, but in bohemian Malibu . . . ."

HEAVEN OR HELL

Her mother dragged the kids to church every Sunday. "I always loved the teachings of Jesus, the simplicity, compassion for the poor, all of it." But she smiles at the question if the sermons rang true to her. "Where I was raised, the hypocrisy was obvious. Jesus taught these wonderful principles, but I just didn't see people practicing them. Little kids notice, don't they?" At home, booze and cruelty overpowered the family's Christian values. One evening her mom served Patricia's pet bunny, Flopsy, oven-roasted for dinner. "How could you possibly do this to a child—my favorite pet!" she recalls. The idea of God eluded Patricia, "because I couldn't find any evidence for it. And then I couldn't get answers to my questions: What happens after we die? Where were we before we were born? The answers I got were too simple: heaven or hell."

These were the fifties. An unlikely advocate of Buddhist wisdom was the American comedian Lenny Bruce. On his record album, he joked: "We know the sound of two hands clapping. What is the sound of one hand clapping?" This famous Zen riddle is designed to lead the student to a contemplation of profound meaning, beyond ordinary logical mind, but the record buyers just thought it was funny. "He recorded a few koans like that, as jokes. And people just started picking it up." When she was a teenager, there were no teachers and hardly any books. "It was hard to distinguish between the different traditions of Zen, Theravada, and so forth. Meanwhile I read Jack Kerouac* and dreamed of going to Japan."

Surf gods, Hollywood stars, and beatniks

Growing up in Malibu, Lekshe discovered another religion: surfing. "Surfing and Buddhism were the only two things that mattered to me. I was totally disinterested in dating and all those sorts of things, but living in California, it was hard to avoid." She joined the Malibu Surfing Association, at a time when Malibu was an epicenter for surf gods, Hollywood stars, and beatniks. Lekshe considers surfing a spiritual endeavor. "When you're out on the ocean, feeling a close kinship with nature and other beings, you have an altogether different perspective on the human experience. Offshore in the vast ocean, it is very clear how minuscule human beings are. Peacefully waiting for the next set, there is time to reflect on life. Surfing is a great way to get in touch with one's own mind, which of course is the whole point of Buddhism." But she is quick to point out that, like anything, the decisive factor is how we go about catching the next wave. "When it is all about *my* wave, surfing can become competitive and vicious. That certainly has nothing to do with spirituality."

---

*American novelist and poet Jack Kerouac (1922–1969), one of the pioneers of the so-called Beat Generation, immersed himself in Buddhism in the fifties. He was the author of *On the Road* and *The Dharma Bums*.

SIMON AND GARFUNKEL IN JAPANESE

Lekshe dropped out of Occidental College in 1964, then nineteen years old, to travel to Japan for surfing and found herself the only woman in Japan's first international surfing competition. During the summer, she chased the waves near Chiba Peninsula. In winter, when the snow mixed with the water, she moved near a Zen temple to meditate. She stayed for a year but searched in vain for a Buddhist teacher.

On a ship from Yokohama to Singapore, she had a lucid dream of herself in robes, surrounded by extremely joyous, loving people. Yet she didn't know where to find such a community. She traveled all over Asia—to Thailand, Cambodia, India, Nepal, Sri Lanka—searching for a teacher and a monastery for women but came up empty. At the time, she did not know that nunneries were few and far between. Only years later did she find some small nunneries in Japan—gems tucked away in remote places with only a few venerable nuns.

"Maybe I hadn't experienced enough of life," she surmised and set about to try "just about everything." She painted, wrote poetry, became a yoga teacher, trained in aikido, even started a folk rock band with friends. She played autoharp and guitar, her strawberry-blond hair down to her waist, rings on every finger and toe. "Too bad my voice was so wimpy. I could never sing blues. So disappointing." She played on the streets of Germany and in clubs in Afghanistan, "enjoying a gypsy lifestyle. We had fun. People always invite you to play and sing." In Japan, her band recorded an album—Simon and Garfunkel in Japanese.

She also visited temples, chanted the mantra of compassion, OM MANI PADME HUNG, and wrote the *Heart Sutra* over and over again in Chinese, but was still searching for the opportunity to study Buddhism in depth. So she returned to California, studied Japanese at the University of California, Berkeley, and got a master's degree in Asian studies from Hawaii. In 1971, she set off for India again and found her way to the Library of Tibetan Works and Archives that the Dalai Lama had opened in Dharamsala.

This center for Tibetan studies in India, where translator Sangye Khandro also studied, was groundbreaking—the first to offer philosophy and language courses for Westerners and Asians alike. Lekshe remembers the day she first ran down the hill to the Tibetan Library. Much to her delight, just as she walked into the classroom, a Tibetan teacher was describing the process of dying. Here were the answers to all the questions about death that had intrigued her as a child. "The teacher, Geshe Ngawang Dhargyey, laid out *exactly* what happens after death, stage by stage. This was precisely what I always wanted to learn."

Lekshe raves about the library as the "fantastic" opportunity to dive into the Tibetan Buddhist science of mind. "We could study with traditional Tibetan teachers, learn the language, and practice in a conducive environment." In Geshe Ngawang Dhargyey, a well-known monk-scholar, Lekshe found her guide. She was so enthusiastic that she eventually stayed for fifteen years, interrupted only when she ran out of money. The first year, she lived on her savings from caring for elderly Japanese in an old folks' home in Hawaii. The second year, she sold her guitar. That must have been a valuable guitar? "Two hundred and fifty dollars," she recalls, "which lasted me a whole year." The third year, things became dire. An American woman offered her lunch every day. Then she began traveling back and forth between India and Hawaii to work as a Japanese translator for tourists in Waikiki.

THE LAKE OF ELOQUENT SPEECH

All the while, Lekshe's ordination dream aboard ship never left her. "For me it was a normal progression. If you're serious about dharma practice, you don't want to get distracted by relationships. Sure, relationships can be fun, but I'd already been through that and didn't find it satisfying. In fact, it was boring." Even as a teenager? "Oh, as a teenager, I wasn't interested at all. I was a surfer," she says decisively. Living in Malibu myself, I swallow the remark that these days, surfing and dating do not seem to be mutually exclusive.

Lekshe finally realized her dream to become a nun in 1977. Pema Chödrön offered her her first set of robes. "Of course, a celibate lifestyle is not for everybody," she says, "but for me, it was ideal." The Sixteenth Gyalwa Karmapa ordained her in France and gave her the name Karma

Lekshe Tsomo. *Karma* indicates the Karmapa's lineage. Very fittingly, *Lekshe* means "eloquent speech." And *Tsomo* is the Tibetan term for "lake," indicating expansiveness. With a twinkle, she explains that men are often named *Gyatso*, meaning "ocean," whereas women get the smaller version. "I was very naïve," she reflects in hindsight. "When I got ordained I did not know that full ordination was not available to women in the Tibetan tradition." There was no training, no website, no nunnery to go to. "We got off to a good start with the Buddha," she remarks. "Monks and nuns were more or less equal. But then patriarchy reasserted itself."

Seemingly by coincidence, she struck up a friendship with a nun who explained the precepts and protocols of full ordination to her. Five years after her novice ordination in France, Venerable Hiu Wan, a legendary nun in Taiwan,* invited her to Taiwan to receive full ordination. Lekshe sees the lack of full bhikshuni ordination for women in many Buddhist countries as a serious drawback. "Why shouldn't women have the same opportunities?" she asks. "More and more, I see it as a human rights issue. Either you have human rights, including religious rights, or you don't. And many women today do not have full religious rights. I think this is unacceptable in the twenty-first century."

As explained in the introduction, Tibetan nuns currently remain novices their whole lives. "There is great resistance from some monks," Karma Lekshe Tsomo says with a sigh. The senior monks would all need to agree on one model for bhikshuni ordination. "We have to be patient," she says, confident that things will strike a balance eventually. "In the end, this is like a great wave that cannot be stopped. The monks may as well ride it. Otherwise, they will go down on the wrong side of history." Not only is higher ordination unavailable to women, but they have not been able to take the final exams in higher studies. "Six of the nuns at our monastery have been ready for years. They have worked so hard. But they have not been able to take the geshe exams because they have not completed their study of Vinaya (monastic discipline). And

*Bhikshuni Shig Hiu Wan (1912–2006) was an outstanding poet and painter who initiated the International Buddhist Studies Conferences and later established Huafan University, one of the leading institutions of higher education in Taiwan.

they have not been able to complete their study of the Vinaya because they are not bhikshunis." She hopes that the recent appointment of a German woman as the first female geshe at the Institute for Buddhist Dialectics, where Lekshe also studied, will open the door for Himalayan nuns to receive the degree as well.

The gender imbalance also makes a grueling economic difference. "Buddhists believe in the idea of merit. Giving to a community of fully ordained monks or nuns is considered meritorious, so donors are happy to support them, feeling that they gain more merit." Keeping the full number of precepts is more meritorious in itself, too. This might be "hard to the Western ear," she continues cautiously, "but Buddhist practice entails clearing out as many distractions as possible and being as mindful as possible, in the broadest sense of the word. Having so many precepts keeps you out of trouble," she says, laughing. "You don't get into compromising situations, and you are free to do what you signed up for."

Too stupid to learn reading

When she studied in Dharamsala, India's first Tibetan nunnery was close by, in the British hill station of Dalhousie. Ironically it had been founded not by an Indian or a Tibetan but by British immigrant Freda Bedi. Another nunnery emerged in Dharamsala in the mid-1970s, but both of these were completely overcrowded. Almost every day, nuns came knocking at the door looking for a place to stay. Lekshe realized that something was seriously wrong with this picture. "The situation was very, very sad. There were lots and lots of nuns coming out of Tibet completely illiterate, ill, and penniless." At the time, she was studying at the Institute of Buddhist Dialectics in McLeod Ganj, near the Dalai Lama's monastery. Zopa Rinpoche gave her the lease to some mud huts in the forest that he no longer needed. Initially, Lekshe thought this might become a nice monastery for Western nuns, "but in the end it was the Himalayan nuns who came. They were really keen on studying." She began with a literacy project for the nuns, because so many of those who fled Tibet could not read or write. "They were so dedicated, so highly motivated, they learned very quickly," she says proudly. "Within two months, all of them could read and were eager to learn more."

At first, the nuns expressed a heartbreaking lack of confidence and kept saying, "Oh, we're too stupid to learn to read." Lekshe wondered, "What does it do to women when they only ever see males on the thrones, in the lineage trees, on the book covers?" But the nuns quickly became motivated to study hard, keen on understanding the Dalai Lama's teachings. "It was quite wonderful to see them blossom, studying sincerely, and eventually debating philosophy. After learning Tibetan, they wanted to learn grammar, so I got a grammar teacher, then philosophy, then English, and before long we had a complete study program."

She started with sixteen nuns, but more nuns soon came knocking. "There was no space, no rooms for them to stay, no funding at all," Lekshe recalls. The pain of having to turn away eager nuns still troubles her. She started another study center in Spiti in the Himalayas and eventually founded fifteen study programs and Jamyang Foundation, a non-profit that focuses on providing education to Himalayan Buddhist women. "Buddhist studies for nuns were unheard of at that time. People thought nuns were not interested in studying. I often heard, 'Oh, it's enough for nuns to just say OM MANI PADME HUNG, the mantra of compassion.' But at night, these nuns would cry their hearts out. They could chant like angels, but they had no clue what they were chanting."

She and a few nun friends decided to get together to talk about the difficulties that Buddhist women were facing. They chose Bodhgaya, the site of the Buddha's awakening in India, for their first gathering in 1987. "I did the best I could to pull together a conference. I had never done anything like this in my life. I remember collecting addresses on index cards and handwriting invitations." This was the pre-internet era. Posting an invitation through the Indian postal system took a month to reach the US and another month for a reply to come back.

IN SEARCH OF A HOLY WOMAN

At this time, Lekshe had already been a nun for ten years. With little support, barely enough to feed herself, she lived in a mud hut without plumbing or heating and only occasional electricity. Late one night, sitting in her hut in the forest near Dharamsala, she heard a faint voice with a strong Southern accent: "Help! Help me, I'm lost!" Venturing out with a flashlight, she bumped into a terrified, elderly woman stumbling around in the forest. Lekshe walked her back to her hotel and thought no more about it. But the next day, in the village market, she again ran into the woman, who turned out to be Elda Hartley, the pioneering spiritual filmmaker and founder of the Hartley Film Foundation. Elda had just returned from Tibet, disillusioned and frustrated about the dire circumstances of the Tibetans living under Chinese occupation, their culture in shreds. On the spur of the moment, over tea with Lekshe, Elda switched gears. Could she turn on the tape recorder and make a film about this unusual nun instead? "Her project was called 'In Search of a Holy Man,'" Lekshe laughs, "but instead of a holy man, she found me." As the conversation turned to the planned nuns' conference in Bodhgaya, Elda Hartley asked, "How much money do you have to organize this conference?" Lekshe responded, "Nothing. My pockets are completely empty."

Elda Hartley spontaneously offered to lend her five thousand dollars, but Lekshe hesitated. What if she were not able to meet the expenses? "In that case," Elda said, "it would be a donation." "But you don't even know me," Lekshe objected one last time, to which Elda Hartley confidently replied, "I know you." That settled it. Incredibly, Lekshe made the expenses exactly and paid Elda back to the penny. "The Sakyadhita conferences have always been like that. We start out with zero, everybody pays their own expenses, we get no support, and somehow we break even every time. It's amazing." She chuckles with delight. From these humble beginnings, the Sakyadhita conferences have generated a worldwide Buddhist women's movement.

Rainbows of robes

Sakyadhita means "Daughters of the Buddha." His Holiness the Dalai Lama opened the first conference in Bodhgaya in 1987, in front of fifteen hundred attendees. A living rainbow of robes fluttered to and fro

A shared understanding across cultures: Karma Lekshe Tsomo with two
Ladakhi women in the Himalayas. Photo courtesy of Karma Lekshe Tsomo

in the tightly packed gathering under a tent: yellow and maroon from
Tibet, grey and black from Korea and Taiwan, yellow and orange from
Sri Lanka, pink from Burma, and white from Thailand.

Every other year, thousands of nuns and monks, laywomen and lay-
men, gather in a different country for a Sakyadhita conference to discuss
the issues. What is the main obstacle? "Sexism," Lekshe candidly sums it
up. She is not afraid to use the F-word. "Feminism," she says, delivering
the punch line with a coy smile, "has been called the radical theory that
women are completely human." The gender imbalance affects Buddhist
women worldwide. "We are talking about more than three hundred
million women dedicated to peace, honesty, loving-kindness, and compassion. Certainly we would want to optimize the talents and potential
of these wonderful women." In the West, more and more teachers recognize this potential, but "women have almost no voice in Asian Buddhist
institutions. For women to move into positions of leadership, they need
to be fully educated and trained."

"MAY THE GODS BE VICTORIOUS!"

This is why Lekshe travels through Ladakh. With her nun friend she has to walk for four solid days on foot, at times trudging through the snow. Fighting the breathtaking altitude on the snowy passes, carrying everything on their backs, she greets occasional cheery villagers and nomads with their herds of yaks along the road. She plows through a panorama of fantasy monasteries, hoary cliffs, army convoys, gaping chasms, and idyllic threading rivers. She crosses a fourteen-thousand-foot pass, shouting "*Lha gyalo!* May the gods be victorious!" like the locals, to celebrate the ascent.

The torrid sun is without mercy, due to the altitude and rarified atmosphere. There are no trees in this mountainous desert, so even with sunscreen, she fries. But by late afternoon when the winds start to howl, after temperatures drop to near freezing, she thanks the sunburn for keeping her warm. Immense compassion floods her heart for these people who have next to nothing and, by some miracle, eke out a precarious existence. "The people's poverty is astonishing," Lekshe remarks. "Their lives are so harsh, yet their faces are beaming and radiant. A picture of His Holiness the Dalai Lama is the most precious possession in every household. His radiant presence on the altar gives them solace and hope."

They have no cars, no appliances, no furniture—just the clothes on their backs and the cherished photograph of His Holiness. Day in and day out, they eat roasted barley flour mixed with thin tea or flat bread or curd, surviving from one short growing season to the next. In the summer, before the harvest, supplies of food are running low. Amazingly, poor as they are, Zangskaris always seem to be joking and laughing, good-natured, serene, and curious.

STRUCK BY A POISONOUS VIPER

"What happened to your arm?" local village women inquire, pointing to Lekshe's severely scarred right arm, visible under the sleeveless robes. "I was bitten by a snake," she answers. They shrink back and gasp, first with expressions of horror, then of merciful concern. "It is karma—the result of my own actions in the past," she reassures them. "For sure, what else could it be but the result of past actions, something like this? Now you are a nun and will create merit in this life, so things will certainly be better in the next life," they say. These four generations of women, unlettered and uneducated in the Western sense of the word, understand a profound truth. Even (or perhaps especially) the two older generations—toothless, clad in animal skins, their hair in dreadlocks—realize the essential principle of the Buddha's teachings with a simplicity and clarity rarely found in sophisticated Western society. They part reluctantly. A bond of understanding that transcends language and culture has been forged.

The snake bite happened near Dharamsala, in 1989. So many nuns wanted to join her study program that Lekshe went looking for a suitable building site in the nearby countryside. While walking under some low branches, a poisonous viper must have fallen from a tree and bitten her. Since Lekshe did not see the snake, she lost eight days before she realized the urgency and got to a hospital. By that time, gangrene had set in and the venom had seriously damaged her arm. She almost died. For weeks, she could hardly move, and the world around her, the doctors, and the noise from the other patients, all melted into one dazed blur. The rural Indian hospital, with its raw poverty, insufficient equipment, and poor hygiene, was hard to survive even without a snake bite, so Lekshe sent out an SOS. A friend in San Diego responded to her urgent call and took her in. The snake bite is, in fact, the reason she now lives in the United States. Too sick to return to Asia, she picked up her studies in Hawaii and completed a PhD. "When in doubt, go back to school, eh?" She had not planned this; she thought she would just always stay in Asia and help support the nuns there. But the snake bite marked a turning point in her life.

She takes the about-face with the characteristic equanimity of a seasoned practitioner. Buddhists believe that nothing happens without a cause. Ultimately, the snake bite forced her to return to the Californian god realm again. A job offer from the University of San Diego as an assistant professor of religious studies came in handy. She points to a stack of students' papers on her tiny wooden desk next to the jammed bookshelf and sighs, slightly amused. "Not enough time to get everything done." Does she miss the kinship of fellow nuns in a more Buddhist environment as she experienced in Asia? In San Diego, she's a curiosity in her red robes. "This is a very good life, a very happy life," she evades a direct reply. "Some people might feel lonely. I like people, but I can stay alone for weeks and months very happily."

THE UNIVERSAL PATH TO LIBERATION

Karma Lekshe Tsomo values the liberal climate at her Catholic university. "They respect someone who is seriously following a spiritual path," she says, applauding the curiosity and openness of her students. She sends them to the Korean and the Vietnamese temples in town to meditate, and they in turn seem to mirror her own openness to various traditions. Lekshe is the only teacher of Tibetan Buddhism I have ever met who feels at home in all traditions, a student of all Buddhist schools, without distinction. Despite the first part of her name, which denotes that she is a disciple of the Karmapa, she refuses to be labeled Nyingma, Kagyü, Gelugpa, or Sakya—the four main traditions of Tibetan Buddhism—or even as a Tibetan Buddhist. "Just Buddhist is enough for me," she says calmly. "Wherever I go, I feel at home, whether it is a Korean, Tibetan, Burmese, or Thai temple." Throughout her Asian pilgrimages, she studied with many masters of various traditions, including S. N. Goenka (b. 1924), a leading lay teacher of the Burmese Vipassana tradition, who impressed her deeply. She adopted Goenka's credo that Buddha never taught a sectarian religion—that the way to liberation is universal. "When you get too attached to your lineage or your teacher, it is just another attachment, isn't it?" And, she is quick to ask, "What does lineage mean for women anyway? The extremely important lineage holders of Tibetan Buddhism are almost exclusively male."

Thus, on her journey through the mountain ranges of Zangskar, she never fails to point out mementos of women's accomplishments. "On this very rock cliff, nuns have meditated for hundreds of years,"

she says. It is easy to see why the solitude of these mountains has produced centuries of saints. With no telephones or TV screens, no blaring
distractions hinder spiritual practice. The valley floor, speckled with
ancient Buddhist reliquaries, stretches endlessly before her as she walks
for four days, sleeping outside in the cutting cold. A fierce wind comes
up late in the day, sweeping dust and sand into every pore. By the time
she finally arrives at the nunnery in Zangla, dusk has long melted into
darkness, while the relentless winds continue to howl, hurling her into
the bluff. But the warmth of the welcome offsets the cold of the night.
In the pitch black, she makes out shadows of the welcoming villagers
as she stumbles along the path to Changchub Chöling Monastery. Soon
she is greeted by a crowd of nuns and billows of incense from evergreen
boughs. Twenty nuns reside in this centuries-old monastery. Leading her
into their guestroom, they fill a bowl with steaming-hot, salty butter
tea, talking across each other to tell her about the latest improvements,
all at once.

There were no living quarters for the nuns until Lekshe began to support them, so they stayed with relatives in the village. Cooking, caring
for children, and working in the fields, they did not live up to the monastic ideal, but that is how they managed. When the study program was
established in 1988, the nuns' lifestyle changed drastically. They went
on special alms rounds near and far to collect donations. With their own
hands, they built small stone-and-mud huts, to begin living together in
community. They convinced Geshe Tenpa Lundrup, a senior Tibetan
lama, to leave his retreat hut in order to teach them the Buddhist texts.

Historically speaking, for women to pursue the monastic philosophy curriculum is unusual. Especially here in Zangskar, where women
typically receive no formal education at all, such an endeavor is revolutionary. In such a harsh environment, the contrast between lives of
household drudgery and full-time spiritual enrichment is stark. Even if
there are no theoretical barriers to women's spiritual realization, Lekshe is very sensitive to the cultural and practical circumstances of the
women's lives in the Himalayas and well aware that Western responses
to gender discrimination must take into account the whole picture.
"Himalayan societies are arranged hierarchically, encompassing gender,

class, education, wealth, ordination status, and even caste, although Buddhism does not recognize caste," she writes in her book *Buddhist Women Across Cultures*.[2] "These societies make no pretense that its members are equal, but their social system is believed to be equitable, flexible, and efficacious, regardless of inequalities." Now the nuns may still help with planting and harvesting, but they concentrate more on meditation and study. The villagers show their appreciation for the nuns by supplying them with barley flour and tea. The relationship has become symbiotic and fruitful, fostering goodwill and respect on both sides.

"Education is crucial," Lekshe insists. "Even as a basis for practice, education is important. And it is indispensable for becoming a teacher. You cannot teach what you don't know." There are still many schools and Buddhist institutes that are not open to women. And women's institutions are usually not equivalent to men's, because they lack the comfortable budgets and good teachers. "Even in the West," Lekshe has found, "we have a harder time gathering donations for nuns. I have often seen donors make the rounds with alms and then stop before they get to the nuns." But here, on the roof of the world, her efforts are making a difference. The next day the nuns invite her to visit the young nuns' class, conducted in the ancient style of memorizing texts by chanting them in chorus. Once the nuns have learned the text by heart, the lama will explain the meaning. His compassion is tender and touching as he shows off his students' prowess.

The gong rings, prompting the nuns to gather in the courtyard for debate, to test their understanding of yesterday's lesson. With keen intelligence and concentration, they enthusiastically examine the topic—the mind state of the enlightened one—from every possible angle. Before the lama arrived here, literacy was rare in Zangla, except among monks. "Today, due to his skillful method and confidence in women's power to learn, the mysteries of Buddhist philosophy are like flowers unfolding," Lekshe says, her round face lit up with a broad smile. "Tomorrow, these women will be able to share the light of the dharma with others."

Venerable Thubten Chodron.
Photo courtesy of Sravasti Abbey

9: THUBTEN CHODRON
(CHERRY GREENE)
A REBEL IN ROBES

*Why a Jewish Californian started one of the most innovative
Tibetan Buddhist monasteries in the United States*[1]

THE ALARM GOES OFF at five o'clock. The sun has just painted the
first faint glimmer of light across the snow-covered mountains on
the horizon, backlighting the expansive panorama. Now the first thing
that hits me in the face, like a cold splash of water, is a printed and taped
three liner on the bathroom mirror:

> All suffering comes from the wish for your own happiness.
> Perfect buddhas are born from the thought to help others.
> Therefore exchange your own happiness for the suffering
> of others.

At five thirty the nine nuns, two lay residents, three volunteers, and a
tired me file into a meditation hall the size of a living room. The rustic
walls in the log cabin contrast with the oriental brocade on the shrine,
the polished-glass water bowls, and the delicate Buddha statue. First we
bow to each other as an expression of honoring each other's good hearts
and buddha nature, then we chant prayers, and finally we sit still with
our spines erect on cushions on the wooden floor for forty-five minutes,
endeavoring to stay in the present moment, mind calm, focused, and
unwavering. Of course, my mind wanders all over: How did a Jewish
woman come to start one of the first Tibetan Buddhist monasteries for

training Westerners in America? Why did she choose the mountains in a conservative part of Washington State for such an adventure? Where did she get the funds?

Shhh! Until a gong rings during breakfast, everybody keeps silence. Every moment, every activity, every detail in Sravasti Abbey is designed to steer the visitor toward mindfulness. Every door sports a tiny printed and taped request that it wants to be shut gently and quietly. The offices in the main building are labeled "right speech" and "right mindfulness"—steps on the eightfold path the Buddha prescribed. I don't think I have ever been to a place where people were so aware of anything I might need at any minute without my asking. Helping hands offer a warm blanket, cups of tea, a copy of the aspiration prayer recited before meals. Except for the prayers that we read together aloud, all of this happens in noble silence; the dance of perfectly choreographed community life unfolds quietly—except for the loud gobbles of three dozen wild turkeys that galumph across the muddy path in expert alignment, racing for one nun's affection in the form of cracked corn. The large birds line up, one by one, as if queuing for a blessing. Venerable Semkye later jokingly calls the turkeys "my disciples."

No snake nest

The woman who made all of this possible is Los Angeles native Cherry Greene, now better known by her Tibetan ordination name, Venerable Thubten Chodron, which roughly translates as "Lamp of the Teachings, Doctrine of the Capable One (the Buddha)." As soon as she enters the bright breakfast room with the floor-to-ceiling windows, everyone rises in unison to pay respect to the abbess. Thubten Chodron's dark brown eyes sparkle with curiosity and piercing intensity. With her head shaven and her fine-boned figure hidden under maroon robes, she has the androgynous look of a true mendicant—yet she speaks as eloquently, fast, and humorously as the California girl that she is. Sometimes people mistake her crimson robes for a fashion statement and stop her in the street to compliment her on her hairdo and outfit. Others have compassionately inquired when the chemotherapy will be over.

"We're going to listen to the BBC," one nun says. It takes me a minute to figure out that BBC does not refer to the British Broadcasting Corporation but to the "Bodhisattva's Breakfast Corner," Thubten Chodron's daily ten-minute dharma perspective on a pressing point. Today she is reading a passage on jealousy from one of her many successful books, *How To Free Your Mind*. "Jealousy ignorantly makes us think we'll be happy if we destroy others' happiness," she teaches. "Like a vicious snake whose venom kills a healthy person, jealousy poisons the happiness and goodness of both ourselves and others."[2]

As soon as the red-cheeked head nun rings the gong after breakfast, we are allowed to speak. Nine friendly faces, most of them in their fifties, turn to me and repeat their names. The nine nuns are aware they all look alike in their maroon robes, their warm, beaming faces framed by grey stubble. To the untrained eye, they aren't easy to tell apart. But the names only help so much—they all start with Thubten, because Thubten Chodron is their ordination master. "Buddha started a community," Thubten Chodron says. "Many people dream of going off on their own and staying by themselves, thinking they will become enlightened that way. But it may be that they don't change their self-centered habits or even notice their habitual tendency to view the world from the perspective of 'me, I, my, and mine.' When you live in a community, you bump up against each other, and you really have to work on yourself." And here is a community that seems to prove that it is possible to live together without becoming a nest of snakes.

MAPPING OUT THE NEXT THREE EONS

Thubten Chodron points to the map that outlines the two hundred and forty acres. Now Sravasti Abbey is home only to a minuscule retreat cabin without running water, the meditation hall, Venerable Chodron's studio (also lacking running water), Ananda Hall (the main building with offices, kitchen, dining room, library, and bedrooms for men), the newly built nuns' residence, and a big old barn. Thubten Chodron paints a grand temple, a new kitchen/dining room/guest house, and a monks' residence—in short, a full-fledged monastery—onto the map with her finger. When asked if she is planning ahead for the next three hundred years, she breaks into her full, deeply resonating laughter. "No, for the next three eons!"

None of the nuns owns anything much, including Thubten Chodron. The abbey, the land, the rickety Subaru, the computers—everything is communal property. Even the black cat, named Manjushri (the Buddha of Wisdom), who hobbles around on three legs, takes turns snuggling on each of the Thubtens' laps as if to show he has no favorites. "None of this is just for us," Thubten Chodron says. "This is for the future of the monastic community in the West." For Buddhism to really take root in the West, "monastics and monasteries are crucial," she says. "Buddha was a monastic. If we forget that, we lose Buddha's own life example of how to live and practice."

Sravasti was the name of an ancient city in northern India, where the historical Buddha Shakyamuni spent most of his monastic life. His Holiness the Dalai Lama personally decided on the name for the abbey, and his letter of endorsement is framed next to the entrance. "The situation for Western monastics is especially difficult because few monasteries have been established in the West," the Dalai Lama's message reads. "The best solution is for Western monastics to develop their own training programs, and we Asians can help from our side. It is particularly pleasing to know that the abbey will be charting a new course as a place where both traditional Tibetan Buddhist teachings and innovative cultural forms will be present."

All the nuns have left behind their jobs, their families, their possessions, their names. "Monastic ordination centers around four root precepts," Thubten Chodron explains, "to avoid killing, stealing, sexual relations, and lying about spiritual attainment."[3] Other precepts aim at maintaining harmonious relations and protecting the monastics from the distractions that destroy mindful awareness: no singing, no dancing, no entertainment. The nuns don't watch TV, and they surf the web just enough to keep abreast with the important topics of the world.

But make no mistake: despite the idyllic setting, monasteries are anything but a sleepy haven for the lazy. There is no staff here. The nine nuns and two lay residents make everything happen: transcribing dozens of hours of teachings every week, communicating with hundreds of students, maintaining three lively websites, organizing retreats, guiding meditation groups, giving dharma talks, filming, recording, editing, cleaning, cooking, chopping wood, patching a leaking roof, you name it. There is always more to do. After breakfast, Venerable Thubten Tarpa, a trim former athletic trainer and physical therapist from Seattle, is grouting the bathroom. "We don't call this work," she says while swiping the top line of the shower, "we call it offering service. People see work as drudgery, but offering service is a chance to contribute to something bigger than ourselves. When people see what we do, they are inspired."

Thubten Tarpa comments that she had "a thing about organized religion" and couldn't imagine joining one. Slowly Chodron's ethics, determination, and vision proved so infectious that Tarpa moved to Sravasti Abbey six years ago. "I need to hear the teachings from a Westerner," she realized, having experienced language and cultural barriers with Tibetan teachers. At Sravasti Abbey, the nuns recite almost all the practices in English. "Venerable Chodron has a fantastic vision and more ideas than an army can take care of. She's one of the smartest people I ever met. She never does not teach. The draw is partly the ethical discipline—when you have it at a certain level, it shines. Thus she attracts people." All of the nuns rave about their abbess' learnedness and skillfulness. "She has no official title of rinpoche, geshe, or professor," another nun, Thubten Chönyi, a former Reiki teacher, tells me in a break, "but Tibetan teachers have told us that we should regard her as such. She is always humble, but whenever you bring a question to her, whether about a Tibetan term or the teachings, she knows the answer."

"WOW, THIS IS WEIRD!"

For the first twenty years of her life, Cherry Greene was a "nice Jewish girl", growing up in Covina, which at the time was more of an enormous orange orchard than the concrete suburb of Los Angeles it is now. A straight-A student, she contemplated going to medical school. Her dad was a dentist and her mom a housewife and bookkeeper. "The embodiment of a protective Jewish mother," Chodron says, "my mother would have been on the phone with the police crying hysterically that her daughter had been kidnapped, if I stayed out one minute past my curfew." She used to call Cherry "Sarah Bernhardt" after the famously melodramatic French actress, Chodron remembers. "I guess it was because I was pretty theatrical with my emotions."

Growing up during the Vietnam War, she had many questions with no answers: "Why are people killing each other in the name of creating a peaceful and safe world? Why do they judge each other based on the color of their skin or what sexual organs they have? What does it mean to love someone? Why do people love each other one year and not speak to each other the next?" She tested her birth religion, Judaism, and her parents would later blame the dry rabbi for their daughter turning away from the family faith. Cherry explored Christianity when she had a Catholic boyfriend, "but none of the answers satisfied me. I could not understand why a compassionate God would punish people, and if he was almighty, why wouldn't he stop suffering? And if he created the whole world, why did he create suffering?" She makes sure to add that these are "obviously religions that benefit millions of people" and that she is only speaking for herself: "They did not satisfy my spiritual yearning."[4]

She abandoned religion at college and laughs when she confesses that she did "what everybody else was doing at the time; you fill in the blanks." After graduation she joined two friends who were traveling around the country in a big yellow bakery van, camping in national parks, and "doing all sorts of things," she says with a wink. At twenty-one, Cherry started working as a teacher in an innovative school and married Bob, a lawyer. Just when her parents thought their buoyant daughter was settling down, a strong desire to "learn what life is about through experiencing it, not reading about it" led the couple to cash in most of their wedding presents. They put on their backpacks, flew to Europe, and spent the next year and a half traveling in Europe, North Africa, Israel, and then overland from Turkey to India and Nepal.

Trekking in Nepal, she toured some Buddhist temples. While she loved the colorful murals, the Buddhist teachings didn't attract her. In hindsight she realizes that she actually visited the birthplace of the man who was to become one of her principal teachers, Thubten Zopa Rinpoche,* but at the time the place was just a quaint Sherpa village to her. In the Himalayas she even met Trulshik Rinpoche (1923–2011), one of the Dalai Lama's revered senior teachers. To illustrate her ignorance at the time, Thubten Chodron recalls in an ironic voice: "For some reason, they took me to his room. I completely ignored him and looked at all the fascinating 'art work' in the room. When a monk came in and bowed to him, I nearly fell over because I had never seen anybody prostrate to another human being before." Making fun of her younger self, she mimics disgust: "I was like, wow, this is weird!"

She did love the art, bought some cheap rice-paper prints, and decorated the walls of their Los Angeles apartment with Buddhist drawings to remind her of the trip. "I had no faith but knew my friends would look at the drawings and say, 'Wow, you've been to India and Nepal? Far out,' and I would smile smugly." She returned to teaching but was still "very much searching for meaning in life. There had to be more to life than having fun, making money, raising a family, growing old, and dying."[5]

BECOMING A *WHAT?*

A flyer announcing a three-week course by Lama Yeshe† and Zopa Rinpoche at the Bodhitree Bookstore in Los Angeles caught her interest. She had just been accepted into a semi-professional folk-dancing group and wore her brown wavy hair down to her waist. "My peasant skirts were either down to the floor or up to just below my rear," she recalls. At the bookstore, everything seemed strange—"a man in a skirt" (a monk in robes), "a woman with shaved head" (a nun), but "the teachings really went into my heart. They made sense. We weren't told these are Truths with a capital T; we were told to check them out for ourselves." The

*Thubten Zopa Rinpoche was born in 1946 in the village of Thami in the Solo Khumbu region of Nepal near Mount Everest.
†Lama Thubten Yeshe (1935–1984) was born in Tibet and escaped to Bhutan in 1959. In 1969, Lama Yeshe and Zopa Rinpoche founded Kopan Monastery above Kathmandu. Its study courses quickly attracted increasing numbers of Westerners.

lamas taught analytical meditation, a thorough process of investigating one's world and oneself. "I have that kind of mind that needs to investigate and understand something. I cannot just accept it because someone says so. So all these meditations really helped me to understand the Buddhist teachings. It was a very deep experience." She was surprised that the Buddhist belief in rebirth and the principle of cause and effect (karma) provided an effective explanation for the questions that had been haunting her. It rang true to her when the lamas said ignorance, attachment, and anger were the cause of all suffering, and when she applied the teachings to her own mind, she felt it calm down. The possibility of removing ignorance and following a spiritual path were the purpose in life for which she had been searching.

There was only one possible conclusion: she had to learn more. Although the next school term was about to start, she decided to go back to Nepal. Bob hesitantly agreed, and so they packed up everything, once again, much to her parents' dismay. By the time they arrived at Kopan, Lama Yeshe's monastery in Nepal, she knew she wanted to become ordained. Hang on, why so fast? If someone had told her just a year earlier that she would be a celibate nun, she would have told them they were out of their mind. "A celibate nun? Certainly not!" Yet, as she puts it, "There was a strong connection, and your life sometimes turns out very different than you thought it would." The dharma made sense to her. In fact, suddenly this was "the only way of life that makes sense. Before that, I had a flat, a job, a husband, everything in place, but I still wasn't happy." She remembers thinking, "Okay, I'll grow old and I'll die, and what good will I have done?" She felt her lack of self-discipline was too great and her attachment too strong to live a dharmic life without the clear structure and ethical discipline of monastic ordination.

"MAY THEY NOT FALL DOWN!"

The Dalai Lama's tutor, Kyabjé Ling Rinpoche (1903–1993), ordained her as a novice in 1977, in a traditional Tibetan ceremony. She confesses with her characteristic humor that she was puzzled by the Tibetan prayers: "I am like, Whoa, what is going on here? My main concern was to keep the clothes on, 'cause it's all held up by one belt." She laughs and gazes skyward as if to invoke heavenly help. "You have to move your robes when you bow, and I was praying intensely, May they not fall down!"

She says she never struggled with her decision. "It was the only logical thing to do. Leading a regular life—there was no purpose, no sense, no meaning to it. But this had purpose, sense, and meaning." Wasn't there anything that was difficult to leave behind? "My hair!" Chodron responds in a flash. "I had spent *years* growing my hair out, *years*!" Her long curls were so spectacular, the thought of cutting them seemed gut-wrenching. She cured her horror by meditating on her own immanent mortality, "imagining what I was going to look like when I was dead, lying in my coffin with my beautiful long hair. I thought, What use is it having beautiful hair when you're dead?"

I am surprised she mentions her mane before her husband. "He was hurt," Chodron admits, and quickly adds, "but he understood why I did it and supported me. He was very kind and did not try to limit my spirituality." Bob even slipped her some money in the first years. Of course it was hard, Chodron confides. "But I also realized that so much of my relationship with him was based on my self-centeredness. He made me feel good. There is a big difference between love and attachment." They have remained good friends. When Chodron visits Los Angeles, she stays with Bob, his wife Sheryl, and their three kids.

GIVING UP THE AMERICAN DREAM

Not everybody took her decision that well. When Cherry told her parents about her wish to become a nun, they asked her to leave the house. "My family didn't speak to me for years. They could not handle it," she says. "When you are Jewish, you stay Jewish. They felt I was giving up my culture. They didn't understand my spiritual interest because they aren't religious. My mother later told me that if I had become a religious Jew, it would also have been difficult for them." It was not only the religious somersault they were struggling with but the horrors of seeing their daughter abandon her career and family life. Chodron's grandparents had fled the pogroms in Eastern Europe; her parents were first-generation immigrants. "As a parent you want your children to have everything you didn't. My parents worked hard to get the American dream, and then their first child isn't interested in continuing it? It was hard for them to understand."

Being the good daughter, she wrote to them every month but never heard back. After a few years her brother's wedding proved a first opportunity to test the waters. Her mother called to invite her to the wedding, but added dryly: "Look normal! And *be* normal!" Lama Yeshe concurred, telling her to "be a California girl" when she was with her parents, which was one of the last things she wanted to be. Recalling the situation, Chodron bends over laughing. She let her hair grow out an inch, stepped onto the plane to America in her robes, and changed into a flowered dress in the restroom shortly before landing. Her parents waited at the gate. "Good thing I changed. If I had come out with a shaved head and in robes, my mom would have gotten hysterical in the midst of the international airport."

Watching her parents' distress, she was sad, but she also understood: "There was nothing I could do about it—other than get married, have babies, and make money, which I didn't want. If I lived the life they wanted, they'd be semi-happy—because you cannot make anybody completely happy. But in the next life we would all be born in the lower realms"—she cites the Buddhist belief in rebirth and several realms of existence—"and then none of us could help anybody else. So while it was hard to see them unhappy, I did what I thought best for the long term, knowing that they would not understand because we had different worldviews." To her, ordination did not mean rejecting her family. "Rather, I wanted to enlarge my family by developing love and compassion for all beings."

Why did she think helping people as a doctor or lawyer wouldn't be enough? "Happiness comes from here," Chodron says, pointing to her heart. "Before I met Buddhism I was completely convinced everything came from outside. The teaching about misery coming from ignorance, attachment, and anger really got me. The bodhichitta teachings, identifying the self-centered thought as the troublemaker and knowing helping others is the thing to do—all this made so much sense. It wasn't like, 'Hallelujah, I believe!'" But when she applied her typically sharp reasoning, "I have to do the only thing that makes sense."

It took her parents many tearful nights, over years, to somewhat come to terms with their daughter's choices. They never asked her what she found in this path, never inquired about her new beliefs. "Part of it was: 'My God, what will our friends think? You did so well in college, now you live in a third-world country where they don't even have flush toilets. Meanwhile, so-and-so's daughter is a lawyer . . . and our daughter is a *what?*'"

As time went on, Thubten Chodron received invitations to teach meditation in many countries around the globe. Her burgeoning success somewhat pacified her parents' disappointment. Through the family grapevine Chodron heard rumors that her mom was bragging about the fact that her daughter was courted and hosted all over the world, from Delhi to Singapore, Jerusalem to Seattle. "My parents weren't aware that Buddhism is one of the world's great religions. It was hard for me to explain it to them. Sometimes when you are very close to somebody, you're not the person they can hear new information from."

This is all the more amazing as one of Thubten Chodron's greatest strengths, as I see it, is her ability to explain the Buddhist teachings in simple, down-to-earth terms, with a great portion of humor and lightheartedness. Her book *Buddhism for Beginners* does exactly what she could not do for her parents: answering everyday questions that curious non-Buddhists and beginners have about her faith. The small volume has become a best-seller and inspires people from all walks of life, many not even Buddhists.

AN INTERNATIONAL PING-PONG BALL

In 1977 Thubten Chodron was among the first generation of Westerners to become a novice nun in the Tibetan tradition; in 1986 she took full ordination in the Chinese Dharmaguptaka* lineage. She readily admits

*The Dharmaguptaka (Skt.), an early Buddhist school, was important in Central Asia

that ordained life is "not clear sailing." Disturbing emotions "do not disappear simply because someone shaves their head." Yet she feels that the precepts, which include celibacy, reduce distractions and allow her to focus all her energy on waking up, working with her "internal garbage," as she calls it. But practically speaking, the living conditions as a Western nun proved difficult. In Christianity, monks and nuns usually enter into a particular order and are given room and board in a monastery. With Western Buddhist monastics, there was no such thing.

"When we got ordained, the Tibetans really did not know what to do with us," she admits. "They were refugees, struggling to reestablish and sustain their own communities in exile." For about fifteen years her teachers sent her around the planet "like an international ping-pong ball" to work in dharma centers in Asia and Europe. Spending a few years at a fledgling nunnery in France, she notes that the nuns were given the horse stables for their lodging, whereas the monks resided in the comparatively lavish Nalanda Monastery a few kilometers away. The nuns had to pay for food and heating, and because she had no money she did a lot of prostrations during the winter to keep warm. "We fixed up the stables, and it was really a wonderful time," she concedes, while also pointing out that they were all quite new, with no senior nun to guide them. "We were out on our own and had to survive financially. Keeping your precepts is very difficult when you have to work for a living. When I ordained, I vowed not to work a job. Sometimes I was extremely poor, but someone would always offer help just before things got desperate." For a while she sewed robes for donations. This experience motivated her to establish Sravasti Abbey, "so that future generations do not have to go through the insecurity we did."

The time at the French nunnery taught her "a lot," she says, listing "the need for structure, discipline, and screening prospective members." Tibetan teachers consider it a blessing for anyone to take vows and rarely reject an aspirant, "but they have a structure already in place.

and China. Their monastic rules are still prevalent in some East Asian countries, including China, Vietnam, Korea, and Taiwan. They have one of only three surviving Buddhist monastic codices (Vinaya), along with the Mulasarvastivada, which is the codex Tibet adopted, and Theravada.

Whereas for us, it really made for some challenges when you have no say who joins your community. You have to take everyone, whether they are mentally and emotionally stable or not. This doesn't work." This observation very much shaped how she has designed life at the abbey.

ON A WING AND A PRAYER

For many years, she was longing to found a place where Western monastics could practice without the need to work ordinary jobs. A couple of early attempts together with other monastics didn't pan out, but she did not give up and kept looking for suitable land. For the first time, her parents were thrilled. "Oh, our daughter is doing something useful now!" she mimics her parents' delight. "I had never owned anything, no car, no flat, nothing. They were thrilled I was doing something *normal*—looking for land."

With a price tag of nearly half a million dollars, the unique property in northeast Washington State was way beyond her means when she first spotted it on a realtor's website. Clearly aware she could only afford half that sum, she decided to check it out "just for the heck of it." Sure enough, she fell in love with its 360-degree view over the hilly countryside. Auspiciously, the seller offered to carry the mortgage. "I just did it on a wing and a prayer, because where would the money come from? I had no big organization behind me." She had saved the offerings she had received from teaching tours and a little money from a few earlier fundraisers; that was it. "I had no big benefactors. But many people believed in what we wanted to do and gave what they could." To this day, many people donate small sums, forming a marvelous mosaic of support.

How she managed to unite thousands behind her is rather amazing. When she moved in, just by herself with her two cats, the neighbors didn't know what to make of her. In the eighties, the popular but controversial Indian guru Bhagwan Rajneesh (later called Osho) had set up a freewheeling community in not-too-far-away Oregon. The headlines about his sex parties, lavish lifestyle, luxury fleet of Rolls Royces, and ugly land battles with the locals were still in the back of people's minds. After all, this is rural America, sparsely populated with farms and deeply conservative. "Our philosophy was to be friendly and kind, to pay our bills on time, and to enter the local community slowly. We went to the county planning and zoning department and asked for their help. They were delighted to help, because often people tried to skirt the rules, whereas we wanted to abide within them." She also taught a series of classes in the local community on "Meditation for Stress" and got to know people that way.

Slowly some Buddhist practitioners were inspired to stay at the abbey. Now the meditation retreats and dharma courses attract about a thousand visitors each year. Even a Carmelite nun who lives a few miles away occasionally joins a retreat. She simply rewrites the Buddhist practices to suit her faith: instead of the Medicine Buddha, she visualizes Jesus the Healer. The mantra Thubten Chodron learned to repeat after her teacher is a universal one that transcends religion: "You are the servant of others."

LIVING ON ALMS

Just like the Buddha's community 2,500 years ago, Sravasti Abbey is willing to provide teachings, guidance, and counseling to anybody who needs help. Last year, when three non-Buddhist locals were diagnosed with cancer, they turned to the nuns for spiritual and emotional support. Everyone is welcome on the land: Sravasti Abbey does not charge for room and board but emphasizes the practice of generosity. Every visitor gives what they can.

Monasteries in Asia traditionally don't buy their own food. The local communities joyfully support the monastics by offering them meals and other necessities. If you ever travel through Thailand, Sri Lanka, or Cambodia, you might see rows of monks, each with his alms bowl in hand, going from house to house in the early morning just after sunrise. This is, in fact, how the Buddha lived and taught his disciples. Begging is as much a practice of renouncing one's likes and dislikes as it is a welcome opportunity for laypeople to support and therefore participate in the merit of a monastic community that is dedicated to meditation

Abbess Thubten Chodron (seated) with her nuns in the Sravasti Abbey
shrine room. Photo courtesy of Sravasti Abbey

and compassion. That this principle works many centuries later, in the
midst of mostly Christian Washington State, is nothing short of a mind-
blowing miracle. "When I first moved here, I thought people were really
backward," admits Thubten Tarpa, still grouting the bathroom. "Boy,
did I have the wrong attitude!"

While the abbey's monastics do not go on alms round—at least not
yet—they do not buy food and eat only what is offered to them. "When
I set the abbey up this way," Chodron recalls, "people told me we would
starve. But look, we're still here and healthy!" Regularly people from
the nearby cities of Spokane, Coeur d'Alene, and Sandpoint come with
offerings of bread, grains, fruit, and vegetables. Many of them met the
nuns due to the meditation classes they give in these cities. They have
since become so intrigued by the radiant nuns that they want to learn
more about the Buddha's teachings at the abbey. People who live too
far to bring food themselves donate money to the food fund. "I worried
about this before I moved here," says Tarpa and mimics panic, "Am I

going to starve?" But in the six years she has lived there, "maybe on one half day there was not a lot of food."

At every meal the monastics eat in silence, mindfully, appreciating every vegetarian bite that the hard work of others has afforded them. They say prayers for the donors' well-being. "It makes you appreciate every little crumb even more," admits Thubten Jigme, a round-faced former psychiatric nurse from Seattle. "We appreciate so much what others give us."

One tenet of the Buddha's teachings is interdependence, and the nuns apply that to their relationship with the environment. They are scrupulous in reusing materials, reducing their consumption, and recycling. They talk about the deer, moose, chipmunks, and other beings as people talk about and care for their neighbors. Contrary to typical American lifestyle, they don't jump in the car and drive to town whenever they need or desire something. "Errands stack up, and then one or two people go in and do them all," explains Venerable Samten. "We even make our doctor and dentist appointments on the same day to reduce our gasoline consumption." The dentist, by the way, has grown to respect the nuns so much that he treats them for free.

FLYING UNDER THE RADAR

Thubten Chodron has won the affection and support of the locals slowly, by keeping things low key. "It's better not to make a big fuss," she has learned. For many years she quietly prepared the ground. Chodron wanted her monastery to be independent. "If you are part of a big organization, people who do not live here establish policies that you have to follow," she observed while teaching at various centers. "That can create difficulties." Some of her ideas on how to set things up were different from how Tibetan masters usually do it, and she wanted to try them out. "Generally Tibetan organizations in the West center around a high teacher," she points to the ceiling, "and everybody else is down here. People tend to listen only to the teacher, who they regard with overwhelming respect, but they do not learn how to work together themselves."

She envisioned the monastery to be a "real" community, with a democratic structure. "Experienced senior monastics make the major deci-sions about the direction the abbey will take, but on practical issues, we aim for consensus." The abbess has to negotiate a fine line between tradition and innovation. "As a Westerner I have been conditioned to believe in democracy and equality," she wrote in the essay *You're Becoming a What?* Yet in the West "some people associate me with an institution they see as hierarchical, and thus negative. There are two challenges here: one is how I relate to the hierarchy, the other is how I am affected by Westerners who see me as part of a hierarchical institution."[6] Ultimately, the real spiritual path leads beyond any divi-sions of culture, gender, or geography, but in the meantime, both Asians and Westerners have their own sets of prejudices and deeply ingrained beliefs about hierarchy and fairness. "Westerners sometimes create their own hierarchy in Buddhism," Chodron has observed. "Some Westerners assume that Asians are holy, while Westerners are ordinary, because they have grown up with Mickey Mouse like you and me. Fascination with the foreign or exotic obscures us from understanding the path. Spiritual practice is about transforming ourselves into kind and wise people, not idolizing a teacher or adopting another culture."[7]

KILLING A VITAL PART OF HERSELF

"For many years I tried to act like the Tibetan nuns: shy, self-effacing, sweet—but it didn't work," Chodron reflects.[8] "I am a college-educated person from the West who had a career. I have to accept myself as such and use my talents instead of pretending to be something else." She readily confesses that she started out on the Buddhist path as a proud, opinionated individual. While some of the downgrading was helpful to counteract the ego, the gender bias in Tibetan society eroded her self-confidence in a way she didn't realize until she returned to America years later. Though Tibetans did not always openly say they thought women were inferior, that certainly was the unspoken message Chodron internalized. She had grown up in a family that believed in the equality of men and women, and after several years of trying to clamp down on her energetic personality, she realized that she was killing a vital part of herself. Now she tries to integrate the "straightforward communication and initiative valued in the West and the humility and gentleness valued in the East to have the best of both worlds."[9] For instance, nuns traditionally sit behind monks no matter their age or qualification. Even the most senior nun has to wait until the youngest boy-monk has taken his share. In Sravasti Abbey, however, one sits and queues according to one's seniority, not according to gender. A small detail, but an important one. Chodron quips, "Male and female are just labels constructed based on where we have bumps on our body."

She is faced with the irony that she is perceived as a feminist rebel in traditional Tibetan circles, while some Westerners automatically marginalize her as part of the "sexist and hierarchical" monastic institution because of her robes. "Curiously, while women's issues are at the forefront of discussion in Western Buddhism, once a woman becomes a monastic, she is seen as 'conservative and traditional,' qualities disdained by some Westerners who practice Buddhism."[10] Chodron comments, unfazed, "You just learn to live with whatever people happen to think of you and continue living your life and practicing the dharma."

How to distinguish between genuine dharma and Tibetan culture? Thubten Chodron has spent a lot of time pondering this question. "And where am I—standing in the middle of it?" After trying to copy the Tibetan nuns, in 1986 she went to Taiwan to receive full ordination. This provided her with a tour d'horizon of the cultural differences. In Taiwan, for instance, instead of sitting down during chanting practices, the monastics stand up. Instead of the sleeveless Tibetan robes, Taiwanese monastics wear many layers. The chanting is different too. "There are some similarities, but at the same time everything was so different. This experience helped me to see much more clearly what the real dharma is. The organizational structure of the monastery or which language you practice in is not dharma but conventional culture. Practicing to free our mind from ignorance, anger, and attachment and to cultivate love, compassion, and wisdom—that is the dharma." She instructs people to do their practices in their native tongue. "When I was in Singapore, I was teaching Chinese people to chant in Tibetan, a language neither of us understood. I thought, 'Something is wrong here.

The Buddha did not speak Tibetan, yet he attained enlightenment.'"
Subsequently she learned that the Dalai Lama advises people to do their
practices in a language they understand.

THE CHALLENGE OF A CLOSELY KNIT COMMUNITY

There are other challenges in the West. For instance, Western culture
celebrates individualism. "Many Westerners prefer to make their own
choices and don't want to answer to anybody," Thubten Chodron has
learned, "but at the same time they feel lonely. Personally, I wanted to
live in a community with people who have the same spiritual intention
and who really want to live as a community, not simply a group of
individuals who share the same residence."

The setting at Sravasti Abbey seems idyllic at first, but the life in
the closely knit community at the abbey is quite demanding for those
who come to stay. "We often get letters from people writing, 'I'm so
inspired, I want to join your community and become ordained immediately.' Well, that's not quite how it works," warns Chodron, who has
seen intense enthusiasm fade away quickly too many times. "We invite
people to come, join in for a month or so, then leave and digest their
experience. Then they can come back again, and gradually, as they are
ready, take the eight lay precepts, which involve avoiding killing, stealing, and lying. After keeping those for a year, they may take the novice
ordination. After two years, they may apply to take full ordination."

In addition to the traditional mind training in love and compassion,
Chodron introduced Nonviolent Communication as taught by Mar-
shall Rosenberg.* The method seeks to balance honest self-expression
with empathy. "We now have a way of giving feedback to each other
without being hurtful," says ex-nurse Thubten Jigme. While she admits
that it is challenging to live full-time within the confines of a small
group, this is exactly what inspired her to join. When old friends come

---

*Rosenberg (b. 1934) is an American psychologist who developed a training that teaches
communication skills to resolve conflicts harmoniously.

to visit, they are stunned by how much their companions have transformed, become gentler, more compassionate.

"In the community, we are so close and transparent, there is no way to hide," Jigme points out. "It is continuous work to smooth your ego mind all the way. Nonviolent Communication is so helpful because we use it as a tool to give feedback without being offensive. Instead of holding back and not expressing our feelings and needs, now we are learning to offer empathy to both ourselves and others. We all hold each other in such a respectful, loving, kind way; it is beautiful. I have never experienced this anywhere else."

Thubten Chodron also talks openly about sexuality, thus pointing to another difference between the East and West. "You have to deal with your sexuality at some time, you can't always avoid it," she states. In Tibetan monasteries the genders are kept entirely separate. "One technique for dealing with sexual attraction is to see the bad side of who you're attracted to, so monks were told that women's bodies are made of filthy substances—which is true, but so are theirs! They were taught that women are lustful and enticing, and so they should avoid them. That may be suitable for them, but I believe we have to be comfortable with our sexuality and find ways of dealing with it, without making whoever we are sexually attracted to into an object of defamation."

A MURDERER NO DIFFERENT FROM US

Thubten Chodron is a rebel disguised as a soft-spoken nun. Her voice sounds sweet, almost childlike. She is always ready to crack a joke, but the punch line might stop you in your tracks. One evening I watched her deliver a speech to college kids in Coeur d'Alene; the next day she delivered a service at the Unitarian Church in Spokane. On both occasions she dropped a few political bombs. Knowing full well that seventy percent of the locals vote Republican, she spoke out against the cutting of education budgets in favor of military expenses and related her insights about the inhumane prison system as she sees it. Both times you could hear people hold their breath. The locals clearly did not expect political statements from a modest nun. "Oh, I am just clarifying how to apply kindness and compassion to the world around us," she says later with a twinkle in her eyes. "I am not telling people how to vote."

Her political views are informed by what she sees in prisons. Several hundred inmates follow her teachings from afar, through her books, CDs, and newsletters. "I never intended to do prison work," Chodron confesses, "it just came to me. One day I got this letter from an inmate in Ohio, and I wrote back. That's how it started." Part of the Buddhist practice is to cultivate love and compassion without bias. "Usually we divide people up into those we love, those we don't like, and those we don't care about," Chodron says, "but the goal of a Buddhist practitioner is to be equally openhearted toward everyone, to wish them happiness and freedom from suffering." There is plenty of suffering in American prisons, and the inmates who write to her have usually caused a generous amount of agony themselves. "The current view in our society is that inmates are evil and irredeemable so we must lock them up to keep society safe." However, after visiting many prisons all over the United States, Mexico, and Asia, the encounters changed her views. "Inmates are no different from us. All of us have made mistakes. Some of the inmates may have made bigger or more damaging mistakes than we have, and many of us think we would never do what they have done." But, Chodron asks, "How do we know that?" She brings up the Rodney King fiasco when the Los Angeles police were videoed beating King up after a high-speed chase. "If I had been brought up in the environment King was, I easily could have acted like him." Acknowledging that the seeds of ignorance, anger, and attachment exist in everyone, herself included, "there is no way I can remain smug, complacent, and think I am above others." Some of her students have done the things we all fear the most—murder, rape, uninhibited brutality—"but after learning about their lives and especially what they experienced as children, I can't put them in a box marked 'evil.' We cannot define the meaning of someone's life by one action they did."

Thubten Chodron recalls some of the most striking transformations she has seen in her inmate students—she mentions two young men who both killed others in a rage when they were sixteen and seventeen years old, respectively. "It is very rewarding to see them acknowledge that they are responsible for their actions. Inmates love hearing about compassion and bodhichitta. They are happy to learn that they can make their lives meaningful for others, that their compassion for others matters." Many of her inmate students are looking deeply at their minds. The lack of other escape routes in the high-security prisons provides some with a heightened urgency to learn how to train and master their minds. When an inmate writes to her that he has been threatened or humiliated by another prisoner or by a guard but has managed to stay calm without retaliating, Chodron celebrates.

The help goes both ways. When a family member of an abbey supporter recently got entangled in drug problems, Chodron asked a convicted drug dealer from Los Angeles to give him advice. His brutally honest letter to the young man proved to be a wake-up call. Chodron's relationship with the men is no longer based on prejudice and fear. "They are more than the incident for which they were convicted. They are living beings whom I respect."

After all, this is what Thubten Chodron is most interested in: teaching forgiveness, including forgiving oneself, and developing compassion and unbiased loving-kindness. In Tibetan Buddhism, every living being possesses "buddha nature," the potential to wake up, regardless of how much confusion and anger they might have lived with at some point in their lives. She carries a message of hope into the prisons and is often the only friendly face they have seen in years. "Some have been abandoned by their families and say they have written to dozens of spiritual groups but never received an answer."

How do you forgive the Nazis?

In the spirit of including everything, life as a Buddhist nun has led her to many unexpected places—Asian countries, prisons, northeast Washington—and finally even to reconcile with her roots. It was important for her to make peace with her birth religion, appreciating what it has taught her. When she was born in 1950, the shadow of the Holocaust still lay over her family, which had lost contact with family members in Europe who were probably killed. "Growing up Jewish, I learned to stick up for the underdog. I learned it's fine to be different, because there were hardly any other Jewish kids at school. You need to stand up for what is right. You need to question deeply and live according to your values." The social aspects of Judaism, compassion and care for society, remind her of some of her Buddhist values too. "These were values in the Jewish community that I grew up with. I am very appreciative of that. At the same time, Judaism did not satisfy me spiritually. Also, I refuse to live with a victim mentality."

Together with her friend Jetsunma Tenzin Palmo she visited the former concentration camp in Auschwitz, Poland, and found herself staring at the suitcases left behind by those gone to the gas chambers. They were inscribed with Jewish names that sounded eerily familiar. She was one of the first Tibetan Buddhists to teach the dharma in Israel. When she gave a talk on forgiveness there, one Israeli asked this Jewish-born Buddhist nun a daunting question: "How do you forgive the Nazis?" She led them in a meditation on Chenresig, the Buddha of Compassion, visualizing healing light permeating the ghettos and the gas chambers. Another time, she visited Gaza and led people there in a meditation on love. These proved to be some of the most powerful experiences for her—practicing compassion in Israel and Gaza, including victims and perpetrators on all sides of the fence.

And finally, after all these years, the practice of forgiveness worked its magic and reached her parents too. Her father visited the abbey for the first time last year. Just like every other visitor, he couldn't help but become enamored with the joyful nuns to the point where he tried to join in their prayers and chant along. Later he was caught bragging to his neighbors back in Los Angeles: "My daughter," Thubten Chodron imitates him playfully, emphasizing every word with the boastful pride of a father, "is – the – CEO – of – the – abbey!"

Roshi Joan Halifax at a wedding blessing.
Photo by Chris Richards. © Joan Halifax

10: ROSHI JOAN HALIFAX

FEARLESS, FIERCE, AND FRAGILE

*A true heroine of engaged Buddhism reflects on living,
dying, and her heart's work*[1]

THE MOUNTAINS IN TIBET stretch toward a sky so immense it can be
intimidating, even unsettling. "The Tibetan landscape exemplifies
a quality of mind that is characterized by vastness," says Roshi* Joan
Halifax. "It's a dark blue that goes on forever. You can almost see stars
in the daytime. The clouds are within reach." Roshi has just returned
from her seventh pilgrimage to Mount Kailash, Tibet's holiest mountain. "The landscape just *is* the mind, and the mind is that landscape,"
she says. "It either makes you completely paranoid—and some people
become very fearful and self-centered there—or something breaks, and
the vastness of the horizon liberates you."

For Roshi Joan, crossing the Tibetan Plateau is an experience like no
other. Not much grows on the boundless stretches of tundra—just modest stubs of vegetation on which the yaks feed. Travelers must cope with
dramatic temperature changes and oxygen-deprived altitudes; fierce
sunlight, wind, and dust; exhaustion and blistered feet. Roshi believes
that such a raw, unfiltered experience of the elements can bring about
deep spiritual transformation.

Roshi is a Japanese honorific title for a teacher.

EVERY DAY IS AN EVEREST

Although she is a priest in a Japanese Zen lineage, Roshi Joan has extensive ties to Tibet and to Tibetan teachers, with whom she has studied
since the early 1970s. Her recent expedition was one of ten journeys
she has made to Tibet. True to her mission of combining meditation
with helping people wherever she can, she invited doctors and clinicians
to join the trip. More than thirty years ago Roshi started the Nomad
Clinics to help alleviate what she calls the "bottomless need" for health
care in these isolated, barren areas.

"We could have arrived and not helped anybody," she says. "We
could have just plowed through here and on to Mount Kailash, but
we have an opportunity to reduce suffering, so let's do it!"[2] Each of
the thirty-one pilgrims brought fifty pounds of medical supplies to dis-
tribute in the mountains of Humla in Nepal. They treated nearly one
thousand patients, many of whom had traveled great distances on foot
in hopes of receiving care. One man had hiked for three days with a
shattered arm. Another man, nearly blind, had walked for two days to
get eyeglasses.

From Humla, the group trekked toward the Tibetan border, stopping
to set up temporary medical clinics in villages along the way and performing "impromptu medical moments." When a trekker from another
group fell and fractured her leg, a physician from Roshi's group set it
right there on the trail. Once inside Tibet, the travelers camped on the
southern shore of Lake Manasarovar, the world's highest freshwater
lake, before advancing into the shadow of glaciated Mount Kailash, a
mountain so holy the locals forbid ascending to the top. Roshi's group
completed the pilgrimage around its base over a period of six days,
crossing one pass at 18,600 feet.

The fact that Roshi, now in her seventies, could make this trip at all
is remarkable, given the physical challenges she has faced over the past
four years. During a trip to Toronto in June 2008, Roshi Joan slipped
and fell on a hard bathroom floor, shattering her greater trochanter. She
spent thirty hours strapped to a gurney in an emergency room, then

another two days waiting for surgery. Two months after the accident, she was walking with crutches, gingerly.

It was not clear that she would ever hike again, much less embark on another pilgrimage to the sacred mountain. She said then, gesturing to the hills outside the window at Prajna Mountain Center in New Mexico, "From this distance, the mountains are a beautiful artifact. I'm pretty sure I'll be able to walk again, but I don't know if I'll be able to walk as I used to. Now, every day is an Everest."

THE TREACHEROUS PATH TO THE MASTER'S CAVE

The road to Prajna Mountain Center in one of the wildest parts of New Mexico can be impassable after a rainstorm. Massive potholes open wide beside slippery ruts, causing the vehicle to lurch and heave. It seemed odd that Roshi Joan would request to be interviewed at "the refuge," as it is known, instead of at her Zen center just five minutes from downtown Santa Fe. Was this a kind of trial, a koan about a treacherous path to the master's mountain cave?

It did make sense, though, that a woman who had once driven a VW van by herself across the Sahara would ask a visitor to make this trek. A woman who, at age sixty-five, had snow-shoed through a blizzard in the dark for four hours to reach the refuge. A woman who in March 2008 had hiked around China and Japan, in the footsteps of Dogen Zenji,* on a foot she didn't realize was broken.

"She's the most fearless person I've ever met," said Peg Murray, her assistant, who graciously offered a ride up the road in Roshi's Toyota 4Runner. Navigating the deep ruts with ease, Murray talked about the first time she had made the drive. Roshi Joan was her passenger, and the spring run-off had dissolved the road to slippery clay muck. Deprived of traction, the knobby wheels slid across the surface as if it were ice. Every time Roshi got out to assess their predicament, she sank up to midshin in mud. "I wanted to turn back," Murray said. "But Roshi

*Dogen Zenji (1200–1253) founded the Soto school of Zen in Japan.

wouldn't let me. She just kept saying, 'You can do this!' She even offered to take the wheel."

Known for embracing challenging, even risky situations, Roshi explained, "Inside me there's this incredible optimist." Roshi's longtime student and colleague Maia Duerr, however, has a somewhat different take. "I think the key to understanding Roshi Joan is seeing her fragility as well as her fearlessness. She is literally fragile right now, her bones breaking. Her mind is brilliant and her heart is huge, but her body is at the breaking point. She has pushed herself to exhaustion."

Fearless, fierce, and fragile: core aspects of a complex woman who is also an academic and an activist, a wild child of the sixties and a celibate priest. Roshi Joan is witty, irreverent, bold, mercurial, sometimes difficult, driven by aspiration and tamed by discipline. You'll catch her without her BlackBerry, iPad, and MacBook Pro—tools of building institutions—only on mountain trails and in the meditation hall. But she is best known for sitting at the bedside of terminally ill patients and pioneering a form of contemplative care. Her 2008 book, *Being with Dying: Cultivating Compassion and Fearlessness in the Presence of Death*, synthesizes lessons from her four decades as a leader in the field. After the accident, this longtime caregiver had to learn how to be, as she put it, "a better care receiver."

At the refuge, it became clear why Roshi Joan had insisted on this venue. Among Prajna's tangle of wildflowers and groves of giant aspens, she was more spacious, at ease. Roshi was reclining beside a plate-glass window, her back propped up by meditation cushions, laptop on lap. Her freshly shaved head accentuated her high cheekbones, her blue eyes flashed with intensity and humor. She spoke about her life's work and about where she was and who she was at that pivotal time while her body forced her to pause.

"I'm a kind of 'plain rice' Buddhist," Roshi Joan said. She described "plain rice" Buddhism as the meditation of everyday life. "When it's time to meditate, you meditate, and when it's time to make a bed, you make a bed. Not very exciting but, actually, exciting. The fierce kind of excitement. Excitement without excitation. It's about being alive."

THE WOUNDED HEALER

After the fall that shattered her trochanter, even as Roshi Joan was speeding in the back of the ambulance on the way to the Toronto hospital, a paramedic poured his heart out to her about his dying wife. "I realized this wasn't about me," she said. "This was always about others."

While she waited for surgery for three days, Roshi Joan practiced *tonglen* for the "numberless beings" streaming through the emergency room and taking priority with their more dramatic wounds. Roshi Joan had learned the sacred compassion practice from Kyabjé Dilgo Khyentse Rinpoche in Bhutan. *Tonglen* translates from the Tibetan as "sending and taking." The practitioner breathes in the suffering of others with every in-breath, then sends out healing, joy, and compassion with every out-breath—all the while acknowledging that both suffering and joy are insubstantial, fleeting, imaginary.

Roshi recalled that her motto in the hospital was "victory over fear." She demonstrated the mudra by holding two fingers in a "V" like a sixties peace sign. She wasn't afraid, she said, and because of the intense pain, she welcomed surgery. But during the operation to insert a metal plate with pins and screws into her upper leg, she lost so much blood that she needed a transfusion. "I could literally feel my heart ebbing."

Roshi Joan is a universal donor, a rare blood type that can donate to everyone but can only accept blood from its own kind—an apt metaphor for a caregiver. "I was in an extremely fragile state," she said. "Kind of an in-between state. There was so much ease. I felt kindness and gratitude."

She canceled some of her teaching commitments and slowed down for a while—only to speed up again as soon as her body allowed her to. One thing is certain, she said. "I can't fall again. I want to keep that fear active. Because that's where I think fear can be extremely useful. That's got to be kept in my foreground: being mindful." She acknowledges that she has "phenomenal drive and a lot of psychophysical energy. So I've been able to push myself over the Himalayas and other kinds of mountain ranges, be they metaphorical or literal. I have to shift into a more balanced perspective." That drive had exacted a physical toll. "I have not directed adequate mercy into my own life," she said. "I haven't taken care of my body that well."

EARLY LESSONS IN LIFE AND DEATH

As a child growing up in Hanover, New Hampshire, and Florida, Joan Halifax learned early lessons in life, illness, and death. She was born "into a Christian family at a navy hospital during the Second World War."³ She describes her businessman father as an introvert who was kind, compassionate, and creative. Her mother, a housewife, went back to college at age forty-four and took great satisfaction in volunteer work. "She spent the last day of her life bringing books and food to people at a hospital," Roshi Joan recalls. As she remarked in a lecture at the Harvard Divinity School,⁴ "History creates the character of a generation; and the qualities of altruism, compassion, and concern for human rights can be found in the lives of many of us who were war babies."

When she was four years old, a virus attacked her eye muscles, leaving her functionally blind for the next two years. "Children tend to be socialized and to form friendships between the ages of four and six,"⁵ she observes. "But because of illness, I was bedridden much of this time, and the absence of conventional friendships during my childhood was quite significant."⁶ She used to lie in her parents' bed listening to her sister and her friends playing outside the window. Instead of romping around with the other kids, she invented "a world inside of myself to compensate for loneliness and disability."⁷

Although she was cared for by her parents, she felt vulnerable, and she found a dear companion in her African-American nanny, Lilla, who told stories at her bedside. Lilla's mother had been a slave, and Lilla had received no formal education, but she was a wise and warm friend to the young child. "I started off thinking of her as a servant, only to discover she was a teacher," Roshi Joan says, adding that this friendship sparked her lifelong quest to understand the roots of social injustice and discrimination. "These feelings, I am sure, grew out of my childhood suffering, the strong presence of ethics in the life of my father, the spirit of service in my mother's life, and my relationship with Lilla."[8]

Rites of passage

Because of this relationship, Joan Halifax eagerly embraced the Civil Rights Movement, and when she arrived in New York in 1963 she was also drawn to the protests against the Vietnam War. She read D. T. Suzuki and Alan Watts, became a "book-Buddhist," and taught herself to meditate. After earning her doctorate in medical anthropology, she was burning to "understand something deeper about culture," and she realized it was "no longer appropriate" for her to "sit in a laboratory or to put chrysanthemums in bayoneted guns at the Pentagon."[9] She set out to drive across the Sahara in order to live with the Dogon people of Africa, a people who were "in the midst of a rite of passage that marked the death and rebirth of their society. If I had known what I was getting into, I would never have attempted it," she noted later.[10] Driving across the desert for almost four weeks became her own rite of passage, sparking a lifelong passion for adventurous travel and the solitude of unfathomable landscapes. Joan returned from Africa quite ill and began exploring new ways of combining alternative healing methods with conventional treatments. Observing that "conventional medical training did not seem to be grounded in compassion,"[11] she began exploring the question, "What does healing mean in our culture?"[12]

Joan's grandmother Bessie was a role model of caregiving, often sitting with dying friends in her Georgia neighborhood. "She normalized death for me," Roshi Joan remembers. But her grandmother's own death in a nursing home was a long, hard, lonely process. "I can never forget hearing her beg my father to let her die, to help her die. She needed us to be present for her, and we withdrew in the face of her suffering." Upon viewing the open casket at the funeral and seeing her grandmother's face finally at peace, Roshi Joan writes in *Being with Dying*, "I realized how much of her misery had been rooted in her family's fear of death, including my own. At that moment, I made the commitment to practice being there for others as they died."

ADVENTURES IN CONSCIOUSNESS

Joan Halifax began working with dying people at the University of Miami School of Medicine. In 1972 she married Stanislav Grof, a psychiatrist from Czechoslovakia. He was the medical director of a project by the National Institute of Mental Health that used LSD as an adjunct to psychotherapy for dying people.

The couple separated after some years of marriage and collaboration, and Joan went to New York to work for her friend, the renowned mythologist Joseph Campbell. The anthropologist in her was called to study indigenous cultures in the Americas and Tibet and explore the healing systems in these remote mountainous areas. Living with the Huichol Indians of Mexico, she witnessed shamans passing through metaphorical experiences of death and rebirth, emerging as wiser and more powerful "wounded healers" after having endured suffering. For several years she studied shamanism and Buddhism in parallel. In her popular 1993 book *The Fruitful Darkness* she chronicles her first trip to Tibet, her work in the Americas, and illuminates connections between these worlds.

Ultimately, Joan chose Zen Buddhism as her path. "The essence of that practice is sitting in stillness and silence and finding the iron pivot in your spine that does not even move in the midst of great suffering. I tasted that stillness and knew that it was medicine."[13] Joan studied with the Korean Zen master Seung Sahn* for a decade, from the mid-1970s and later received dharma transmission from the Vietnamese Buddhist monk Thich Nhat Hanh† in 1990.

Meeting Thich Nhat Hanh and exploring his convictions about peace as social action marked her transformation from a confrontational and provocative activist to a gentler kind of radical. "Here was a man who could see and feel the suffering on both sides and would not take

---

*Seung Sahn (1927–2004) was one of the first Korean Zen masters who taught in America. He founded the international Kwan Um School of Zen.
†Thich Nhat Hanh (b. 1926) is a Vietnamese monk and Zen master whose extensive writings have greatly influenced the understanding of Buddhism in the West. He founded Plum Village Monastery in France and the Order of Interbeing.

either,"[14] Roshi Joan says. "I realized that what he had been teaching about meditation in action means that everything can be an experience of practice. Our daily lives are the vehicles for awakening, for freeing ourselves and others from suffering."[15] She identified the missing ingredient in her life as the relationship between service and contemplative practice.[16]

STRONG BACK, SOFT FRONT

She founded the Ojai Foundation, a Buddhist-based California retreat center, in 1979. For eleven years she lived "on the earth," in a canvas dwelling without electricity, running water, or plumbing. She describes the tight, experiential community life as a "life of porosity," with a thin and transparent membrane and practically no privacy. The Foundation was nicknamed "the Wizard's Camp" for the extraordinary faculty that Joan invited, ranging from indigenous teachers to Western academics. Ojai hosted some of Thich Nhat Hanh's first meditation retreats in the United States, as well as workshops on chaos theory, ethnobotany, neuroscience, and dream research. In parallel with Zen, Joan also studied Tibetan Buddhism, most intensively with Chagdud Rinpoche, a Nyingma master* whom Roshi describes as "an exemplary human being and a powerful teacher. I felt very close to him, and I loved him for his transparency."

At age forty-two, she had to have tumors on both eyes surgically removed. Thereupon, a medical accident with radiation severely burned her eyes, and she had to wear eye bandages for several months. This sent her inward again.[17] The enforced isolation, together with her mother's death, prompted her to question her constant involvement in the community and to long for solitude, wanting to "be nobody, doing nothing."[18] And yet, after two years of travel, staying no longer than five nights in any place, her calling emerged clearly, once again: to be with the dying.

*See chapter 7.

BEARING WITNESS

Over the following years, Joan Halifax sat with dying people, in silence and in conversation, a practice she continues to this day. She has tried to help patients meet their challenges with awareness; both she and the patient "bear witness" to whatever emotions and experiences arise. In an initiative to also support caregivers, she founded the Project on Being with Dying, a training program for professionals in end-of-life care, now in its seventeenth year. One of the core messages in her book *Being With Dying* is "strong back, soft front," which, she explains, "is about the relationship between equanimity and compassion. 'Strong back' is equanimity and your capacity to really uphold yourself. 'Soft front' is opening to things as they are." Acknowledging that most suffering is rooted in fear, part of her life's work is to try to be "a kind of role model of what it's like to be free of fear. The only way one can actualize compassion is through the medium of fearlessness," she says, "because to really let yourself feel the suffering of another person—and then to allow the awakened heart to resolve to serve and transform the field of suffering—takes so much courage." Roshi speaks of the deeply ingrained Buddhist practice of opening up to another's suffering. "Whatever illness and suffering they are enduring, we are also experiencing, even though it may not be directly afflicting our body.[19] We are on the journey together."

Her fearlessness includes the courage to acknowledge her vulnerability: "At times I do feel rather fragile," Roshi admits. "No surprise—my life has been challenging in many ways. For the most part, the difficulties have strengthened my back and tenderized me. And yet, most of us suffer from bouts of 'strong front, soft back.' That includes me, when I am tired or feel as though I have not been quite right in my speech or actions." As her longtime friend, the writer Natalie Goldberg, puts it, "She's fearless, yes, but I also know her underbelly. She's vulnerable and tender and also scared like everybody else. That's what makes her fearless. She's not fearless like a brick; hers is a fearlessness that comes out of tenderness for the world."

GETTING DOWN IN THE STREET, GETTING DIRTY

In 1992, philanthropist Laurance Rockefeller and Richard Baker Roshi*
gave Joan a house in New Mexico, between the Santa Fe River and
Cerro Gordo Mountain. She set about building a new retreat center
from scratch, regreening the trodden desert land. She named the center *Upaya*, Sanskrit for "skillful means." The Upaya Institute and Zen
Center is now a sprawling complex of adobe buildings with a spacious
meditation hall and lush gardens. Her living room at Upaya exemplifies her ties to many cultures: the thick adobe walls are adorned with
elaborate Tibetan cloth paintings; presiding over the Native American
kiva fireplace is a Chinese bodhisattva carved from a bamboo root,
and beside the fireplace is an ancient statue from Cambodia. In Upaya's
meditation hall, a large painting by Japanese artist Mayumi Oda depicts
Roshi Joan as a wild green Tara of compassionate action, with blond
hair flying and vivid blue eyes, surrounded by the landscape of Prajna,
her beloved late dog Dominga by her side.

Joan continued to practice with Thich Nhat Hanh and his community while Upaya's community grew. But in 1995 she asked Roshi Bernie
Glassman† to be her primary teacher—a sea change in many ways. A
Jewish New Yorker, Glassman is known for leading "street retreats"
in the Bronx, in which participants live among homeless people for
weeks at a time. Joan explains her shift: "Thay [Thich Nhat Hanh] is
just an extraordinary force for good and for Buddhism in the world. I
was deeply enriched by his dharma. But Thay is nice. I am not a 'nice'
Buddhist. I'm much more interested in a kind of get-down-in-the-street-
and-get-dirty Buddhism."

She cur her long, thick hair, and Glassman ordained her as a roshi
in the order of Zen Peacemakers. This lineage does not require celibacy of priests. However, Roshi Joan says, "In the mid-90s, when I was

---

*Zentatsu Richard Baker (b. 1936), an American Soto Zen roshi, served as abbot of
the San Francisco Zen Center for thirteen years. He is the founder of Dharma Sangha.
†Tetsugen Bernard Glassman (b. 1939) is an American Zen Buddhist author and
cofounder of the Zen Peacemakers.

preparing for ordination as a Zen priest, I chose to be a celibate because I wanted to only serve the dharma. As the abbot of a Zen center and someone who's teaching all over the world, to be in a primary relationship would not serve that individual, my partner." Formalizing her vow of celibacy has made it possible for her to move in a more unfettered way, she feels. "A man approaching me knows I'm a celibate because that's public knowledge. It just becomes simpler. You're handing your life over to the world. You're a servant to all beings."

As abbot of Upaya, Roshi Joan merges the dharma of compassionate care with the cross-cultural and political elements of her work. She invites guest teachers as diverse as tribal leaders, former prisoners, environmental activists, Catholic priests, Jane Fonda. An admitted "addict" of Internet news and an active user of social media, Roshi often weaves current events into her dharma talks and speaks out against the US occupations of Iraq and Afghanistan. She has invited several Tibetan Buddhist teachers to lecture at Upaya; the monks from the Drepung Loseling Monastery in Atlanta fill the meditation hall with their primordial OMs every holiday season. "I think it's very useful for us in Buddhism to have a big roof," Roshi says, "and to understand that there are 84,000 dharma doors." She adds that stepping into another school of Buddhism "helps us see our own school through different eyes."

"By bringing all the elements of her rich background into Zen, she makes the practice very current and alive," confirms Natalie Goldberg. Roshi Bernie holds that what makes Roshi Joan exceptional is "her ability to create new forms of practice that are needed for this time and place."

When Roshi teaches health-care providers about the *bardos*—transitions between states of consciousness—she uses language accessible to non-Buddhists. "You can experience an intermediate state just falling asleep," she says. "Every breath we take, in a way, is a bardo." However, she adds, "I don't think we can verify the moment-of-death and after-death bardos. I don't know if they're veridical. But they're comparable to processes that one experiences in fainting, going through the anesthesia experience, falling asleep, and so forth."

She doesn't recommend that Christian or Jewish caregivers use the

Roshi Joan Halifax at her Nomad's Clinic in Humla, Nepal, with a Nepali man and his baby. Photo courtesy of Joan Halifax

traditional Tibetan manual for dying, *The Tibetan Book of the Dead*, in a literal way. She doubts that the visions it explicates for the transition period after death, such as deities holding skulls full of blood, would appear to a Westerner because every culture is conditioned to its own cultural images. In her opinion, the visions in this book "actually refer not so much to particular deities appearing, but to states of mind."

DECONSTRUCTING THE MYTH OF THE "GOOD DEATH"

Roshi acknowledges that over the years, losing friends and patients has gotten a little easier for her to handle. "I look at death as part of life. For people who are very close or special to me, I grieve. I don't reject the grieving at all. I wouldn't take one minute of sorrow away from me." She likes to deconstruct the myth of the "good death," pointing out that some people depart in denial, defiance, even misery. "I think the term 'good death' is a big problem. Every death has its own narrative, and I feel one has to respect the unique journey each individual takes to that destination we call death."

In her work with dying people, Roshi shares Theravada, Zen, and Tibetan practices. She emphasizes bodhichitta practice (the Tibetan practice of the compassionate, awakened mind), noting that Tibetan

Buddhism articulates bodhichitta in a more granular way than Zen. Health-care providers can use the wisdom of the compassionate mind to cultivate a deeper sense of meaning in their work and to increase their own resilience, just as it has helped Roshi stay engaged when working in challenging environments, such as Tibet, Burma, Nanjing, and the hospital and prison systems. "Bodhichitta has given me strength to carry on in this world," she says. "And to work with diligence, and a lot of love, and also a lot of joy in bringing the dharma forward in difficult situations."

HUMOR FROM BEYOND THE GRAVE

At her Ojai Foundation Chagdud Rinpoche led workshops on the practice of phowa, which he considered a profound, effective practice for health-care practitioners. They learned the practice "in a transmissional way," she says, because of Rinpoche's own proficiency. In this practice, the dying person's consciousness is transferred along the central channel of the body and out the top of the head. Roshi says that almost all of Rinpoche's students of phowa, including her, showed signs of accomplishment in the practice, such as "a tender swelling in your fontanel, a slight moisture or dew point at the top of the head, and sometimes even blood on the crown of the head." Roshi says her faith in these techniques has grown over the years "because I've applied them in real-life situations. This is not theoretical."

When people ask Roshi why, as a Buddhist teacher, she has a leather couch in her living room, she relates the story of Patrick, a young man who was dying of AIDS in Santa Fe. She had spent many hours keeping vigil by his bedside, practicing together. "He had gone through many different phases, some characterized by a lot of agony, some characterized by a lot of joy and even bliss," she recalls. One night, after nearly twenty-four hours of sitting a vigil at Patrick's house, she left at three o'clock to get some sleep. "I fell asleep and into a deep dream," she says. "In the dream I walked into Patrick's room and there he was. He was like a four- or five-year-old boy, and he had a kind of condom coming out of the crown of his head. Emanating from the condom was this white, luminous powder that was going up into the atmosphere. In my dream I became lucid, and I realized he had died at that moment." She woke up and the phone began to ring. It was Patrick's hospice nurse, who told her that Patrick had just died. Roshi drove back to the house. "I did phowa with him again. I say 'again' because I felt I had done it already in the dream. Or he had done it."

Regarding the symbol of the condom, she says, "He'd been a very sexually active young man. In the dream state, you associate things."

Patrick left Upaya the leather couch, brown and cushy, in his will. "It was a gift from Patrick," she says. "Maybe it was a joke."

"I WON'T HAVE IT!"

People sometimes ask her if it is difficult to be around death and dying, to bear witness to sick bodies and grieving hearts. She readily admits to experiencing some fear when she began this work. "I felt as if I would get what they had. Breast cancer, colon cancer, uterine cancer, AIDS. One day, I realized that I already had what they had. I was not separate from this one with cancer, that one with AIDS. How could I be afraid of getting what I already had?"[20]

Roshi is convinced that her childhood experience with illness taught her to see life as transient when she was very young. "I just don't want to waste any time." A few years ago, while giving a lecture in a Santa Fe theater, Roshi quoted writer Annie Dillard in resonant tones. "There is always an enormous temptation in all of life to diddle around making itsy-bitsy friends and meals and journeys for itsy-bitsy years on end . . . and then to sulk along the rest of your days on the edge of rage." Her voice rose, fierce. "I . . . won't . . . HAVE IT!" The last words echoed in the concert hall as the audience drew a collective shivered gasp. She made the audience repeat the words back to her in unison, forcefully: "I won't HAVE IT!"

Her outcry was inspiring and scary, a refusal to stay asleep any longer, a vow to do something about a world in crisis. Some audience members looked surprised to see an older woman—and a monastic with a shaved head and priest's robes at that—speak with such untamed emotion. They may have expected a demure nun, someone more tender and tranquil. She continued in a voice reedy with ardor, "The world is wilder than that in all directions, more dangerous and bitter, more extravagant and bright."

A TREMENDOUS AMOUNT OF FIRE

Roshi's direct style can get her into trouble. Her assistant, Peg Murray, found her "really scary" at first. "There's a tremendous amount of fire in her," Murray says. "People don't expect that. Because she's a woman, people expect her to lecture on loving-kindness and to be in a soft place all the time. She does have that side, but she can be undiplomatic, and some see that as a fault. She doesn't sugarcoat things. She has said strong things to people and freaked them out. But to me, that's the point. I want a teacher who can kick my butt and show me to my edge."

Over the years, several people have left Upaya because of conflicts. "Roshi Joan trusts her own judgment," notes Marty Peale, one of Upaya's earliest residents. "But you don't have to agree with her, and you don't have to stay." After a falling out with Roshi Joan in 1999, Peale left the community. Six years later, however, the death of a mutual friend brought them together again. For several years recently, Peale was a caretaker at "the refuge" and a mentor in the Chaplaincy Program. Even while their relationship was strained, Peale knew that Roshi's love for her was still strong. She acknowledges such challenges as very human. "We have to know that we do cause suffering—she does cause suffering—and not be discouraged by that," says Peale. "Such ups and downs can serve us; they are part of the path."

When asked about Roshi's difficult side, Natalie Goldberg admits, "Once or twice, she has been confrontational with me in a way that wasn't so skillful. But we talked about it, and it was fine." She adds, "I'm not afraid of her power. I'm proud of her as a woman. I root for her. She stands up and believes in herself. Women don't know how to support women in success, and that's hard for her."

Roshi agrees that her approach is quite direct, "which isn't always a comfortable thing for anybody." She laughs. "Moreover, I'm not always right. You can be direct and off two degrees, and you can really make quite a mess of things. Or you can be direct and be really accurate, but your timing could be really wrong. Or the person can't sustain what you're reflecting. It's tough. People don't like that in a woman."

Roshi Joan thinks that if she had been born into a man's body, "I'd be looked on as a gentle person. But I ended up in a woman's body. I'm glad I was born into a woman's body, and that at times people find it very difficult to digest how I am. That's been good to live with because it has precipitated a lot of examination of my own behaviors."

IDOLS AND DEMONS

Noting that students often project their own issues onto teachers, Roshi differentiates three stages of the student-teacher relationship: "Idealization, demonization, and if you're lucky, normalization. If somebody's idealizing me, I send that energy back to them. One way is to recognize their own basic goodness, to really feel it within yourself. Another is to show them what a doofus you are. I don't walk around my Zen center like Cardinal Richelieu," she quips. "I'm constantly making fun of myself, showing my worst side to everybody, and talking about my failures."

She describes her hospital room in Toronto, where three students sat at her bedside. "The back of my hospital gown was wide open, so when I had to get out of bed, my ass was hanging out. I was thinking, 'I've got to sit in front of these students in a month in full priest robes.' They really got to see my feet of clay, so to speak. That's why I feel such aversion to the term 'death with dignity.' It's hype. Who should be dignified? Sickness is a very undignified process."

A STRONG STAND AGAINST SEXUAL MISCONDUCT

Perhaps every teacher has feet of clay, but sexual misconduct is another matter in Roshi's eyes. In 2010, a scandal broke about Zen teacher Eido

Shimano's* sexual affairs with students over more than forty-five years, as documented in an archive kept by Robert Aitken Roshi.† (Shimano has publicly denied the allegations but has resigned from his abbacy of the Zen Studies Society in New York.) Roshi Joan posted an open letter on the Upaya website expressing her concerns about what she calls "violations of boundaries and faith."[21]

Regarding the sexual misconduct of male clergy in general, she writes,

> If you want to deepen the shadow of any religion, turn wisdom and compassion into hypocrisy, and stand by, conflict averse, as its male clergy disrespects women, has sex with female congregants, dominates women, abuses women, degrades or rapes them. . . . I have been waiting for years for a concerted response to such violations against women in our Buddhist world. Many of us women have brought these issues to the attention of the wider community and have been shamed and shunned.

However, she writes that now,

> Buddhists are finally getting it. You have to take a stand, a strong and vocal stand, against the predatory behavior of its religious figures. You have to speak truth to power, and speak it loudly. And you have to act.

In response, Roshi received a deluge of emails and letters. Most supported her position while a few judged feminism as outdated or accused Roshi of being self-serving. Some of the messages were written by women (or the partners of women) who had been involved with

---

*Eido Tai Shimano (b. 1932), a Japanese-born Rinzai Zen Buddhist teacher, established the first Rinzai lineage in the United States. He founded a Zen center in Manhattan and a monastery in the Catskills.

†Robert Aitken Roshi (1917–2010) was a Zen teacher in the Harada-Yasutani lineage who chose to live as a layperson. A social activist, he was one of the founders of the Buddhist Peace Fellowship.

Chögyam Trungpa Rinpoche, another teacher known for having had affairs with students. Although some women who wrote to her asserted that their involvement with Trungpa was beneficial, she says that by her estimation, "most of the people who have written to me experienced deep suffering around these encounters."

DRINKING POISON

Roshi had much contact with Trungpa in the seventies and eighties. She taught at Naropa, the university he founded, invited him onto the faculty of a program she produced, and she traveled to Japan with him. She openly acknowledges that he acted inappropriately toward her on several occasions. "Trungpa was a person of immense imagination, magnetism, and vision," Roshi recalls. "He was a pioneer in thinking, an artist who hit the American scene at just the right moment. A lot of us were very attracted to his community, his writings, his teachings. We were fascinated by him."

However, she decided not to be his student. "I felt that his teachings were compromised by his behavior. Which some people said *was* a teaching. But it wasn't the kind of teaching I wanted or needed." As a civil rights worker, antiwar activist, and feminist, she found his behavior to be highly problematic. "I had lived a pretty wild life too," Roshi continues. "But I didn't want to drink the same poison. I didn't feel I could straighten my life out with someone who had an addiction to alcohol and seemingly to sex."

One factor in the dynamic was "this idolization and idealization of spiritual teachers, which is unrealistic," she says. "In the end, I don't think that did him any good at all. Because he embodied the shadow in a way that actually harmed quite a few people." A number of his students would not agree with her on this point and have told her so. "But at my age, I can look back with some sense of regret that he didn't have peers, colleagues, and teachers who would help him see things in a more global way. As a person, as a woman, I've made my share of mistakes," Roshi concedes. "But as a feminist, I'm very clear that religion is no excuse for the violation of the teacher-student boundary." When that boundary, based on trust, is violated, "it's a direct assault on the three jewels, the Buddha, dharma, and sangha."

Rather than idealize their spiritual teachers, Roshi recommends that students "retrieve their projections, see their own enlightened nature and their own deluded nature, and see the deluded and enlightened nature of every human being." Our longing for a perfect parent makes us willing to justify dysfunctional behavior in spiritual or educational settings, she suspects. "In Tibetan Buddhism, practices like taking life vows to a teacher—*samaya* vows—which serve to make you ever more faithful and under the wing of your teacher, these can possibly diminish the kind of discernment that we value in our culture."

She honestly discusses the "cultural bias" she has experienced with Eastern teachers. "The Eastern pattern is more towards seeking harmony; the Western pattern is to seek transparency." She feels that what she brought to the path as a Westerner and as a woman "was not always appreciated. There is a gender bias in Buddhism, which perceived women as somewhat lesser." Though she acknowledges that Thich Nhat Hanh has since empowered many women, she longed to have "a straightforward communication from Westerner to Westerner"—a wish that informed her decision to take American Roshi Bernie Glassman as her primary teacher. "Many Eastern teachers think they are always right, whereas Bernie's first tenet is 'always not knowing.'"

She believes that teachers have a responsibility to embody wholesomeness, following the example of His Holiness the Dalai Lama. Roshi considers the Dalai Lama to be a "very significant influence" in her life, particularly because of his teachings on ethics and universal responsibility. "He wants to see a secular ethics that really cuts through the religious differences." She joins the Dalai Lama for meetings of the Mind and Life Institute, a nonprofit organization that since 1987 has hosted dialogues between scholars, scientists, and representatives of the world's contemplative traditions. One of the founders of Mind and Life, Roshi Joan serves as a board member as well as a moderator and presenter at the meetings, which are often held in Dharamsala.

"It's been inspiring to sit in His Holiness's living room every year, sometimes twice a year, in this fairly intimate situation." She cherishes

His Holiness the Dalai Lama with Roshi Joan Halifax.
Photo courtesy of Joan Halifax

"the opportunity to be educated by the neuroscientists and philosophers. We've seen the whole field of contemplative neuroscience emerge out of these dialogues." Faculty members often present new scientific evidence for the efficacy of meditation, findings that deeply influence Roshi's own work in medical settings. From Mind and Life has sprung Zen Brain, Upaya's lively annual gathering of neuroscientists, psychologists, and philosophers.

Although early Mind and Life gatherings were heavily male dominated, Roshi has spoken privately with the Dalai Lama and the board to advocate for gender parity in the meetings. His Holiness has been receptive to these requests, and the gender balance is rapidly changing as the organization invites more women to participate, including nuns. Advocating for others—women, patients, prisoners—is a thread that runs throughout Roshi's work.

Marty Peale notes that today Upaya is a strong center for women, with several women in leadership roles. But, she says, "We're all realizing that someday, and it might be twenty years from now, we'll have to go on without Roshi. We are thinking about how to keep her legacy alive. No one of us can do what she has done. It will take a team."

ARDUOUS, TIRING, INSPIRING, AND FUN

After her accident, Roshi looked carefully at her priorities. She decided that when she got her health back, she would work on a more global level. Now she is traveling and teaching almost constantly, all over the world, returning to Upaya only to lead occasional retreats. She is about to leave for the World Economic Forum in Switzerland, where she will be featured as a panelist in several discussions, such as "Neuro-ethics: A Marriage between Morals and Matter" and "The Science of Mastering Emotions." She now also teaches in Thailand, Burma, Japan, India, and Malaysia, an interesting process for her as a Western Buddhist woman bringing the dharma back to its geographical origins.

Roshi Joan has let her hair grow out in short, steely waves. Energetic and in good spirits, she talks about her rehabilitation process after the accident, which she calls "arduous, tiring, inspiring, and fun." She used her recent trip to Tibet as an incentive to recover her physical strength. "It was a spiritual light at the end of a very long tunnel."

Since her accident, she has gone through varying degrees of pain. "I try to have the approach, 'I'm in pain, but I'm not suffering.' I'm walking like an older person—much more slowly and carefully." For a good part of the Nepal/Tibet trek she rode on horseback, which she describes as "at times quite terrifying," given the narrow mountain trails with high exposures. "It's much scarier than walking. But the horse didn't want to die, and I had to just let go."

Roshi says that the ego does strange things in a boundless landscape like the Tibetan Plateau—it tries to reify itself by attaching to the next visible object, such as a cairn strung with prayer flags or a monastery in the distance. "Some people want to retreat to their tents and fuss with their duffel bags," Roshi observes. "It's just too much space. You lose all sense of reference points." She continues, "What is rich is to take a walk, a long walk on the Plateau, not toward anything, and watch the mind slowly, slowly relax. And then lift your eyes to the sky. And just open yourself to that vastness."

Lama Tsultrim Allione at Tara Mandala in Colorado.
Photo by Laurie Pearce Bauer. © Laurie Pearce Bauer

11: Tsultrim Allione
(JOAN ROUSMANIÈRE EWING)
THE ENLIGHTENED FEMINIST

*A mother of three and best-selling author follows in the
footsteps of an eleventh-century Tibetan saint*[1]

THE LOFTY TIBETAN THRONE has been exquisitely carved by traditional artists, but the master occupying the throne in full brocade robes is anything but traditional. Tall and blue-eyed, she wears
the pointed red dakini hat on her straight blond-grey hair, confidently
playing the bell and the two-sided hand drum. Lama Tsultrim Allione
is about to give Machig Labdron's initiation for *chöd*, or "cutting
through." As Tsultrim performs Machig's signature ritual, she reminds
us who this extraordinary eleventh-century Tibetan mystic was: one of
the most revered yoginis of Tibet.

The triple grandmother born in Maine in 1947 and Machig Labdron,
the yogini born in Central Tibet in 1055, could hardly be further apart
in time and space, yet they are sisters in spirit: a few years ago, Tsultrim
Allione was recognized as an emanation* of Machig.

With a wailing, eerie sound, Tsultrim expertly blows the *kangling*, the
flute made out of a thigh bone, then confers the blessings of Machig's
practice. In a reversal of common wisdom, Machig Labdron's chöd ritual

---

*An emanation is not exactly the same as a reincarnation, but scholars and lamas give
widely varying answers about what the difference is. To simplify greatly, *reincarnation*
refers to a realized master choosing to be reborn in a human body, whereas the term
emanation is used in a more general sense to indicate that the blessing of a deity or a
realized master has entered another being's mind.

switched the logic of how to deal with what we fear. Machig instructed us to open ourselves to our inner enemies, "to feed our demons," instead of running away. In Machig's definition, demons are not bloodthirsty monsters but reside within us: "Demons are our obsessions and fears, chronic illnesses, or common problems like depression, anxiety, and addiction,"[2] Tsultrim explains. "They are the forces that we fight inside ourselves."[3] Paradoxically, embracing the demons weakens their power and they loosen their grip. In the temple, Tsultrim reiterates Machig's promise: "This empowerment transforms all obstacles into the path of good fortune. The sick person attains bliss through sickness. Adverse conditions become companions on the path. A single 'eat me, take me' is better than a thousand 'protect me's.'"

The age-old empowerment ritual ends with a stunning contemporary encore as if to prove that the dharma has finally arrived in the West with a bang. A handsome young student pays homage to another female hero: Lady Gaga. Soon two hundred students are rapping and clapping to the rhythm of 'Born This Way,' cleverly revamping the pop icon's lyrics to suit the occasion:

> We're gonna practice
> 'Till we're awake!
> Don't be a meany,
> Be a dakini!

A CELEBRATION OF THE ENLIGHTENED FEMININE

Tsultrim gives the empowerment in her temple, Tara Mandala, which she calls "a template of the awakened mind, a celebration of the enlightened feminine." A mandala is a symbolic representation of a sacred world, in Tsultrim's definition "a primal centering tool that maps the psyche's journey of transformation. The mandala interfaces between the yet-to-be-perfected world, or encumbered emotions, and the dimension of luminosity of the sacred ideal world."[4] Twenty-one golden statues of Tara sit on ledges around the bright yellow sixty-foot octagon. Dakinis dance atop every entrance door. Finely carved dragons wriggle around delicate red columns. Yet a basic fixture of any Buddhist temple is missing: a male buddha. She laughs when I point out the absence of anything male. "I know! If the Dalai Lama walked in here, the first thing he would ask is, 'Where is the Buddha?'" Therefore she has commissioned one more statue, and Buddha Shakyamuni is on his way from Nepal.

I cannot think of another female teacher who has taken the idea of the "enlightened feminine" quite so far. "This tradition is still so massively patriarchal that we need quite a substantial change," she states forthrightly in her deep, raspy voice. Before she built Tara Mandala, she asked many people what a temple dedicated to the feminine should look like. "All came up with a round shape. You wouldn't really build a square temple for the feminine." For pragmatic construction reasons, the architect made it octagonal.

The morning after the empowerment, at seven o'clock, she hikes with me to tour the land. Under a stainless sunrise, Tsultrim Allione, her son Costanzo, and twenty students file on the ridge below a breast-shaped peak. Because of its shape, she has dubbed the mountain "Ekajati" after the one-breasted, three-eyed wrathful protectress of the Great Perfection teachings. "Walk every step mindfully!" she instructs, as she starts on the steep incline. "Dedicate every step to someone who is ill or needs help!" Seven hundred acres unfold in soft green hilly waves around us as we walk. There is no path as she forges her way uphill, through scrub and brush. Maybe this is a fitting image for a woman who is blazing a new path for the dharma in the West.

Tsultrim Allione has created a magical yet modern Tibetan oasis in the midst of Colorado, at the southern end of the San Juan Mountains, near Pagosa Springs. With meager funds to begin with, she managed to raise six million dollars to build a soaring twelve-thousand-square-foot temple. Bhutanese wood carving, Nepalese paintings, Tibetan geomancy, and Western eco-technology blend seamlessly, creating a unique three-storey celebration of spiritual feminism.

Like so many things in her life, the land "came" to her in a vision, with the temple "descending from the autumn sky as blue, then 'out of the blue' came the rest of the design." Tsultrim says that she instantly recognized the land from her dreams when a real estate agent showed it to her. The red temple juts out of the soft valley below, while to the north a vast, green, bowl-shaped meadow curves like a womb. This particular stretch of the Colorado basin is considered sacred to the Native Americans. From Tara Mandala's highest peak we spot one of the Indians' holiest places, Chimney Rock, a natural rock crag that sticks vertically into the sky. From the beginning Tsultrim Allione has invited the Native Americans to her ceremonies. "I always felt that in order to establish the dharma in America, we needed to ask permission from the native people, because they are really the caretakers of the land, and they know the energies here."

With her back to the rising sun, she instructs the group to sit down and read aloud the powerful aspiration prayer of the primordial Buddha, Samantabhadra:

> I shall purify oceans of realms;
> Liberate oceans of sentient beings;
> Understand oceans of dharma;
> Realize oceans of wisdom.

A DAKINI AS BOSS

After returning from the mountain, we speak in her tiny, bright yellow room on the first floor of the temple, where she secludes herself most of the time now. How would she explain what it means to be recognized as an emanation in the twenty-first century? Lama Tsultrim reflects for a second, then breaks into laughter, "I'm still trying to figure that out. The way I see it, I am working for her." Tsultrim defines an emanation as "a being who comes into the world to further that lineage in some way, so Machig Labdron is my boss."

During a retreat in 2006, "Machig appeared to me in a vision on a white lion," Tsultrim recalls. "She transmitted teachings to me, and then she said, you have to gather my lineage and establish it here, at Tara Mandala. 'It's urgent,' she said with such intensity, I almost left retreat." The dream encounter led Tsultrim in 2007 to visit the cave and monastery at Zangri Kangmar in Central Tibet, where Machig Labdron lived from age thirty-seven until she passed away in her nineties.[5] After Tsultrim and her group sat down to practice chöd in the main temple, the resident teacher, Karma Nyiton Kunkhyab Chökyi Dorje Rinpoche, made an unexpected announcement. "I want to make it clear to all of you, and there should be no doubt, that Tsultrim is an emanation of Machig Labdron." The lama gave Tsultrim some of Machig's objects, among them a crystal *purba** and the only remaining *tsa tsa*† of her ashes. He said that his mission was the same as Tsultrim's—to establish Machig's lineage. "Machig actually had a direct lineage in itself, which had dispersed into the other lineages," Tsultrim explains. "So we both tried to collect her actual lineage and bring that out again. That's what I was doing already."

While Tsultrim was still in Tibet, a master in Kathmandu who had focused on Machig Labdron's practices for most of his life had a vision. Machig Labdron appeared to Lama Tsering Wangdu and prophesied that she would arrive in three days. Three days later, on her way back from Tibet, Tsultrim arrived unannounced. This lama too wrote a recognition letter. Lama Tsultrim thinks that the purpose of the acknowledgments was "for me to develop confidence, because I have a really hard time accepting this. I knew things, but I doubted them, and then I allowed myself to know what I already knew, if that makes sense."

For Tsultrim, the recognition explained her lifelong bond with Machig's teachings. Long before she was recognized, in 1983, she had already translated Machig's biography from the Tibetan language, embraced and taught her practices, especially chöd, and collected every text about and from Machig Labdron she could find. The recognition ceremony validated her efforts. "It allowed me to trust my visions more." If she was an emanation of Machig, then suddenly so many inexplicable turns in her life made sense.

In the eleventh century, only the teachings that came from Buddha's native land, India, were regarded as authentic. Yet in her autobiography

*A ceremonial dagger.
†The molded shapes, in Tibetan called *tsa tsas*, are usually miniature buddhas formed out of clay. Often, the ashes and pulverized bones of deceased masters and great practitioners are mixed into the clay.

Tsultrim Allione during a joyful celebration with her students
at Tara Mandala in Colorado. Photo courtesy of Tara Mandala

Machig stated that her teaching came from Tibet, not India, thus pro-
voking intense scrutiny. "The Indian scholars were very suspicious, so
three speed-walkers* from India came to test Machig," Tsultrim explains.
"They couldn't defeat Machig in debate, and they were impressed by
her personal insight into the Buddhist teachings and their history. Then
Machig directed them to the corpse from her previous life in India,
which had remained undecayed in a cave. She predicted that particular
relics would emerge when the corpse was burned, such as five buddhas
on the skull and a relief of the Great Mother, Prajnaparamita, on the
collarbone, and so on. After the scholars returned to India, everything
occurred as she had predicted, and any doubts were settled."

Already Machig's life story begins with a miracle. She started out
in the body of a man who transferred his consciousness into Machig's
female figure. "In order to understand this kind of story, we must surrender our Western frame of reference, which limits our ideas of what

---

*Realized yogis are said to have mastered the art of walking at an extremely high speed.
Thus they are reported to accomplish the journey from India to Tibet, which would
usually take months, within days.

is possible and what is impossible," Tsultrim Allione writes in the prologue to her translation of Machig's biography. "At higher levels of spiritual development, the material world can be manipulated by the consciousness, and many things become possible."[6]

A thousand years later, Tsultrim Allione too asks us to believe in developments outside of the ordinary. Tsultrim also has been criticized for writing her own practices and passing them on to her students, thus establishing new aspects to this old lineage in a new country—an almost unheard-of endeavor for a Western woman. Like Machig, she had been a nun but disrobed in her twenties. Like Machig, she has three children. Like Machig, she felt the need to return to intensive practice when her children had grown out of their diapers. Like Machig, she has adapted the teachings to the country where she was born.

A FAMILY OF ADVENTURERS

Tsultrim Allione has always been a visionary and let herself be guided by dreams and intuition—a trait she believes has carried over with her family history. "My ancestors were seers and visionaries. They lived at the mountain of Tara in Ireland, which was sacred to the pre-Christian pagan religion, before they moved to Scotland and continued to be seers and lawyers there."

Her grandfather had been to Tibet decades earlier, trekking into the Himalayas from Darjeeling. "We have a family history of adventure. My mother walked all around southern Russia at nineteen, with just a friend, and got her pilot's license a few years later." When not exploring the world physically, her grandparents tested it intellectually. Both obtained doctorates in philosophy. Her grandfather taught at Harvard and her grandmother at Smith and Mount Holyoke after getting her PhD from Harvard, in an era where this was extremely unusual for a woman. The same grandmother had given Joan Rousmanière Ewing, as Tsultrim was known then, her first Buddhist book, on Zen poetry, when she was fifteen.

Both her parents were liberal-spirited Unitarians. Her father published small independent newspapers in Maine and then New Hampshire.

Tsultrim describes him as "a really good father, very present, very pro-tective. He wasn't very emotionally close, but he was always *there*." Given this background, "It wasn't so strange for my family that I went to India," Tsultrim says, "but becoming a Buddhist was different."

At nineteen years old, Joan Rousmanière Ewing traveled to Calcutta with her best friend, Victress Hitchcock. Victress' parents were in the diplomatic corps; her father was the Consul General of Calcutta and had arranged for the teenagers to volunteer at Mother Teresa's orphan-age, in the hope "that this would get the fantasies of the 'mystic East' out of our heads," Tsultrim says. But the opposite happened when the parents sent the girls to help Tibetan refugees in Kathmandu. "As soon as I met the Tibetans in 1967, I felt this real coming home. It was a very dramatic feeling, a real longing that I hadn't realized I had until I met them."

One morning a Nepalese family that she visited brought her onto their rooftop. In the distance, she saw a white, glowing globe on a pointed hill, like an island: Swayambhunath, one of Nepal's most ancient places of worship. She was instantly mesmerized. When she first climbed up the 365 steep steps to the temple, she felt her life "had been completely altered."

She moved into a small hut on the neighboring hill to join the rhythm of the Tibetan pilgrims, from their early morning rounds to their sunset chants. With more pigs and cows on the street than cars, the sporadic presence of electricity, and an unending stream of pilgrims, she felt as if she had traveled in a time machine. "Part of myself, which had up until then remained empty, was being filled," she describes the experience in *Women of Wisdom.* "A joyful sense of being in the blessings which were almost tangibly present began to steal over me."[7] She stayed for a few months, hitchhiked across India, and met the Dalai Lama, before her parents beckoned her with a plane ticket to come back to New Hamp-shire. She complied but found herself miserable when she tried to go back to school. Though her family was open-minded, they were very skeptical about her new path. Reflecting about her older sister and one younger brother, Tsultrim says, "We are not super close. My journey was just very foreign to them."

Becoming Tsultrim

Searching for ways to keep her newfound connection with the Tibetans, she continued to recite the mantras she had learned in Nepal and traveled to Chögyam Trungpa's center in Scotland, Samye Ling. He was recovering from a car accident and hardly teaching, so she leaped at the chance to take a Volkswagen bus from London back to Kathmandu. "This was the time when you could go overland, through Turkey, Iraq, Iran, Afghanistan, Pakistan, to India and then Nepal—imagine that today!" she beams. Before she left, Trungpa gave her a copy of a practice that he had written, the *Sadhana of All Siddhis*, and during the dusty six-week bus ride she kept reading it over and over.

Auspiciously, her arrival at the Swayambhunath temple in Kathmandu coincided with a visit of one of the most revered teachers from Tibet, the Sixteenth Karmapa. "I started to get very agitated," Tsultrim says. "I was unable to sleep or eat much. I felt there was something I was supposed to do, but I didn't know what it was." Suddenly, a line from Trungpa's sadhana spoke strongly to her:

The only offering I can make is to follow your example.

Since the practice paid homage to the Karmapa, who was residing next door at Swayambhunath, and he was a monk, Joan Ewing took this as a clear sign that she too should take robes. Losing no time, she went directly to the monastery, offered the Karmapa flowers and told him she wanted to become a nun. He laughed, and according to Tsultrim later admitted he had seen her in the crowd before and had already told his attendant this Western woman would become a nun. "I was wild," she says. "I've always just done things without thinking too much. I didn't even really know what a Buddhist was, and I hadn't even taken refuge when I became a nun."

Only a few weeks later, in January 1970, the Karmapa ordained Joan Rousmanière Ewing in Bodhgaya, India, and gave her the name Karma Tsultrim Chödron, the "Discipline Lamp of the Teachings." While her family could hardly fathom their daughter's rapid transformation,

Tsultrim was on spiritual autopilot. The Karmapa said she had been his disciple in a previous lifetime. Tsultrim moved into a room so small she could touch all four walls while sitting on her bed. Since the cell was right next to the Swayambhunath temple, it was the perfect launching pad for her to embark on a path of serious study and retreat. She sees the time she spent as a nun as an "invaluable experience. It is important for women to have the experience of living a 'virgin' existence: a maiden alone, complete in herself, belonging to no man."[8]

She was already dreaming of establishing a retreat center in America. While she was doing her prostrations and reciting the traditional mantras, her mind was admittedly "obsessed" with designing a dharma center in the West where Westerners could find the same solitude as in the Himalayas. But when she finally returned to America after a few years, to see her family in New Hampshire, the culture of the seventies didn't welcome a shaven-headed girl in foreign habit. "When I came back, my family was really nervous, because they lived in a small town." She might have been the only Tibetan Buddhist nun in America at the time. Attracting curiosity and comments, the robes became "more of a hindrance than a blessing. To me, the point of the robes was to simplify one's external appearance so that one could concentrate on one's inner development, [yet] the novelty of the Tibetan robes in America seemed to have the opposite effect."[9] She had almost died of hepatitis in Nepal shortly after her ordination and was reluctant to go back to an unheated shack without running water. But she could not see herself keeping the robes in the midst of the "wild scene around Trungpa Rinpoche" in Vermont and Boulder where she landed. Besides, she was young and pretty, even with a shaved head. "I was only twenty-two at the time of my ordination," she says. "I was not formed enough to resist being swept away whenever I fell in love."[10]

"COOKING IN THE CAULDRON OF MOTHERHOOD"

Within a year of returning her vows, Tsultrim went from being a nun to a married mother, from the silence of morning prayers to nursing her baby girl, from a rather rigid meditation schedule to having no time of her own. Nine months after her first daughter, Sherab, was born, she gave birth to her second baby, Aloka. The radical life change led Tsultrim to question: How exactly did motherhood fit in with Buddhism? When she looked at the life stories of the great saints of her lineage, almost all of them were male, and the few women had either abandoned their children or were celibate nuns. "I had no role models for women in my position, no stories to follow," she says. "It seemed that because of my choice of disrobing I had lost my path."

She attempted to transform motherhood into her path instead, taking nursing as a training in altruism, with her children revealing her self-clinging when she longed for the comfort of silence. "As I cooked in the cauldron of motherhood, the incredible love I felt for my children opened my heart and brought me a much greater understanding of universal love. It made me understand the suffering of the world much more deeply. This has been an important thread for me, both as a practitioner and as a human being."[11]

Around the same time, Trungpa Rinpoche authorized her to teach, and she started teaching at Naropa University and in the Buddhist community in Boulder, Colorado. A black-and-white snapshot of her laughing with Allen Ginsberg at a kitchen table hangs outside her room in the Tara Mandala temple and reminds her of the years when she was the beat poet's meditation instructor. Community life in Boulder proved both inspiring and challenging. "Although I enjoyed living in a Buddhist community, after several years I felt unhappy with the patriarchal, hierarchical, structured organization there."[12]

A DOWNWARD SPIRAL OF DEPRESSION

Allen Ginsberg introduced her to an Italian filmmaker, Costanzo Allione, who was in Colorado to shoot a movie about the poet. Within a year, Tsultrim entered her second marriage, moved to Rome, and became pregnant with twins, Costanzo and Chiara. Unable to speak the local language, feeling cut off from her spiritual roots on their remote farm in Italy, she and her husband soon were struggling with marriage problems that sometimes erupted in domestic violence. After a taxing pregnancy and a traumatic hospital experience with the preemies, Chiara's sudden death at two-and-a-half months propelled her into a downward spiral of depression and grief. "It's not like one has all these beautiful revelations, and everything is easy," she admits now, three decades later. "I've gone through very difficult trials."

Chiara means "clarity" in Italian, and clarity was what Tsultrim Allione was missing most. After her infant's death, out of "this moment of extreme descent, confusion, loss and grief, I began to feel my way back into a relationship with the sacred feminine."[13] She says, "I do not feel my search for my path as a woman conflicts with practices I have done before but, rather, it is bringing forth other kinds of awareness. I realize now that, for me, spirituality is connected to a delicate, playful, spacious part of myself which closes up in militantly regimented situations."[14]

More than ever, Tsultrim was desperate for guidance. "I needed to turn to teachers, stories, *anything*, that would guide me. I was a full-time mother from morning 'til midnight. I couldn't see anything ahead of me but a life full with babies, fatigue, and loneliness. As a serious practitioner, I didn't know where to turn."[15] When she could find no comfort in the traditional texts or teachings, she made a decision: "Okay, I have to create this for myself and for all these women in a similar situation."[16]

SEARCHING FOR A SPIRITUAL MOTHER

Seeking out life stories of Buddhist women from the past, she longed to discover "some thread that would help me in my life—which was, of course, very different than the lives of the ancient yoginis and yet I felt, their stories would begin to feed me."[17] She was looking for "a spiritual mother, a model," to benefit both her life and develop a blueprint for others.

Machig literally means "one mother," and Tsultrim "met" her the following year. During a retreat in California her teacher, Namkhai Norbu Rinpoche, taught chöd. He invoked the presence of Machig Labdron as she is described in the text: a dancing, white, sixteen-year-old dakini. One evening Namkhai Norbu Rinpoche kept repeating the invocation for hours, well past midnight. "This night, I suddenly had this experience of another female form emerging out of the darkness, from a cemetery." Tsultrim didn't see her as a youthful teenager but as old: "She had long, pendular breasts that had fed babies. Her grey hair was streaming down, and she was looking at me in this incredibly intense way, with immense compassion in her eyes. It was like an invitation, and at the same time, a challenge. I was shocked, because this wasn't what I was supposed to be seeing, yet there she was, and she came very close to me."

After going to bed, she dreamed about getting back to "her" mountain, Swayambhunath, in Nepal. The dreams kept recurring the following nights and carried an immense feeling of urgency. Tsultrim finally realized that this probably was "not just a metaphor about returning to my center in some way, but that I actually had to go back there."

Getting back to Swayambhunath was not easy; a civil war was raging in Nepal, and she was caring for her three young children. She ended up going alone, leaving the children with her husband. Ascending the steep stairs to Swayambhunath again, she found her old monk friend waiting for her. When she told him about her search for women's stories, he joyfully returned with a huge volume of loose Tibetan leaves, wrapped in orange cloth—Machig Labdron's biography. Translating the work together with the monk, she laid the foundation for her best-selling book *Women of Wisdom*, the biographies of six female Tibetan mystics. The research connected her with the role models she had been longing for but also with a bigger picture: "When I found the dakinis, I found an access point for the empowered, enlightened feminine."[18]

She describes dakinis as having "a quality of playfulness, expressing emptiness. This feminine quality of seduction and play makes you insecure and yet open, pulling the rug out from under you. These dakinis embody and activate the powerful, active transformative energy of the feminine." Fittingly, they appeared when she was at her lowest. "Dakinis tend to push us through blockages," Tsultrim says. "They tend to appear during moments of transition when we might not know what to do next. The dakinis will remove the blockage. Sometimes that energy needs to be forceful, so the wrathful dakini appears. The dakinis also traditionally show up when you're between the worlds, between life and death, between sleep and waking. The twilight. In fact, the language of the dakinis is called the twilight language."[19]

Tsultrim experiences being guided by Machig in a very intimate way, receiving practices directly from the vision. Tsultrim soon relied on Machig as her primary guide. She deeply reflected on how to make Machig's teachings relevant for a modern Western audience. The practice of cutting through helped her to let go when her failing marriage with Allione turned into a raging custody battle over baby Costanzo. She also learned about Machig's recipe for dealing with grief: embracing it. "I decided, I am not going to try to be brave and try to not feel the pain, or not cry. I intuitively felt that suppressing my feelings would be bad for my health. The emotions would go inwards, and something would crack inside my body."[20]

Tsultrim Allione combines Western psychology with traditional Tibetan rituals. She finds that psychological work is useful to avoid bypassing or suppressing emotional issues that might not be addressed by chanting mantras and visualizing deities. In *Feeding Your Demons*, her reinterpretation of chöd, she incorporates her knowledge of Jungian psychoanalysis. With a simple five-step process for dealing with foes like addiction, abuse, or depression, she tries to make the ancient practice accessible even to modern non-Buddhists.

Tsultrim's practice texts are stripped of the elaborations found in many Tibetan originals. "They are almost skeletal," she says, "because the nature of mind is the key for Western practitioners." She calls her practice texts "kind of revelations, but I would not want to be too inflated about it. They came out of my extensive experience with practice, feeling into how to transmit that in the West. Machig also wrote her practices from her meditation experience."

"AUTHENTIC SACRED SEX"

Around the same time that she embraced the "enlightened feminine," Tsultrim took a stand against sexual abuse by some lamas. "That was very difficult. It wasn't popular, even amongst so-called feminist Buddhists," she remembers, "so I was criticized a lot for that too. But ethically, I couldn't sit back and watch it."

Tsultrim Allione distinguishes between "authentic sacred sex," where wisdom realization is shared with an equally empowered partner, and "that underground thing that is not really beneficial or where there is maybe a huge power difference, when somebody is just used and then thrown out." Tsultrim cautions that it is "not automatically bad when a teacher has sex with a student, it really depends." Because sexual energy "is a beautiful thing, a powerful meeting," she wishes that teachings on authentic tantric sexual relationships in the Tibetan tradition were less secret. "I think that could be an interesting development, because everyone is having sex, and it is a powerful experience to bring the path to it." She would like to see "more enlightened energy around the topic. Let's bring it out in the open, let people be trained and elevate the experience into a practice of nonduality and liberation through the senses."

HEALING CANCER

On the daybed in her room, she sits under a Tibetan scroll depicting the blue Medicine Buddha. In recent years, she has developed a reputation as a healer. When she was in one-year retreat several years ago, she caught a lung infection that would not go away. While walking in the forest, she "saw" the herbs that would help her and started to "communicate" with the plants. She made teas and tinctures for herself, and sure enough, drinking the concoction cured her ailment. When she came out of that same retreat, a neighbor had been diagnosed with terminal cancer. Determined to just face death calmly, he refused to follow his doctor's advice for surgery and chemotherapy. Again, Tsultrim "saw" the herbs that would help him. After three months he stopped by on the way back from the clinic to thank her: his doctors could not find a trace of the cancer anymore. Since then Tara Mandala has developed a full-blown herbal remedies program. In traditional mythology, the land of Tara is said to have healing properties. Ann Hackney, a full-time herbalist, spends most of her days scouting the vast land for medicinal herbs like balsam root, burdock, mullein, red clover, barberry, or dandelion, then distills them in the long row of glass containers that line the entrance of her office. The formula against cancer, Contra-Can, has since become Tara Mandala's most successful herbal product.

MEETING THE DEMON OF DEATH

Yet while the recent years were a time of fruition—the temple finished, the paint dried, a strong community established—the woman who was most famous for feeding her demons now had to meet her biggest demon yet. Though she still radiates that magnetic presence that has attracted thousands of students, she looks visibly fragile underneath. Her eyes tear up when she revisits the events that lie so recently behind her. Unexpectedly she had another encounter with one of the most uncompromising demons of all: death. One beautiful summer morning in July 2010, she found her husband of twenty-two years motionless in his bed. The previous night he had been dancing; now he lay dead after a heart attack cut his life force in his sleep.

"I am still reeling from that shock," she admits. She must have taught on impermanence innumerable times, yet thirty-one years after the death of her baby, the unexpected demise of another most beloved put her strength to a test once again. "We have all heard a thousand times that we really don't know when death will strike, but it is still shocking."

At fifty-five years old, David Petit was in the prime of his life, "a lion of a man" with a flowing, shoulder-length grey mane. He combined the gracefulness of a professional dancer with the creativity of an abstract painter, the courage of a daredevil horseman with the softness of an accomplished Dzogchen practitioner. Tsultrim describes him as "wild, due to that Native American part in him. He loved to dance, to party, to laugh, to drink good wine, and he was an advanced Dzogchen yogi, much more advanced than most people knew until his death. He could do *anything*." Almost all the dozen staff at Tara Mandala have their own stories how they almost got killed when they went horseback riding with David, jumping off the cliffs and galloping across the largely untouched land. "Protector" is the word Tsultrim thinks describes him best. He was watching over her, her vision, the land. "He had the power to communicate with the wild animals, he kept the bears at bay," says Allione's daughter-in-law, Cady Allione. "It was uncanny. He was also the only one who could stand up to Lama Tsultrim and tease her."

Tsultrim Allione had found her match in 1989 when her and David's shared love of Native American rituals had brought them together in the sweat lodge of a mutual friend. As the fire keeper David brought in the hot rocks. "Once we found each other, that was it," Tsultrim says. "From then on we were together." In fact, David had first heard Tsultrim's name at the school where he taught her daughters theater and dance. "When he heard my name, the hairs on his body stood up, and he had never had that experience before. When he finally met me, he was very nervous; sometimes he would even run away. He knew his destiny was coming at him." Tsultrim laughs as she recounts the story. They treated each other like old soul mates reconnecting again in this lifetime, and though he was a Christian when they met, he soon acknowledged Tsultrim as his teacher, studied with many Tibetan masters, and slowly accomplished advanced Dzogchen practices.

When David and Tsultrim first moved out to the deserted hills in southwest Colorado in 1993 with a few students, there was only earth: no buildings, no running water, no electricity. "There were competitions who could go the longest without a shower," managing director Cady Allione jokes. Living in tents and tipis at first, Tsultrim says, "we got to know the land. We invited the native elders to teach us about the sacred geography of the area. I couldn't have done it without David. He was key at every step of the way."

David Petit helped fulfill Tsultrim's dream of a "physical manifestation of feminine enlightenment" in adobe and stone, mineral color and wood carvings. "Lama Tsultrim had the wisdom and the vision," says her son, Costanzo, "but without David, it would never have manifested, without any doubt. As much as there is enlightened feminine, there has to be the enlightened masculine. One cannot be without the other. You need both."

Costanzo, thirty-one, is the only one of Tsultrim's three children who has embraced Buddhism as a full-time path. Within hours of David's death, Costanzo abruptly left his retreat hermitage in Tibet on the other side of the world. He called his mother from the Himalayas, assuring her: "Mom, I'm going to man up. David was preparing me for this for years. I can do this." Traveling at breakneck speed over precipitous rain-slicked roads, Costanzo arrived just after the cremation. He now supports his mother in running Tara Mandala, taking care of maintenance and teaching meditation classes.

A PASSAGE OF GRIEF THROUGH TIBET

After David's death, Lama Tsultrim couldn't bear to stay in the haven they had built together. David was everywhere, yet nowhere. Hoping that her intense grief would fade into the vast space of the Tibetan plateau, she packed her bags and took off to the Himalayas for half a year. This time, she went by herself, seeking solace in a pilgrimage to familiar remote places, an outer passage to help her with the inner passage of grieving. She carried a tiny tsa tsa from David's ashes close to her heart. In winter, few tourists travel the Tibetan plateau because the

Tsultrim Allione visiting Machig Labdron's temple at Zangri Kangmar in Central Tibet in 2007, where she was recognized as an emanation.
Photo courtesy of Tara Mandala

biting cold is just too inhumane, but this is high season for the hardy local pilgrims. "That was very powerful. I met Dodasel Wangmo, who is the last family holder in the Dzinpa Rangdrol lineage that we are establishing here." At eighty-three, she is still working as a doctor. Tsultrim spent six weeks with her and her disciples, learning the ancient tunes for her favorite chöd practice, receiving transmissions, and interviewing the people around her. Before leaving, the senior lineage master bestowed on Tsultrim the entrustment for the whole lineage—a very rare occasion. "The lama who brought us there said he had been with her for thirty years, and he never saw her give it. He himself had never received it," Tsultrim remarks. "We didn't even realize when we were getting it what was happening. She just pulled this book from the top shelf and gave it, and the lama said afterwards, you won't believe what just happened."

SURFING ON WAVES OF SUFFERING

Since her return from Tibet and India, she is slowly reentering her responsibilities as a teacher. When Chagdud Khadro, one of her best friends, visits, she suggests for Tsultrim to start teaching again by sharing how she deals with grief. In Lama Tsultrim's first teaching since David's death, Chagdud Khadro offers her the traditional white silk scarf, then sits back down at the front of the temple, next to Lama Tsultrim's throne, as Tsultrim searches for the right words. "Grief really reminds me a lot of birth, of being in labor. When you're in labor, you're subject to something beyond your control, and you have to submit to it." Tsultrim Allione reaches for a glass of water, to calm her hoarse voice, before she speaks about her "ocean" of grief. "I am surfing," she says. "I am not trying to stop the waves, because I realize I can't stop them. I feel them coming, then, okay, am I going to be able to get up on my board and ride it? Or am I going to get tumbled? Both things happen, because every wave is different."

The woman who gained a vast following by teaching the Tibetan practice of chöd now has to cut through her own pain, which, as she admits, is eating her up. "It is really a principle of chöd practice to open up to that which devours you. That which devours you becomes that which can heal."

What helped her most in the time immediately after David died were lyrics from a traditional song, and she chants them softly, with the age-old tune:

If I am in sorrow, I am happy
Because I take the sorrow of all.
May the samsaric ocean of suffering
Be completely emptied.

The verse speaks to Tsultrim "so completely, because I was feeling sorrow, and this line was telling me what to do with it. I invited sorrow into me." As she had taught a hundred times, she took all the sorrow of all the women who had lost their beloved, expanded the opening to all the men who had lost their beloved, and gradually moved out to all sorrow in the world.

"Grief is very self-focused in a way," she concedes. "You are kind of lost, collapsed inward. When you take on others' suffering, you have to open your heart to all other people who are feeling the same." Her voice breaks as she says these words in the temple, and she does not wipe away a few tears that roll down her cheek. "It is paradoxical," she admits. "You think, if I take on theirs on top of mine it is going to be unbearable, because it is already unbearable, how can I take more than what this already is? The paradox is that it takes the grief away. It is actually impossible to take on the sorrow of everyone if there is a self. To be there, you have to let go of self-clinging and realize your true nature is incredibly vast, completely perfect, lucid, and compassionate. It can accommodate everything."

At the end of the teaching she recalls how Machig once stripped naked during an empowerment. "If you know Tibetan women, this is a much bigger deal than it is in California," Tsultrim quips, then goes on to relate the lesson to learn from this unconventional behavior: "There is nothing real to hold on to. Just let it go, who cares? Who are we protecting, anyway?"

She is now able to acknowledge all the good things in her life, the twenty-two years with a loving husband, her three children and three grandchildren, the fulfillment of many aspirations. "David never left the land, he died here and was cremated here," Tsultrim says, pointing outside the window of her tiny temple cell to the surrounding hills. "In that sense, it was perfect. His work here was finished." Her work must go on.

Forty-two years after meeting and getting ordained by the Sixteenth Karmapa, his successor granted Tsultrim Allione a historical request: for the first time, the Seventeenth Karmapa, Ogyen Trinley Dorje, bestowed the empowerment of Tsultrim's heart practice, chöd. "Karmapas have maintained a close connection to this practice," the young Karmapa said at this occasion in October 2012 in a crowded temple near Dharamsala, India. "I myself feel a deep bond with these teachings coming from Machig Labdrön. She is the perfect embodiment of wisdom and compassion and has inspired Buddhist practitioners for many centuries." With Tsultrim Allione, Jetsunma Tenzin Palmo, and many female students filing past one by one with auspicious scarves and bowls full of offerings, the Karmapa went on to praise Tsultrim's dedication in front of a mainly female audience of more than a thousand students. "She has been doing a lot of work to preserve and maintain the continuity of the teachings and practice of chöd," he acknowledged, "and she has a very pure heart motivation in doing this, which I deeply rejoice in." The Karmapa emphasized specifically how pleased he was to "offer this encouragement and support to female practitioners from around the Himalayan region and the world."

And so another element of Machig's life story repeated itself in the twenty-first century: Lama Tsultrim won the support of the head of her lineage.

Khandro Tsering Chödron in France.
Photo by Graham Price. © Graham Price

12: Khandro Tsering Chödron

THE QUEEN OF DAKINIS

*A tribute to a hidden master who taught through her sheer
presence, beauty, and example and lived through some of the most
dramatic periods of Tibetan history*[1]

W HEN DZONGSAR KHYENTSE RINPOCHE lights the torch to begin
the elaborate fire puja, he marks the end not only of one woman's
life but of an era. Thousands have gathered outside Lerab Ling, the
magnificent three-tier temple in the south of France that was Khandro Tsering Chödron's last home. Devotees as far away as Bhutan and
Sikkim, following the funerary rites via live streaming on screens, say
farewell to one of the last dakinis who grew up in pre-Communist Tibet.
In her honor, hundreds of thousands of butter lamps are alight in sacred
sites like Bodhgaya and in her homeland of Tibet. Hundreds of monks
across the Himalayan regions have been practicing intensively in the
three months since her passing in May 2011, not because Khandro Tsering Chödron needed the prayers, but because the demise of a highly
realized practitioner marks a passage for her followers as well.

Khandro Tsering Chödron's name literally means "Dakini Lamp of
the Teachings and Long Life." The wife of Jamyang Khyentse Chökyi
Lodrö, one of the most eminent masters of the twentieth century, she
was universally regarded as one of the supremely realized female Buddhist practitioners of our time. Tibetans called her a "hidden master"
because throughout her life she refused to preach with words, yet she
taught by her sheer presence, beauty, and example. At her memorial

service, her nephew, Sogyal Rinpoche,* searches for words to express his admiration of her: "There was no-one quite like her in this world. She was the greatest woman master, respected by all the lamas. She lived an exemplary life, a life of pure devotion that was legendary among the masters and their students alike. Anyone who had the good fortune to meet her was blessed."² He adds, fighting tears, "For me she was my spiritual mother, the most precious person in the whole world, the one I loved the most. That is because in Vajrayana Buddhism, we consider the lama and his consort are indivisible."³

Sogyal Rinpoche's retreat center, with one of the largest Tibetan Buddhist temples west of Asia, is tucked into this hidden valley on top of a mountain plateau in Languedoc, less than an hour away from the buzzing beaches of the Mediterranean. In prior years I watched this tiny, slightly hunched lady in her traditional wraparound dress circumambulate the temple several times daily. She would meticulously set one foot in front of the other, her eyes hidden behind oversized Chanel sunglasses, her arm seeking support from one of the monks. Khandrola, as she was affectionately called, looked as though she had stepped right out of a medieval painting. Her traditional floor-length Tibetan dress was of the fine blue cotton that aristocratic Tibetans have worn for centuries; an ocean-blue silk shawl enveloped her shoulders; her long gray hair was gathered in a knot and crowned with a floppy green cap. This the princess of Sikkim had knitted for her, and Khandro was rarely seen without it.

THE LUMINOSITY OF ABSOLUTE SPACE

Dilgo Khyentse Rinpoche called her "the queen of dakinis,"⁴ and while one of her most notable qualities was her utter humility, upon her death she is given a memorial ceremony worthy of a queen. A dozen eminent lamas have taken their places on thrones under make-shift tents, surrounding the bell-shaped white stupa in the four cardinal directions

---

*Born in East Tibet around 1947, Sogyal Rinpoche has been teaching in the West for more than thirty years. He is the spiritual director of Rigpa, an international network of Buddhist centers.

under the azure September sky. To the East, His Holiness Sakya Tri-zin, the head of the Sakya school, together with his wife and youngest son, Gyana Vajra Rinpoche, sits in the shade outside of the big three-storey temple to perform the practice of Vajrayogini in her honor. He met Khandro Tsering Chödron for the first time in Lhasa, Tibet, in 1955 when he was eleven years old. To the South, Dzongsar Khyentse Rinpoche, who is the incarnation of Khandro Tsering Chödron's late husband, is immersed in intensive prayer. "She was like a mother to me," he says, "and she first taught me to read." To the West, Sogyal Rinpoche performs a purification practice, framed by Orgyen Tobgyal Rinpoche* and Alak Zenkar Rinpoche,† as well as Khandro's sister, Mayumla Tsering Wangmo. To the North, Sakya Trizin's eldest son, Ratna Vajra Rinpoche, and his lamas wield vajras and ring bells. Filing in a procession around the temple, a hundred of Khandro's friends, students, and caregivers each hold up offerings: incense, guitars and flutes, exuberant flowers, bowls filled with lush fruits. The shiny copper roof of the quadratic, golden three-tier structure gleams in the morning sun. Finally, eight bearers carry her remains in a golden palanquin. As the long procession comes to a halt before the white stupa, Dzongsar Khyentse Rinpoche tenderly lifts her remains. Wrapped in brocade, embalmed with the traditional solutions, her body has shrunk to the size of an eight-year-old child.

The departure of a realized master is not like any ordinary death. When he heard of Khandro's passing, the Seventeenth Gyalwa Karmapa spontaneously said, "She did not die. She has flown off."[5] Buddhists believe that leaving this life is an opportunity for meditators to merge their awareness with the luminosity of absolute space. "A great prac-titioner such as she was merges the clear light of the path they have recognized during their practice in life with the clear light of the ground

---

*Orgyen Tobgyal Rinpoche, born 1951 in Kham, East Tibet, fled Tibet in 1959 with his father, the late Third Neten Chokling Rinpoche. He has been a member of the Tibetan Parliament in Exile for many years and mainly oversees his monastery in Bir, North India, but also teaches internationally.
†Alak Zenkar Rinpoche, born 1943 in East Tibet, currently lives in New York. An emi-nent scholar, he has been instrumental in reviving Buddhism and preserving Tibetan texts in East Tibet.

that dawns at the moment of death," Orgyen Tobgyal explains.⁶ "It's like breaking a vase."

At the peak of the ceremony, Khandro Tsering Chödron's melodic voice resounds through the mountains from the loudspeakers as lively as ever. Her chanting the mantra of Padmasambhava stirs many of the students to silent tears. The lamas and students meditate to merge their minds with hers, to recall her beautiful spirit and her example of profound spiritual achievement. As the fire blazes, monks evoke the haunting sounds from the long horns and clash the cymbals. Photographs from her life are projected onto the large video screens, a last homage to a woman who witnessed some of the most dramatic vicissitudes of Tibetan history. The early pictures show a tender teenager smiling into the camera with a slightly shy gaze. On one black-and-white image she is holding a bunch of flowers, standing alone in the vast landscape of Tibet. Just then, the wind picks up and a gentle gust wafts over the gathering, a precursor to an imminent summer storm, as if to disperse the sorrow about her demise.

A FAMILY OF UNRIVALLED GOOD FORTUNE

Khandro Tsering Chödron was born in a small village in East Tibet around 1929. Nobody knows the exact time or year, for who would have kept a record? Khandro was part of an ancient family renowned throughout Tibet both for their immense wealth and for their generosity. Legend has it that her ancestors descend from a magical emanation of Nyenchen Tanglha, protector deity of Tibet. Villagers also tell how the family received the name of "Lakar" from the founder of the Gelugpa tradition of Tibetan Buddhism, Jé Tsongkhapa (1357–1419). When Tsongkhapa first made his way from the far northeast to Central Tibet, he journeyed through the Trehor region and was welcomed by a man who offered him a white (in Tibetan *kar*) woolen shawl (*la*) to protect him from the cold and rain. Tsongkhapa saw this immaculate shawl as an auspicious sign. Full of joy, he predicted, "From now on, for generations to come, your family will know unrivalled prosperity and good fortune. You shall even take 'Lakar' as your family name."

To this day nearly every Tibetan knows the Lakars' name, since they sponsored many of the great prayer festivals.[7]

Khandro's mother, Dechen Tso, was the daughter of the King of Ling. She married the two Lakar brothers, Tutob Namgyal and Sonam Tobgyal. During those times, it was not unusual for a woman to marry several brothers. In fact, the age-old custom of giving a daughter in marriage not just to one man but to several or all of his brothers is still practiced in some isolated Himalayan regions.

Khandro had one elder brother and one elder sister, but her brother did not live long. Before Khandro's birth the Fifth Dzogchen Rinpoche, Thubten Chökyi Dorje (1872–1935), prophesied that "a jewel" would be born in that family. Khandro was immediately regarded as a special child, even considered a reincarnation of Yeshe Tsogyal, the foremost female master of Tibetan Buddhism in the eighth century, and also an emanation of Tara, the most revered female buddha.

Those who knew Khandro during her early years say she was shy and reserved but endowed with a wild, playful, and independent spirit. Despite the wealth of the family and many servants, Khandro learned household chores, including cooking, milking the sheep, and weaving yarn, as was the custom in this remote area that had no electricity or running water. To indicate her status both as a daughter of a wealthy family and as an unmarried girl, a Khampa girl would usually wear amber, coral, and turquoise woven into her hair, but Khandro always preferred simple dresses and hardly wore jewelry. To this day her elder sister, Tsering Wangmo, never leaves the house without a thick layer of porcelain-colored makeup, a long-standing fashion in the circles of the high-ranking aristocratic Tibetan women. Khandro, however, never used makeup, fancy jewelry, or elaborate clothes. Her beauty lay much in her naturalness and simplicity. Her high cheekbones, and most of all, her deeply penetrating, warm eyes made her a stunning sight far into her eighties.

Her home village is in an area known as the Four Rivers and Six Peaks, nestled at the foot of glaciated mountain ranges. A nearby river added beauty and majesty to the sparsely populated valley. The Lakar family house might have been one of the biggest in East Tibet. Khandro's sister, Tsering Wangmo, says jokingly, "The house was so big, when a person fired a gunshot in one end of the house, you could hardly hear it at the other." Horses and sheep lived on the ground floor to prevent the biting cold from creeping up from the ground and to keep the two upper floors warm. The Lakars constantly accommodated yogis and masters who performed elaborate rituals in the nine shrine rooms. Tsering Wangmo remembers the house continually ringing with the sounds of bells and drums, prayers and mantras, but it was destroyed after the Communist invasion in the 1950s. Today only a large pile of rubble remains, and villagers still circumambulate the sand-colored clay out of reverence for hallowed ground.

"The connection is made"

Jamyang Khyentse Chökyi Lodrö (1893–1959) sometimes came to stay at the Lakar house. Authority on all traditions, he was the heart of the nonsectarian movement in Tibet. Sogyal Rinpoche lived with him like his son until he was nine years old and remembers him as handsome and so tall that "he always seemed to stand a good head above others in a crowd."[8] An ordained monk in robes, his silver hair cropped close to the scalp, his elongated face glowed with a kind, profoundly wise gaze. "What you noticed most about him was his presence," recalls Sogyal Rinpoche. "His glance and bearing told you that he was a wise and holy man. He had a rich, deep, enchanting voice. . . . And for all the respect and even awe he commanded, there was humility in everything he did."[9] He spent many years in solitary retreat and came to be regarded as an encyclopedia of knowledge and, in Sogyal Rinpoche's words, "a living proof of how someone who had realized the teachings and completed their practice would be."[10] Many of the younger generation of masters who would later bring Tibetan Buddhism to the West revered him as their master.

Once there was a great treasure revealer* living in the Lakar mansion

---

*Tib. terton. Especially in the Nyingma tradition, teachings are believed to have been hidden by Padmasambhava and other enlightened masters until the time was ripe. Particularly gifted or realized masters might then reveal these teachings centuries later.

and Chökyi Lodrö came to receive teachings. At this time Chökyi Lodrö collided with seven-year-old Khandro Tsering Chödron in the narrow doorway. The unorthodox treasure revealer burst out, "Ah, the auspicious connection has now been made!"[11] According to Dilgo Khyentse Rinpoche, Chökyi Lodrö seemed embarrassed and ignored the treasure revealer for several days.[12]

When she was sixteen years old Khandro saw her future husband again while visiting a temple. Chökyi Lodrö's students were offering him a Tara statue for his long life. Just as they were checking for auspicious signs, Khandro Tsering Chödron lost her way and inadvertently walked in on the ceremony. People present suspected this incident was a sign that she was destined to become his companion.

SAVING THE MASTER'S LIFE

Jamyang Khyentse Chökyi Lodrö fell seriously ill in 1943 when he was forty-nine years old. His attendants summoned the best doctors, but no cure would help. Attempting to accumulate healing merit, monks recited the "Words of the Buddha" (Tib. *Kangyur*) a hundred times, but nothing improved his condition. Several renowned masters advised that he needed to marry in order to remove obstacles to his longevity. In Tibet, dakinis are considered a source of inspiration who give life and support, especially to treasure revealers. Chökyi Lodrö, however, insisted on keeping his monk's vows. This went on for five years.

Khandro remembered how one summer day in 1948 messengers arrived out of breath. She was called in from the fields. The messengers urged her to get on a horse immediately, still in her work clothes, and rush to Chökyi Lodrö's monastery in Dzongsar, which was a good two days' ride away. His condition had become critical, and he needed her help. Matters of life and death were determined by astrology in those days, and the planets did not tolerate any hesitation. Declining help to such an outstanding master was out of the question. She hastily gathered a few clothes and set off on horseback with her sister. "At least," Khandro said later in a teasing spirit, "they could have given me time to clean and dress up!" Khandro's friend Dagmola Sakya, herself married to the great Sakya lama Dagchen Rinpoche, remembers, "There were many rainbows and other auspicious signs when Khandro arrived at Dzongsar. The locals said, 'Dakinis are landing. She definitely is the emanation of someone who is benefiting sentient beings and the long life of a lama.'" Chökyi Lodrö married Khandro later that year, and his health started to improve.

"Many people were surprised," Chökyi Lodrö's disciple, Dilgo Khyentse Rinpoche, recalled, but "there was no criticism from any of the monks at the monastery or at the monastic college."[13] Even today, Tibetans don't look at their union as a common marriage, nor do they regard Khandro as an ordinary woman. Khandro Tsering Chödron was known as Khyentse Sangyum, which means "Khyentse's sacred consort." "This is for religious purposes, not an ordinary marriage," Dagmola Sakya explains. "That's also why it was only a small wedding, not a big celebration."

TALES OF WONDERS

For the next eleven years Chökyi Lodrö imparted countless teachings and transmissions to his devoted companion. He even composed a four-line prayer in which he praised her as the emanation of the "Dakini of great bliss who is no other than Yeshe Tsogyal" and as the incarnation of Shelkar Dorje Tso, an accomplished eighth-century female master who was said to cross rivers as if they were meadows.[14] To the Tibetans, the tales of mystics and wonders are their daily bread of inspiration, and while these might be harder to believe for Westerners, certainly everybody could get a glimpse of Khandro's heartfelt expressions of devotion.

"Jamyang Khyentse Chökyi Lodrö was the inspiration of Khandro's entire life," recalls Dzongsar Khyentse Rinpoche. "Her immense devotion to him never changed. I never even heard her refer to him as her husband. She considered herself as a student. When I was young, I would wonder why every time we came to the passage in the chants that contains a praise to Jamyang Khyentse Chökyi Lodrö, tears would just stream down her face."

Whenever a master had a difficult request, he would try to get Khandro to bring it to Chökyi Lodrö, for he hardly ever refused any wish of hers. She often put her questions "in the form of a song, and he would write songs back to her, in an almost teasing and playful way."[15] She had an amazingly pure tone to her voice, and her rendering of the famous mantra of Padmasambhava inspires even the toughest skeptic. No matter how busy Chöyki Lodrö was, how many months he spent in solitary retreat, or how long the never-ending queues were of villagers and high-ranking officials who requested his advice and blessings, he would always make time to be with Khandro and take his meals with her, just the two of them. "He was very, very loving with her," recalls Khandro's friend Dagmola Sakya. "It was a very special and close relationship."

Dagmola Sakya is four years younger than Khandro and also from East Tibet. When Dagmola was twenty years old, the Dalai Lama requested her husband join him on a trip to meet with Mao Zedong in Beijing. While her husband was gone, Dagmola and her first baby son moved into Khandro's room at Dzongsar Monastery for a year. "She was shy, but once we became friends she was extremely funny, constantly joking," recalls Dagmola. "I admired her sweet, playful nature and sense of humor, and she could draw so beautifully. We laughed a lot together!"

The extraordinary atmosphere around Chökyi Lodrö

Dagmola remembers the atmosphere around Chökyi Lodrö as "so warm and extraordinary that I always wanted to stay a little longer. Whenever we ate together one felt like one had received a blessing. There was so much energy there that one felt completely different."

Dzongsar Monastery was in a comparatively mild area where wheat, barley, and vegetables were harvested. The mountains above were wild and untouched. Mountain lions and leopards stalked deer in the woods. Hundreds of monks lived in the eighty rooms of the monastery compound, which accommodated an endless stream of visitors. Even when Chökyi Lodrö went to remote places, people would still continue to seek him out, and he would never close his door to them. "I never once

Khandro Tsering Chödron in Lhasa, 1956.
Photo courtesy of the Estate of Gyalyum Kunzang Dechen Tsomo Namgyal

saw him angry or scold anybody," says Dagmola. "No matter what, whether it was a master from any school or an ordinary visitor, he was always able to give all the answers right away. From the first moment of meeting him, I saw him as special. I was even a little bit afraid, as I didn't want to displease him at all."

Chökyi Lodrö appointed one of the best calligraphers and writers, the secretary of the King of Dergé, to teach the two young women writing, spelling, and drawing. The abbot of Lhagyal Monastery taught them Tibetan grammar. "Today I wish we had done a little better," says Dagmola, recalling that unusual opportunity. "We played more than we really studied." Both Khandro and Dagmola enjoyed the freedom of being ordinary more than the pleasures of wealth and status. Being wives of high-ranking masters, they were often required to dress and act according to protocol, but privately they showed blatant disregard for the rules. While Dagmola had to wear the traditional Sakya head-dress and brocade robes, Khandro would just put on a simple long silk dress. By others they were perceived as so noble that ordinary activities like sewing were out of the question. Secretly, they purchased a Chinese sewing machine at the market and began to sew aprons for their servants, as well as hats and belts. One day a high master, Tulku Kunzang, entered without knocking, carrying a beautiful Chinese bowl decorated with auspicious signs and filled with fruit. He respectfully performed three prostrations to Khandro and Dagmola before frowning angrily at the sewing machine. "A master's wife is supposed to study, read, and pray," he began scolding. "You are wasting time! Stop sewing and recite prayers!" While they were being scolded, Khandro poked Dagmola. "Though I was the younger one, she would hide behind me and have me speak," says Dagmola, who seemingly gave in. Of course this did not stop them. They posted one of their attendants at the door as a sentinel, and whenever anybody came they just covered the machine.[16]

Khandro's and Dagmola's memories let us glimpse the long-gone pastimes of a Tibet yet unconquered. Many times the family, visitors, and monks went for a picnic on the banks of a nearby river, playing traditional Tibetan games, running, or racing horses. Chökyi Lodrö had one particular favorite game that Khandro enjoyed watching: candy was placed in a big bowl of yogurt and then put in front of a yak's saddle on a rock. Horsemen had to gallop hanging upside down and try to take the candy from the bowl with their teeth. Many times riders slid off the saddle, face first into the yogurt bowl.[17]

MAGIC AND MIRACLES

Pewar Rinpoche (b. 1933), another contemporary who witnessed their unusual bond, says: "By taking Khandro Tsering Chödron as his companion, he was able to live much longer, and it is really due to that fact that I and many of the disciples were able to receive incredible amounts of teachings, transmissions, and empowerments. This would not have taken place if Jamyang Khyentse Chökyi Lodrö had not married Khandro." Pewar Rinpoche, who still lives in Tibet, wears his black hair braided in a plait that frames his forehead. He rushed to the south of France to participate in Khandro's memorial ceremonies, where he speaks of an even more profound consequence after Chökyi Lodrö's marriage: "It was after Khandro Tsering Chödron had come that he started to perform miracles." According to Pewar Rinpoche, Chökyi Lodrö once blessed a large cloth painting from a distance, with grains of rice that fell from the sky. People saw a rush of grains coming from the north and hitting the painting, yet the grains did not fall to the ground. Those present realized that the blessing rice was coming from the direction of Jamyang Khyentse's place, and when they looked in that direction, a second and third set of blessings flew through the sky like clouds of grains. Pewar Rinpoche attests, "They again got stuck on the painting, and not a single grain fell on the ground."

As his name reveals, the late Dzongsar Ngari Tulku (1945–2008) was trained in Dzongsar Monastery as a young boy. While living as a white-haired yogi in Sikkim, he remembered one occasion in 1952 when Jamyang Khyentse Chökyi Lodrö was visiting a sacred place above Dzongsar Monastery. Ngari Tulku recalled that Chökyi Lodrö, together with the great female master Gyalrong Khandro, Khandro Tsering Chödron, and Sogyal Rinpoche all left their handprints in the solid rock—a sign they had accomplished power over matter. In Tibetan

Buddhism the world is not as solid as it seems to the ordinary eye; once they have realized the true, open nature of everything, the wise are said to be able to go beyond the limitations of mind and matter.

A NARROW ESCAPE

Khandro's and Chökyi Lodrö's happy days in Tibet were not to last. The year after their wedding, Chinese troops started to mass at the borders. Mao Zedong summoned Chökyi Lodrö along with other high-ranking masters to Beijing in 1955. Chökyi Lodrö must have had premonitions that several of these masters would not return alive, because he quietly decided to travel in the opposite direction. Khandro, her sister Tsering Wangmo, the seven-year-old Sogyal Rinpoche, and a small party of family and attendants set off on horseback together for the treacherous three-month journey to Lhasa, the capital of Tibet. Dressed in the disguise of a simple monk, Chökyi Lodrö slipped out of the Chinese grip. Leaving almost all their possessions behind as if they were just going away on pilgrimage, the party was extremely careful not to give any hints that they would go beyond Lhasa.

Even without Communist dictators, traveling in remote Tibet was scary. Robbers and burglars, mountain lions and avalanches could easily wipe out a traveling party. As Sogyal Rinpoche recalls, they would rise early each morning before dawn and break down the tents. By the first light rays, the yaks carrying the baggage and food moved out of camp. A scout went ahead and chose a good campground for the next night. During the day, Khandro rode next to her husband. Chökyi Lodrö would give teachings, tell stories, and practice, and everybody tried to ride close enough so as not to miss a word he said.

Chökyi Lodrö was not keen to leave Tibet immediately. Around the time of the New Year celebrations of 1956, following a divination, the Sixteenth Karmapa, Rangjung Rigpa'i Dorje, strongly urged him to seek refuge in Sikkim. During his stay in Lhasa his fame had spread throughout the holy city, and many members of the aristocracy had begun to request blessings and teachings.[18] This gathering of influential personalities raised an alarm with the Chinese authorities. After spending a month at Sakya Monastery, Chökyi Lodrö saw no other way than to turn south for Sikkim.[19]

Crossing the rugged terrain of the Himalayas that took them from the high, arid plateau of Tibet across mountain trails, glaciers, and snow-bound passes, Chökyi Lodrö and Khandro at least were able to take advantage of the dire circumstances by traveling on a pilgrimage to the sacred places of Buddhism in India and Nepal before reaching the tropical rainforests of Sikkim. Chökyi Lodrö had a special connection with Sikkim. Like the King of Sikkim, Chögyal Tashi Namgyal, he too was considered an incarnation of Lhatsün Namkha Jigme, a widely revered siddha who had established the teachings of the Great Perfection in Sikkim in the seventeenth century. At the king's invitation, Chökyi Lodrö and Khandro moved into Gangtok's Royal Palace. This handsome, two-storey white cube with its elaborately painted windows and doors became once again a great spiritual center, attracting hundreds of Tibetans and pilgrims to camp nearby. Chökyi Lodrö gave teachings and empowerments to increasing numbers of disciples who had crossed the border. Many Tibetans took his decision to leave as an omen that Tibet's future was dire, and they followed his example by escaping before Mao Zedong turned Tibet into a torture chamber.

Losing Tibet and the teacher

Was it pure coincidence that Chökyi Lodrö fell ill at the same time as the news came from Tibet that the Chinese had completely taken over? With Khandro always at his side, senior masters, heads of lineages, and pilgrims filed in to visit him, imploring him to live on. As Sogyal Rinpoche recalls, his death was eventually to occur just after they heard that the three great monasteries of Tibet—Sera, Drepung, and Ganden—had been occupied by the Chinese.[20] Around the beginning of June 1959, Jamyang Khyentse Chökyi Lodrö entered his final meditation in his palace temple, and his remains were enshrined in a small golden stupa in the Royal Palace.

No matter how often her sister and her family entreated her to move to the Lakar residence just half an hour from the palace, Khandro

Jamyang Khyentse Chökyi Lodrö and Khandro in Tibet.
Photo courtesy of the Estate of Gyalyum Kunzang Dechen Tsomo Namgyal

insisted she could not leave her teacher's relics. Khandro was then only thirty years old. "She was still very young when Dzongsar Khyentse Chökyi Lodrö passed away," says her friend Dagmola, "but she remained at the palace temple and didn't want to move. Of course many other consorts would have remarried, and I am sure many lamas have tried, but she never did and that shows how strong she is and really an extraordinary human being." Khandro always said that there was no separation between her and Chökyi Lodrö.

HER GREATNESS IN HER ORDINARINESS

For almost five decades, Khandro lived by herself in Chökyi Lodrö's shrine room in Sikkim, spending most of her time in prayer. Every morning she would get up early, around three thirty or four, and start meditating. After a light breakfast, maybe just tea and Tibetan bread, she would clean the shrine room and set out the offerings. She loved flowers and her window sill was covered with red begonias. She also cared for animals and always had several dogs and cats. She even kept a ram with curly horns in the palace garden; everywhere she went it followed her like a pet. Sometimes she liked to draw, but most of the time she was content to just sit there, on the low mattress, which was also her bed, and practice. "You felt the simplicity of her mind, which was also very sharp," says Mauro de March, an Italian student who knew her for twenty-three years. "If you have been introduced to the nature of mind, then you realized that she was the personification of that awareness. You have to have some understanding of meditation to see who she is. Just to be able to sit in her presence was quite a strong teaching in itself." Occasionally, she would meet visitors, but it was close to impossible to get her to give a teaching or a blessing.

Her simple room was filled with the many gifts visitors left her. The Princess of Sikkim, Tenzin Tashi, remembers adoring "tiny red robins, delicate glass deer, swans, other birds, many small idols, dolls, . . . and a multitude of other tiny wonders all jostling for space in her room."[21] As a child, Tenzin Tashi eagerly awaited the moments when Khandro would open a fat little porcelain duck and take out the duck's "eggs," usually chocolate or other goodies.

Khandro Rinpoche too recalls visiting Khandro Tsering Chödron as a child. "She was very loving, very kind, and I remember she gathered a palmful of sweets and put them in my hands. Her exceptional wisdom, grace, and compassion inspired so many of us, and in offering our respects and prayers, we aspire to follow her example. The wives of these great lamas are not just called sangyums ("sacred consort"), but they embody everything you see in the teachers themselves, they are equal in their practice, their realization, capability, and love. They are extraordinary women, very humble, discreet, helpful, never putting themselves forward. Khandro might have been very shy, but in her shyness so brave."

Her caregiver Australian nun Kunga Gyalmo says, "Khandro-la demonstrated devotion in a perfect way. At the same time, she was completely ordinary, unfabricated, natural. In her, I saw a gracious example of my ultimate potential." Khandro didn't really care if anybody thought she was realized or not. "In her presence, all concepts of what realization is fell away," Kunga Gyalmo goes on to say. "The fact that she was so humble and unassuming seems to demonstrate a profound confidence she had in an ordinary simplicity. Through this, she affected so many people. We may expect a great master to sit on a high throne and expound on wise words, but she contradicted such concepts. She simply taught through who she was." Khandro firmly believed in the power of heartfelt prayer. So this is what she did. She prayed and taught by being an example. Chagdud Khadro calls her "transcendent. She was a dakini manifesting in an ephemeral human form. The rest of us are human."

COMING FULL CIRCLE

After Sogyal Rinpoche's mother came to live with him in France, her sister, Khandro, joined her there in 2006. Chökyi Lodrö's incarnation, Dzongsar Khyentse Rinpoche, took his predecessor's relics to Bir, North India, and Khandro moved to France, where I first met her in 2006.

There the Mediterranean evaporates in the distance as the path climbs up a steep ascent onto a breathtakingly high and arid plateau built on precipitous cliffs and deep red earth. If it was not for a few lone olive trees and some bright red poppies, one could mistake the vast landscape, with its juniper forests, for Tibet. On top of the plateau, the sky opens, and the bluffs give way to a jaw-dropping 360-degree view. The Pyrenees rise in the far distance in the west; there are unusual creature-shaped cliff formations in the east, the ancient castle ruin of Caylar in the north, and in the distance to the south shimmers the silky, deep blue of the Mediterranean. Some vultures, blown around by an unexpectedly brisk wind, hunt the sky as if to strengthen the reminiscence of Tibet.

As buses unload school classes and tourists stream down the footpath, their ears pressed against the multilingual electronic tour guide, the recorded voice explains the uniqueness of this authentic Tibetan temple that has been modeled after the centuries-old temples of the Himalayas. The place is humming with the sounds of drums and bells and the voices of Westerners singing the mantra of the Buddha of compassion.

Sometimes the tourists, moving backward with their cameras to get the best view of the magnificent building, bumped into Khandro, muttered a "sorry" or "excusez-moi" and moved on to capture the next exotic detail of the hand-painted magical birds and dragons that writhe on the crimson walls. If only the tourists knew that the real sight worth seeing was not the spectacular golden twenty-two-foot Buddha, not the thousand glittering buddhas in the main hall, nor the meticulously painted frescoes. If only they had had the time to stop for a moment, they could have seen real beauty right before them in human form—Khandro Tsering Chödron.

I watched renowned masters hastily jump off their high thrones when they realized that Khandro was about to walk in. It is Asian custom to denote one's rank by the seating order and the height of the throne. None of the teachers, no matter how big their title and how elevated their rank, would want to be seated higher than Khandro. Yet Khandro never spoke about her realization. Regardless of how fervently students and other teachers requested her to teach, nobody ever heard her boast of her wisdom. She always looked slightly amused when someone bowed to her with folded hands or otherwise treated her with the utmost respect and veneration. "Oh, I think I finally figured out why everybody stands up and bows to me when I walk in," she said matter-of-factly one noon, when she stepped out into the courtyard and dozens of students simultaneously jumped up from their lunch to fold their hands and bow. It seemed like a choreographed dance of devotion to her, but Khandro deferred the veneration to Mayumla Tsering Wangmo, Sogyal Rinpoche's mother: "These poor beings must mistake me for my sister."

Despite the constant stream of love and admiration that flowed her way, it was obvious that she honestly did not think of herself as anything special. "Humility is probably the single most important attribute of a dharma student," says Dzongsar Khyentse Rinpoche. "It would be an understatement to say that present-day dharma students are lacking humility—it does not even exist. Her humility is her teaching."

Buddhist practice, understood in all its profundity, is not about being special but about being truly natural. The absence of any sense of ego is indeed the greatest and most fundamental accomplishment. This very selflessness bestows the freedom to simply be, uninhibited. It grants an inner confidence without any need to show proof of anything. It added grace and dignity to everything Khandro did and had nothing to do with the self-denigration we like to practice in the West. Despite her humbleness and silence, people could not help but be moved by her presence. "Khandro was such an enigma," Kunga Gyalmo says haltingly, searching for words how to best describe her. As her caregiver in India and France, Gyalmo often took Khandro for little excursions or medical examinations and observed how she would attract people like a magnet. "Everybody was affected by her presence, even people who have no background in Buddhism. For instance, we would go to a little Hindu gathering in a common park, or enjoy the local gardens. Inadvertently people would feel the need to show veneration to this old Asian lady in a wheelchair or on the park bench, not knowing anything about her. People would walk up to us and ask, 'Who is this woman? The moment I saw her, I felt something special.' Even in a French hospital, she made a huge impression on the doctors, and they came to love her."

Occasionally, a splinter of Khandro's sharp wisdom sparked through a casual conversation, or her eyes suddenly shot you a knowing look. Toward the end of her life, Khandro became like a child, in the very best sense of the word: wide open, always completely present in the moment, exuding purity, innocence, and love. There was no posturing and positioning, and this total lack of vanity brought with it an immediate ease and poise when in her presence. Unlike with many other masters, I never felt intimidated—only in awe as if encountering a powerful yet tender force of nature. Throughout her life she refused to take the seat of a lama and give blessings. When Dilgo Khyentse Rinpoche wanted to receive a blessing from her, he had to gently take her hand and place it on top of his head.[22] But in the last years of her life, she became more open and would often softly stroke the cheek of a visitor as a blessing.

THE FLEDGLING IN HER HANDS

The last time I saw her, I had found a tiny fledgling, helplessly wiggling its wing-stumps on the steep staircase that leads away from the temple. No nest or mama bird were anywhere to be seen. I picked it up though I knew that chances for its survival were slim. "Take it to Khandro," said Yonten, the resident monk. "We take all injured animals to her." Seriously, he wanted me to disturb the most respected female master of our time because a baby bird had fallen out of its nest? He nodded reassuringly. Yes, while Khandro was not ordinarily seeing any visitors, she was always available for matters of life and death. Ahead he went. Up the stairs, on the first floor of what was once an abandoned French farmhouse, Khandro and her sister sat on the cream-colored sofa in Sogyal Rinpoche's former living room, rolling their rosaries through their hands and murmuring mantras as they always did, almost all day long. Their square room with the beautiful old hardwood floors and the precious Tibetan carpets overlooked the Hérault Valley. Sogyal Rinpoche redecorated it for his mother and his aunt Khandro with the exquisite golden furniture and Tibetan cloth paintings that would remind them of their long-gone Tibetan home. Khandro smiled at the tiny bird, then reached out to gently touch its head and gestured at her attendant monk to bring some medicinal nectar. She muttered some prayers in her soft, high voice, then motioned for her sister to touch the bird with a few drops of the blessed substance. A few hours later the fledgling died, but at least, or so Yonten believed, it passed on with the blessings of the greatest woman master, assuring the connection had been made and would continue in its next life.

Despite being in her eighties, she often sat through a whole day of rituals and chanting in the big temple with hundreds of Sogyal Rinpoche's students. While Khandro had a comfortable chair at the feet of the golden Buddha, her sister, Tsering Wangmo, would spend whole practice days sitting cross-legged on the floor. Moving the beads of their rosaries one by one, saying a prayer with each clicking of the beads, the two sisters were vibrant models of grace, dedication, and compassion. The two watched out for each other and were very close yet also very different in style and character. While Tsering Wangmo liked to have everything in perfect order, Khandro was completely relaxed and could not care less about her appearance or the arrangements in her room.

At least once a year, the reincarnation of Khandro's former husband, Dzongsar Khyentse Rinpoche, visited her in France. When he affectionately took her hand to guide her to her chair, she looked up at him with her eyes full of love, and the intimacy and warmth between her and the young incarnation spoke of their former bond.

MASTERY OVER MIND

Thus Khandro had come full circle. From living like a revered master's wife in the snow mountains of Tibet, to being a refugee in India and Sikkim, she finally found her home in one of the most influential Buddhist communities in the West. "Khandro did not teach formally. In fact, she did not speak a great deal; but what she did say was penetratingly clear and often even prophetic," Sogyal Rinpoche reminisces. "To listen to her fervent and blissful chanting, or to practice with her, was to be inspired to the depths of your being. Even to walk with her, or shop, or simply sit with her was to bathe in the powerful, quiet happiness of her presence."[23] She enjoyed having children around and liked to dance with them or hear them sing. Her humor was hilarious, blunt, and "politically incorrect," as one of her nurses put it. One of the first English words she picked up was "naughty girl," and she liked to use it whenever she had her own mind about something. Her attendants admired her playful nature, and none of them ever heard her complain about all the friends and fortunes she lost in Tibet. When other Tibetans lamented the terrible loss that has befallen them, she simply stood up and walked away.

At that time, it became increasingly clear that for her, like a great Dzogchen yogini, ordinary perceptions had dissolved, and she had transcended the attachments and concerns of this world. "Although she spoke less and less towards the end of her life, it seemed to me that with her incredible humor, she was always giving us an important teaching about the ironies of life," Sogyal Rinpoche says. "Perhaps we don't need to take everything so seriously, she seemed to say. Even this whole cycle of existence, birth, and death that Buddhists call 'samsara' looks quite ridiculous when viewed from an enlightened perspective."[24]

Khandro's health started to deteriorate in the spring of 2011. After a fall, she injured her hip and had to be hospitalized. She insisted she wanted to return home to Lerab Ling. Dzongsar Khyentse Rinpoche cut short his teaching program in Australia and rushed to France. Reading an important Dzogchen text to her, Longchenpa's *Treasury of Dharmadhatu*, he noticed her trouble breathing. "But when I was looking at her, I could see absolute awareness in her eyes, total awareness," he says. "Even before that, she did not wish to have any treatment or stay in the hospital. Ordinary beings like us will do anything even to live one more minute, but for her the reality was very clear. Even an ordinary person cannot miss that kind of quality she had in her last days."

Fifty-two years after her husband left his body, Khandro too demonstrated mastery over her mind at the moment of death. Orgyen Tobgyal Rinpoche and Sogyal Rinpoche both witnessed Khandro's final moments. "When ordinary people come close to death, they lose consciousness, or they cannot recognize who is talking to them, or they fail to hear what you are saying. She was not like that at all," Orgyen Tobgyal Rinpoche observed.[25] "Her mind had a distinct clarity to it, and her gaze was exactly as described in the Dzogchen texts: her eyes, which were always quite alert, were sharper than ever." When Sogyal Rinpoche asked if she was in pain, she would just shake her head. If he asked if she was feeling well, she would nod. "This made me think that she had reached the point where, for her, all delusory appearances, all the ordinary perceptions of life and death, had dissolved, and that's why she did not feel pain," Orgyen Tobgyal says.[26]

The day she passed away Sogyal Rinpoche came to her room around five thirty in the evening. He saw that her eyes were different. "She was just gazing into the sky. I called her, 'My aunt, I'm here.' She didn't respond. I felt she was in meditation."[27] About an hour later, with Sogyal Rinpoche and Orgyen Tobgyal Rinpoche present, her breathing stopped. But her heart was still warm and stayed warm for three-and-a-half days. Her body showed no signs of disintegration. When a practitioner remains in meditation for several days after the body has stopped functioning, this is called *tukdam* in Tibetan. Orgyen Tobgyal Rinpoche emphasizes how he continued to feel Khandro's presence. "According to Dzogchen, after a great practitioner passes away, they actually stay in meditation for three days, so it is extremely important to keep secrecy and not to disturb the meditation by touching the body. Her mind merged naturally into the great expanse, like water merging into water."[28] He observed that even Khandro's hands and feet were still warm for several days. "It is said that a Dzogchen practitioner who is able to merge the luminosities in tukdam is accomplishing eons of practice in a single instant and goes on to attain enlightenment."[29]

Sogyal Rinpoche describes the death of a great master in *The Tibetan Book of Living and Dying*, which now seems like a reference to Khandro's passing as well:

Besides their perfect poise, there will be other signs that show they are resting in the state of the Ground Luminosity: There is still a certain color and glow in their face, the nose does not sink inward, the skin remains soft and flexible, the body does not become stiff, the eyes are said to keep a soft and compassionate glow, and there is still a warmth at the heart.

Great care is taken that the master's body is not touched, and silence is maintained until he or she has arisen from this state of meditation.[30]

This was the last silent lesson she taught her students: "For beings who have a connection with the person in tukdam, this is extremely powerful," Orgyen Tobgyal Rinpoche explains. "This is why it is so important to merge one's mind strongly with the mind of an enlightened being in prayer. Like a fire, the wisdom mind is so powerful at that time, if one gets closer to the fire, one can't get cold."[31] Students from all over the world came to sit with her body in Sogyal Rinpoche's tiny personal shrine room, making aspiration prayers and uniting their minds with Khandro's. The Lamp of the Teachings might have left this world, but her light continues to shine.

Epilogue

IN THIS VOLUME I focus deliberately on some of the most successful female pioneers in the West, but of course there are many more
amazing women in Tibetan Buddhism who deserve to be honored and
praised. Think of all the unsung practitioners in Tibet, such as the
Nangchen nuns in East Tibet, who continue their steadfast practice
under unimaginable pressure. I aspire to one day visit these accomplished practitioners who still carry out the traditional three-year
retreats in the most remote locations, sitting in their customary three-
by-three–foot wooden meditation boxes. Though they are rare, a handful of female lineage holders were given the opportunity to head up
lineages dedicated to empowering female practitioners in Tibet, such
as the current Samding Dorje Phagmo, abbess of Samding Monastery
in Tibet, or Jetsun Shugseb Lochen Rinpoche, whose followers are
now reinvigorating her tradition both in Tibet and in exile. Among the
women currently taking responsibility in Tibet, Khenpo Jigme Puntsok's niece Jetsunma Mumso comes to mind; she carries on the vision
of her late uncle in directing Larung Gar in East Tibet, the renowned
study center that attracted several thousand monks and nuns before the
Chinese government crackdown in 2001.

Then there are the tens of thousands of Tibetans who continue to
work for their compatriots in exile. To name just a few, the Dalai Lama's
sister, Jetsun Pema, has dedicated her life to creating a safe refuge for
Tibetan children who have been sent by their parents across the ice-
covered passes to India, in the hope of finding a better future in exile.
The Tibetan Women's Association has worked since its founding in
1959 to support Tibetan women and raise awareness for the education

of nuns. Ani Chöying Drolma has used her successful singing career to sponsor more than a dozen charities in Nepal and establish Arya Tara School, the first school in Nepal to bring Western and Tibetan educations to nuns. Other Tibetan women, such as Ngawang Sangdrol, survived decades of torture in Chinese prisons and now use their voices, unafraid, to tell others the truth about the hell beneath the Chinese "kingdom of heaven."

Increasing numbers of Western women are inspired to follow the path forged by the Asian trailblazers. The first Tibetan Buddhist nunnery in America, the Vajra Dakini Nunnery, is fledging in Vermont under the American abbess Venerable Khenmo Nyima Drolma. Women continue to excel in studies, for instance, Venerable Kelsang Wangmo, the first female geshe; and myriad women, ordained and lay, are seeing their possibilities broaden as a direct result of the efforts of a few courageous pioneers.

Innumerable women and men all over the world organize meditation retreats, teach, study, cook, clean, drive, and keep centers flourishing. And the dharma would be nothing without the many wonderful practitioners who don't sit on thrones and don't write books but just quietly light up the world.

The website www.dakinipower.com is dedicated to celebrating the accomplishments and life stories of the women featured in this book and many more. Please visit the site and share your story of how Tibetan Buddhist women have inspired you.

DEDICATION

May you live long and realizef your fullest potential.
May your spirits soar high, and may you always have the
courage to follow the truth.
May all your aspirations be fulfilled and goodness prevail.
May every being on earth find peace and happiness, shelter
and refuge.
Don't let anybody tell you it can't be done.

Acknowledgments

I OWE HEARTFELT THANKS TO all the teachers interviewed in the book who generously opened their hearts and homes to me. Dzigar Kongtrul Rinpoche, Dzongsar Khyentse Rinpoche, Gyatrul Rinpoche, and Sogyal Rinpoche gave their valuable time to contribute their insights. So did David Khon, Jetsunla Dechen Paldron, Lama Chönam, Dungse Jampal Norbu, B. Alan Wallace, Carol Moss, Rita M. Gross, Basia Turzanski, Jann Jackson, Tenzin Lhamo, Costanzo Allione, Geshema Kelsang Wangmo, Naomi and Marvin Mattis, Bel Pedrosa, and Helen Berliner.

I thank Gayle Landes, Barbara Wadkins, Tami Carter, Ann Hart, and Patty Waltcher for editorial counsel and proofreading. Matteo Pistono kindly mentored me at all stages of the writing process and gave invaluable feedback. Editors Susan Kyser and Sudé Walters polished the manuscript with great finesse. The chapter about Khandro Tsering Chödron would certainly be incomplete without Volker Denck's mountain of research which he selflessly passed on to me, as well as the big-hearted efforts of Patrick Gaffney, Mauro de March, Lotsawa Adam Pearcey, Ani Kunga Gyalmo, Kimberly Poppe, Lena Raab, Daniela van Wart, Barbara Lepani, Ingrid Strauss, and the Rigpa transcribing team.

I genuinely appreciate writer Vicki Mackenzie, who kindly allowed me to use her research from her best-seller *Cave in the Snow* for the chapter about Tenzin Palmo. Jurgen Gude and Sasha Meyerowitz were great companions in filming our documentary about Elizabeth Mattis-Namgyel for the Dutch Buddhist Broadcast Foundation, which also provided the perfect opportunity to conduct some of the interviews with her for this book. Kristin Barendsen contributed her writing proficiency in the chapter on Joan Halifax. I thank Greg Seton for his friendship and scholarly advice over the years.

Many volunteers and staff worked tirelessly behind the scenes at the dharma centers to facilitate the interviews: Ani Jigme Chödron, Sravasti Abbey's office manager Zopa, Venerable Thubten Tarpa and all the other Venerable nuns, John Owens, Heather Conte at Dongyu Gatsal Ling nunnery, Scott Globus at Yeshe Nyingpo, Pema Chödrön's assistant Glenna Zirkel, Cady Allione, Mary Klinghammer, Ann Hackney, and Robin Ösel Drimé at Tara Mandala.

The very kind and talented photographer Amy Gaskin not only took marvelous pictures of Dagmola Sakya but went out of her way and beyond in offering her unique artistic skills to improve the photo selection for the entire book. Artists Karin Krüger and Noa P. Kaplan, and photographers Gayle Landes, Jurek Schreiner, Graham Price, Liza Matthews, Ronai Rocha, David Gordon, Diana Blok, Laurie Pearce Bauer, Sasha Meyerowitz, Buddy Frank, Volker Dencks, and many others contributed their wonderful talent to render the book aesthetically beautiful.

Having received so much, I want to give back a little to the women who need it most. A percentage of my profits from the book will be donated to grassroots organizations dedicated to the education of girls and women in Asia, such as the Jamyang Foundation (www.jamyang .org) and Lotus Outreach (www.lotusoutreach.org).

NOTES

PREFACE

1. All proper names are spelled in accordance with the teachers' preferences and therefore deviate in some instances from the standard spelling of Tibetan terms in this volume. For example, Chagdud Khadro prefers to have the second part of her name spelled without the "n."

INTRODUCTION: THE DAKINI PRINCIPLE

1. For an alternative translation, see Gyalwa Changchub and Namkhai Nyingpo, *Lady of the Lotus-Born: The Life and Enlightenment of Yeshe Tsogyal* (Boston: Shambhala Publications, 2002), p. xxxiii.
2. *Reflections on a Mountain Lake: Teachings on Practical Buddhism* (Ithaca, NY: Snow Lion Publications, 2002), p. 78.
3. Tenzin Palmo, as quoted in Vicki Mackenzie, *Cave in the Snow: Tenzin Palmo's Quest for Enlightenment* (New York: Bloomsbury, 1999), p. 133.
4. Judith Simmer-Brown, *Dakini's Warm Breath* (Boston: Shambhala Publications, 2001), p. 9. This is a very thoroughly researched scholarly exploration of the dakini principle.
5. Some of the teachings Tsultrim Allione has given on the topic have been recorded and distributed as *The Mandala of the Enlightened Feminine* (Louisville, CO: Sounds True, 2003). I quote from the recording here.
6. Jamyang Sakya and Julie Emory, *Princess in the Land of Snows: The Life of Jamyang Sakya in Tibet* (Boston: Shambhala Publications, 2001), p. 13.
7. Ibid., p. 54.
8. *The Mandala of the Enlightened Feminine.*
9. *Reflections*, p. 78.

10. *Reflections*, p. 77.
11. For a more detailed explanation of the complex historical issues, see Karma Lekshe Tsomo, ed., *Buddhist Women Across Cultures* (Albany, NY: SUNY Press, 1999), pp. 167–189.
12. See Hildegard Diemberger, *When a Woman Becomes a Religious Dynasty: The Samding Dorje Phagmo of Tibet* (New York: Columbia University Press, 2007), p. 133.
13. *The Progressive*, January 2006 issue. For the full interview see www .progressive.org/mag_intvo106.
14. Jerome Edou, *Machig Labdrön and the Foundations of Chöd* (Ithaca, NY: Snow Lion Publications, 1995), p. 5.
15. *Reflections*, p. 78.
16. From *The Mandala of the Enlightened Feminine*.
17. *Reflections*, p. 41.
18. Ibid.
19. Ibid., p. 42.
20. http://www.ted.com/talks/joan_halifax.html.
21. Rita M. Gross, *Buddhism After Patriarchy: A Feminist History, Analysis, and Reconstruction of Buddhism* (Albany, NY: SUNY Press, 1993), p. 25.

CHAPTER 1: JETSUN KHANDRO RINPOCHE

1. The primary sources for this chapter are two extensive interviews with Khandro Rinpoche, conducted at the Verizon Center in Washington, DC, in July 2011, during the Dalai Lama's visit. With her approval, the interviews were supplemented with statements she has made elsewhere in her teachings and other interviews, most notably a radio interview by Walter Fordham (www.chroniclesradio.com/sound/dispatches_2006_09_28 .mp3). Additional information was provided in interviews with her sister Jetsun Dechen Paldron, and her students Tenzin Lhamo, Rita Gross, Jann Jackson, Helen Berliner, and others.
2. www.chroniclesradio.com/sound/dispatches_2006_09_28.mp3.
3. A transcript of this talk is available at http://lotusgardens.org/teachingson line/documents/JKR-LovingKindnessIsRealistic-110713.pdf.
4. The last sentence is quoted from her interview in www.chroniclesradio .com/sound/dispatches_2006_09_28.mp3.

5. Khandro Rinpoche told this story at a talk at E-Vam Institute in Cha-tham, NY, in 2010, and the account here is given from the transcript of her talk as it appears in the E-Vam Institute Newsletter, Fall 2010.
6. Tulku Urgyen, *Blazing Splendor: The Memoirs of Tulku Urgyen Rinpoche* (Berkeley, CA: North Atlantic Books, 2005), p. 56.
7. http://www.chroniclesradio.com/sound/dispatches_2006_09_28.mp3.
8. Quoted from Ken McLeod's translation of Tokmé Zangpo's (1297–1371) Tibetan verses. See http://www.unfetteredmind.org/37-practices-of-a-bodhisattva.
9. From Khandro Rinpoche's contribution to the "Life as a Western Buddhist Nun" conference. Full text available at http://www.thubtenchodron.org/BuddhistNunsMonasticLife/LifeAsAWesternBuddhistNun/living_the_dharma.html.

CHAPTER 2: DAGMOLA KUSHO SAKYA

1. The primary sources for this chapter are several extensive interviews I conducted with Dagmola in Malibu between 2008 and 2012 as well as interviews with her son David Khon and her students Carol Moss, B. Alan Wallace, and others. I also consulted the transcripts of Volker Dencks's two unpublished interviews with Dagmola about her life, which he conducted in Seattle in 2007. Especially for the description of her years in Tibet, with Dagmola's approval, I rely heavily on her own two biographies which chronicle her life in much greater detail. In particular, I highly recommend her English autobiography, *Princess in the Land of Snows*, by Jamyang Sakya and Julie Emery (Boston: Shambhala Publications, 1990). Copyrighted material from *Princess in the Land of Snows*, ©1990 by Jamyang Sakya and Julie Emery, is reprinted here by arrangement with Shambhala Publications, Inc., Boston, MA; www.shambhala.com.
2. Jetsun Kusho took novice ordination at the age of seven and completed her first retreat at age ten. Most unusually, in 1955, when she was only seventeen years old, she gave the full transmission of the important "Path and Fruition" (Tib. *lamdré*) teachings to Tibetan monks over a period of three months when her brother was unavailable. In 1959, Jetsun Kusho escaped from Tibet to India, before settling in Vancouver, Canada, with her family in 1971. In order to provide for

her five sons, she worked as a farm laborer, knitwear designer, and in other jobs, while trying to maintain her spiritual practices. Heeding the repeated requests of her brother and other eminent masters, Jetsun Kusho started teaching in the West in the early 1980s. A more detailed biography can be found at www.sakya-retreat.net/sakya_he.html.

3. Dezhung Rinpoche's life story and accomplishments are chronicled in the very informative book *A Saint in Seattle* by David P. Jackson (Boston: Wisdom Publications, 2003).

4. The book has so far only been published in Tibetan. See Jamyang Dagmo Sakya and Tulku Yeshi Gyatso, *bDag mo 'jam dbyangs dpal mo'i mi tse'i lo rgyus* [The biography of Jamyang Dagmo Sakya] (Taipei: Kathog Rigzin Chenpo, 2009).

5. *Princess in the Land of Snows*, p. 12.

6. Ibid., p. 70.

7. Ibid., p. 74.

8. Ibid., p. 75.

9. Ibid.

10. Ibid., p. 77.

11. Ibid., pp. 79–80.

12. See Mikel Dunham, *Buddha's Warriors* (New York: Penguin, 2004), p. 60. For an in-depth account of Tibet at the time of the Chinese invasion and the Tibetan resistance, Dunham's book is an invaluable resource. His research provided background information for this chapter.

13. *Princess*, p. 97.

14. Ibid., pp. 112–113.

15. Ibid., p. 117.

16. Ibid.

17. Ibid., p. 170.

18. Ibid., p. 179.

19. Ibid., p. 188.

20. Ibid., p. 308.

21. *A Saint in Seattle*, p. 273.

22. Gene Smith talks about his years with the Sakya family in the documentary *Digital Dharma* by Dafna Yachin. More information about him is available at www.tbrc.org and at www.digitaldharma.com.

23. *A Saint in Seattle*, p. 292.

24. *Princess*, p. xv.
25. "Tibet Was Never Like This," *Seattle Magazine* (February 1967), p. 14. Quoted from *A Saint in Seattle*, p. 309.

CHAPTER 3: JETSUNMA TENZIN PALMO

1. The primary sources for this chapter are my interviews with Tenzin Palmo in 1999, 2001, and 2009 in India. I also draw on the first chapter of Tenzin Palmo's book *Reflections on a Mountain Lake*, in which she gives a personal account of her upbringing and her retreat in Ladakh. The details of Tenzin Palmo's extraordinary life and her quest to find enlightenment in a female body are told in full in the best-selling biography *Cave in the Snow* by Vicki Mackenzie, which I wholeheartedly recommend. With Vicki's kind permission, I draw on her research here, particularly in the passages about Tenzin Palmo's earlier years and her time in Ladakh. Based on *Cave in the Snow*, director Liz Thompson made a fabulous documentary film with the same title that served as an additional source for this chapter.
2. *Reflections*, p. 21.
3. See also *Reflections*, p. 19, and *Cave in the Snow*, p. 4.
4. *Reflections*, p. 19.
5. See also similar quotes in *Cave in the Snow*, p. 4 and p. 121.
6. *Reflections*, p. 20.
7. From the film documentary *Cave in the Snow*.
8. *Reflections*, p. 11.
9. Based on *Cave in the Snow*, p. 31.
10. *Reflections*, p. 13.
11. *Cave in the Snow*, p. 42.
12. See also similar quotes in *Reflections*, p. 14, and *Cave in the Snow*, p. 43.
13. Based on *Cave in the Snow*, p. 43.
14. From an interview she gave Lucy Powell for *The Guardian*, 14 May 2009.
15. *Cave in the Snow*, p. 45.
16. See also similar quotes in *Reflections*, p. 14, and *Cave*, p. 46.
17. *Cave in the Snow*, p. 63.

18. *Reflections*, p. 28.
19. A detailed report about the pilgrimage and photos can be found at www .tenzinpalmo.com.
20. See also *Reflections*, p. 58 and p. 163.
21. This encounter with His Holiness is shown in the film documentary *Cave in the Snow.*
22. The enthronement ceremony can be watched at tenzinpalmo.com/index .php?option=com_content&task=view&id=50&Itemid=34.

CHAPTER 4: SANGYE KHANDRO

1. Lama Chönam and Sangye Khandro, trans., *The Lives and Liberation of Princess Mandarava, the Indian Consort of Padmasambhava* (Boston: Wisdom Publications, 1998).
2. The interviews took place over several days in Alameda during breaks in an elaborate Buddhist empowerment ritual that lasted for many months. Sangye Khandro was engaged in translating and training translators in Orgyen Dorje Den, Gyatrul Rinpoche's temple in the Bay Area. During this visit, I also spoke with Gyatrul Rinpoche, Lama Chönam, Sangye Tendar, and several of Sangye Khandro's longtime friends and students who all kindly provided additional anecdotes and insights.
3. The classic guide of the eighth-century saint Shantideva. Its ten chapters are designed to develop the compassionate mind of enlightenment, bodhichitta. One of the many translations of *The Way of the Bodhisattva* has been published by Padmakara (Boston: Shambhala Publications, 2003).Pema Chödrön wrote a contemporary commentary on it, called *No Time to Lose* (Boston: Shambhala Publications, 2007).

CHAPTER 5: PEMA CHÖDRÖN

1. My encounters with Pema Chödrön took place over a period of ten years. When I met her, I met her as a student and fellow retreatant, not in the role of a book author, and therefore did not document our exchanges as a reporter would. Thus I felt it would be more accurate in some instances to quote very similar statements from interviews she had given elsewhere rather than quoting from memory. Additional information was provided in interviews with her students and friends. Pema Chödron read and approved the use of her quotes for this chap-

ter. I gratefully acknowledge permission to reprint copyrighted material from *Tricycle: The Buddhist Review*, Vol. III, No. 1, Fall 1993, pp. 16–24. © 1993 by Helen Tworkov. Reprinted by permission of *Tricycle*.

2. The title refers to Chögyam Trungpa Rinpoche's teachings as published in *Smile at Fear* (Boston: Shambhala Publications, 2009).

3. In this paragraph I rely on her statements as they appear in *Crucial Point* Fall/Winter 2004: http://www.mangalashribhuti.org/pdf/cp_fall_winter04.pdf.

4. Helen Tworkov's interview with Pema Chödrön was first published in *Tricycle: The Buddhist Review* 3, no. 1 (Fall 1993): 16–24. The full interview is available at www.tricycle.com/feature/no-right-no-wrong. Here it is quoted from the edited interview in *Buddhist Women on the Edge*, p. 296.

5. Leonore Friedman, *Meetings with Remarkable Women: Buddhist Teachers in America* (Boston: Shambhala Publications, 2000), p. 106.

6. From an interview with Bill Moyers for "Bill Moyers on Faith and Reason," PBS, August 4, 2006; available at http://video.pbs.org/video/1383845135.

7. This paragraph is quoted and paraphrased from *When Things Fall Apart: Heart Advice for Difficult Times* (Boston: Shambhala Publications, 2002), p. 10, with the author's approval.

8. Moyers, Faith and Reason interview.

9. Ibid.

10. Ibid.

11. Ibid.

12. Ibid.

13. *When Things Fall Apart*, p. 10.

14. *Meetings With Remarkable Women*, p. 115.

15. *Tricycle: The Buddhist Review* 3, no. 1 (Fall 1993): 16–24. Quoted with permission.

16. Ibid.

17. Moyers, Faith and Reason interview.

18. Ibid.

19. Ibid.

20. See Introduction and chapters 3 and 8 for details on the difficulties surrounding full ordination in the Tibetan tradition.

21. *Meetings With Remarkable Women*, p. 108.

22. Ibid., p. 109.

23. Ibid.

24. Ibid., pp. 109–110.

25. *When Things Fall Apart*, p. 6.

26. www.pemachodronfoundation.org.

27. Fabrice Midal, ed., *Recalling Chögyam Trungpa* (Boston: Shambhala Publications, 2005), p. 245.

28. Ibid.

29. Ibid., p. 246.

30. Ibid., pp. 251–252.

31. Pema's description of life at the Abbey can be found on her website pema chodronfoundation.org/video/.

32. *When Things Fall Apart*, pp. 6–7.

33. Ibid.

34. *Tricycle: The Buddhist Review* 3, no. 1 (Fall 1993): 16–24.

35. *Places That Scare You*, p. 33.

36. *Tricycle* interview. Quoted from *Buddhist Women on the Edge*, p. 295.

37. *Buddhist Women on the Edge*, p. 294.

38. Ibid.

39. Ibid., p. 298.

40. *Tricycle: The Buddhist Review* 3, no. 1 (Fall 1993): 16–24.

41. Ibid.

42. Ibid.

43. Ibid.

44. Ibid.

45. Ibid.

46. Ibid.

47. *When Things Fall Apart*, p. 12.

48. *Cultivating Openness When Things Fall Apart*, interview with Pema Chödrön by bell hooks, *Shambhala Sun*, March 1997.

49. Ibid.

50. Moyers, Faith and Reason interview.

51. Ibid.

52. *Let's Be Honest*, interview with Dzigar Kongtrul Rinpoche and Pema Chödrön by Elizabeth Namgyel, *Shambhala Sun*, January 2006.

53. Moyers, Faith and Reason interview.
54. *Crucial Point* Fall/Winter 2004, p. 14.
55. The following account is quoted and paraphrased from Pema's accounts in *Let's Be Honest* as well as *Crucial Point*.
56. *Let's Be Honest*.
57. Ibid.
58. Ibid.
59. Ibid.
60. *Crucial Point*, p. 14.

CHAPTER 6: ELIZABETH MATTIS-NAMGYEL

1. The main sources for this chapter are my interviews with Elizabeth, her family, and students. Apart from an in-depth interview I conducted with her for *View Magazine* at Lerab Ling in 2009, most of the interviews happened in Crestone and Boulder over a weeklong period while shooting the thirty-minute documentary *The Power of an Open Question* for the Buddhist Broadcasting Foundation.
2. Patrul Rinpoche, *The Words of My Perfect Teacher* (Boston: Shambhala Publications, 1998), pp. 144–145.
3. Elizabeth often uses these examples in her teachings and also in her book *The Power of an Open Question*, p. 105.
4. Ibid., p. 97.
5. Ibid., p. 101.
6. Ibid., p. 104.
7. Diana Mukpo, *Dragon Thunder: My Life with Chögyam Trungpa* (Boston: Shambhala Publications, 2006).
8. Ibid., p. 85.
9. She uses a similar description in the introduction to *The Power of an Open Question*, pp. 1–2.

CHAPTER 7: CHAGDUD KHADRO

1. The main interview with Chagdud Khadro took place in Los Angeles in 2011, when she visited on a teaching and fundraising tour.
2. Chagdud Tulku, *Lord of the Dance* (Junction City, CA: Padma Publishing, 1992), p. 201.
3. *Red Tara Commentary* (Junction City, CA: Padma Publishing, 1986).
4. *Ngondro Commentary* (Junction City, CA: Padma Publishing, 1995).

5. *P'howa* (Junction City, CA: Padma Publishing, 1998).
6. *Lord of the Dance*, p. 218.

CHAPTER 8: KARMA LEKSHE TSOMO

1. This chapter is the result of a collaboration by Karma Lekshe Tsomo and Michaela Haas. Lekshe Tsomo has contributed the travel stories and reflections about the situation of Himalayan nuns from her own description of her journey. With Lekshe Tsomo's approval, her Himalayan adventures have been edited and updated for this chapter. The full account of her first journey to Zangskar can be read at www.jamyang. org. In addition to the extensive interview with Lekshe Tsomo in San Diego in 2010 that forms the basis of this chapter, her many publications on the situation of nuns and papers from various Sakyadhita conferences provided invaluable additional background information.
1. Karma Lekshe Tsomo, ed., *Buddhist Women Across Cultures* (Albany, NY: SUNY Press, 1999), p. 175.

CHAPTER 9: THUBTEN CHODRON

1. The primary source for this chapter was a three-day visit to Sravasti Abbey, during which Thubten Chodron granted me an extensive interview and I attended several of her public teachings, observed life at the abbey, and spoke to the residents. With Thubten Chodron's approval, occasionally additional material has been supplemented from her own writings, particularly her essay "You're Becoming a What? Living as a Western Buddhist Nun," in Marianne Dresser, ed., *Buddhist Women on the Edge: Contemporary Perspectives from the Western Frontier* (Berkeley, CA: North Atlantic Books, 1996), pp. 223–233, which I brought to our interview to discuss and clarify. In addition, I consulted many of her own books; a short autobiographical piece from her contribution to an international conference as published in Peter N. Gregory and Susanne Mrozik, eds., *Women Practicing Buddhism: American Experiences* (Somerville, MA: Wisdom Publications, 2007), pp. 191–196; many of the essays she has published on her website, www.thubtenchodron.org; and an unpublished draft of a foreword she wrote for a forthcoming book on her prison work.
2. *How to Free Your Mind* (Ithaca, NY: Snow Lion Publications, 2005), p. 47.

3. Thubten Chodron. "You're Becoming a What? Living as a Western Buddhist Nun," in Marianne Dresser, ed., *Buddhist Women on the Edge: Contemporary Perspectives from the Western Frontier* (Berkeley, CA: North Atlantic Books, 1996), p. 226.

4. See also ibid., pp. 223–233.

5. See also ibid., p. 223.

6. Ibid., p. 228.

7. Paraphrased from ibid., p. 229, and my own interview with her, with Thubten Chodron's permission.

8. From Chodron's essay "Finding Our Own Way," in Thubten Chodron, ed., *Blossoms of the Dharma: Living as a Buddhist Nun* (Berkeley, CA: North Atlantic Books, 1999). Retrieved from http://www.thubtenchodron.org/BuddhistNunsMonasticLife/LifeAsAWesternBuddhistNun/finding_our_way.html.

9. See also Dresser, ed., *Buddhist Women on the Edge*, p. 230.

10. See also ibid., p. 231.

CHAPTER 10: ROSHI JOAN HALIFAX

1. This chapter has been contributed by Kristin Barendsen and arranged by Michaela Haas. With the kind permission of the *Shambhala Sun* editors, Kristen's article "Joan Halifax: Fearless and Fragile" (*Shambhala Sun*, May 2009, pp. 57–63, © 2009 by Kristin Barendsen; reprinted by permission of *Shambhala Sun*) has been adapted here and significantly expanded. Kristin conducted two additional interviews with Roshi Joan for this chapter; Michaela conducted one additional interview with Roshi Joan; and with Roshi Joan's permission, Michaela added further information about her early years from the autobiographical lectures she delivered at the Harvard Divinity School, published as *A Buddhist Life in America: Simplicity in the Complex* (New York: Paulist Press, 1998).

2. *Lucky Dark*, a film by Fabrizio Chiesa, documents Roshi Joan's pilgrimage to Tibet.

3. *A Buddhist Life in America*, p. 7.

4. Ibid.

5. Ibid., p. 8.

6. Ibid.

7. Ibid., p. 9.

8. Ibid., p. 10.
9. All quotes in the previous sentence from *A Buddhist Life in America,* pp. 10–11.
10. Ibid., p. 11.
11. Ibid., p. 13.
12. Ibid.
13. Ibid., p. 17.
14. Ibid., p. 20.
15. Edited, with Roshi Joan's permission, from *A Buddhist Life in America,* p. 20.
16. Ibid., p. 21.
17. Ibid., p. 22.
18. Ibid., p. 23.
19. Ibid., pp. 35–36.
20. Ibid., p. 35.
21. http://www.upaya.org/news/2011/01/02/why-buddhism-violations-of-trust-in-the-sexual-sphere-roshi-joan-halifax/.

CHAPTER 11: TSULTRIM ALLIONE

1. The primary source for this chapter was a three-day visit to Tara Mandala, where I conducted extensive interviews with Tsultrim Allione, her family, and several of her long-term students. In addition, Tsultrim Allione pointed me to an unpublished video recording of teachings on grief she had given earlier, and one audio recording, *The Mandala of the Enlightened Feminine* (Louisville, CO: Sounds True, 2003). She also gave her permission to quote from her extensive biographical introduction to *Women of Wisdom* (Ithaca, NY: Snow Lion Publications, 2000).
2. *Feeding Your Demons: Ancient Wisdom for Resolving Inner Conflict* (New York: Little, Brown and Company, 2008), p. 3.
3. Ibid.
4. *Women of Wisdom,* p. 50. Order of quote changed with Tsultrim Allione's approval.
5. The Tibetan sources provide widely varying dates for her, but there is evidence that Machig Labdron lived at least to age ninety, possibly longer. For a discussion of the various dates see Dan Martin, "The Woman Illusion? Research into the lives of spiritually accomplished

women leaders of the 11th and 12th centuries," pp. 52–53 in *Women in Tibet*, edited by Janet Gyatso and Hanna Havnevik (New York: Columbia University Press, 2005).

6. *Women of Wisdom*, pp. 165–167.
7. Ibid., p. 15. In her book Tsultrim Allione chronicles this phase of her life in much more detail.
8. Ibid., p. 23.
9. Ibid., p. 22.
10. Ibid., p. 23.
11. Ibid., p. 41.
12. Ibid., p. 24.
13. Quoted from the recording *The Mandala of the Enlightened Feminine*.
14. *Women of Wisdom*, p. 28.
15. Quoted from the recording *The Mandala of the Enlightened Feminine*.
16. Ibid.
17. Ibid.
18. Ibid.
19. Ibid.
20. From Tsultrim Allione's teachings on grief at Tara Mandala, 2011.

CHAPTER 12: KHANDRO TSERING CHÖDRON

1. Apart from my own encounters with Khandro Tsering Chödron at Lerab Ling in France and watching the online streaming of the commemorative fire puja, the primary source for this biographical chapter are interviews with her family, students, and friends, and oral teachings given by Sogyal Rinpoche, Orgyen Tobgyal Rinpoche, and Dzongsar Khyentse Rinpoche. Dzongsar Khyentse Rinpoche and Dagmola Sakya kindly granted me interviews to clarify various aspects of Khandro's biography in Los Angeles in 2011. Khandro's students Mauro de March, Kunga Gyalmo, and Lena Raab, among others, contributed their memories. As part of a greater effort to assemble the biography of Jamyang Khyentse Chökyi Lodrö and the history of the Lakar family, a team of Rigpa students under the guidance of Adam Pearcey and Volker Dencks has interviewed dozens of eminent masters over a period of several years and has given me generous access to transcripts of the interviews, most notably an in-depth interview with Mayumla

Tsering Wangmo from 13 August 1996, translated by Ringu Tulku, and interviews with the late Dzongsar Ngari Tulku and Pewar Rinpoche. Some of their research has been edited and published online at www. rememberingthemasters.org, www.lotsawahouse.org, and www .rigpawiki.org. I have also consulted *View, The Rigpa Journal*, July 2011, which is a commemorative issue dedicated to Khandro's life and passing; Sogyal Rinpoche's *The Tibetan Book of Living and Dying*; Dilgo Khyentse Rinpoche's autobiography *Brilliant Moon*; Tulku Thondup's *Masters of Meditation and Miracles*; and Tulku Urgyen's *Blazing Splendor*.

2. From his speech at the memorial service, here quoted as edited in *View, The Rigpa Journal*, July 2011.

3. Ibid.

4. Ibid.

5. From the Karmapa's condolence message, as published on http://khandro. tseringchodron.org/2011/06/08/his-holiness-the-17th-karmapa/.

6. *View, The Rigpa Journal*, July 2011.

7. The Lakar history in this and the following paragraphs is here largely told according to Mayumla Tsering Wangmo's and Orgyen Tobgyal's accounts, which have also been published at www.lotsawahouse.org/lakar.html.

8. *Tibetan Book of Living and Dying*, p. xv.

9. Ibid.

10. Ibid., p. xvi.

11. From a teaching by Sogyal Rinpoche at Lerab Ling, 21 April 2008. Another version of the story is given in *Brilliant Moon*, p. 128.

12. *Brilliant Moon*, p. 128. Orgyen Tobgyal Rinpoche gives a slightly different account: "At this point [Ati Terton] touched the heads of the two young girls, Tsering Chödrön and Tsering Wangmo, who at that time were very young, and said, 'Later on when Jamyang Khyentse becomes a great vajradhara, these two will be part of his assembly of dakinis, and at that time even I might have the good fortune to be of some small service. It has all been very auspicious.' Jamyang Khyentse was completely taken aback by this. 'What is this person saying?' he asked. 'I have never heard anything like it!' But years later when he looked back on this, he said, 'That terton

must have really known something.'" From www.lotsawahouse.org /tibetan-masters/orgyen-tobgyal-rinpoche/biography-khyentse-lodro.

13. *Brilliant Moon*, p. 128.

14. See *Masters of Meditation and Miracles*, p. 92.

15. www.huffingtonpost.com/sogyal-rinpoche/khandro-tsering-chodron -in-memory-of-an-extraordinary-buddhist-master_b_968647. html?ref=buddhism and *Tibetan Book of Living and Dying*, p. 143.

16. Accounts as given in interviews with Dagmola. See also *Princess in the Land of Snows*, pp. 172–173.

17. See also *Princess in the Land of Snows*, pp. 173–174.

18. *Blazing Splendor*, pp. 297–303.

19. www.rememberingthemasters.org.

20. For Sogyal Rinpoche's detailed account of his master's passing see *Tibetan Book of Living and Dying*, p. 273.

21. From her article "Missing Sangyum Kusho" in *Talk Sikkim* Magazine, April 2009.

22. From a teaching by Sogyal Rinpoche in Berlin, 3 June 2011. See also www.huffingtonpost.com/sogyal-rinpoche/khandro-tsering-chodron-in-memory-of-an-extraordinary-buddhist-master_b_968647.html ?ref=buddhism and *Tibetan Book of Living and Dying*, p. 143.

23. www.huffingtonpost.com/sogyal-rinpoche/khandro-tsering-chodron-in-memory-of-an-extraordinary-buddhist-master_b_968647. html?ref=buddhism.

24. Ibid.

25. From oral teachings given by Orgyen Tobgyal Rinpoche at Lerab Ling, 30 May 2011, and *View, The Rigpa Journal*, July 2011.

26. Ibid.

27. From oral teachings given by Sogyal Rinpoche in Berlin, 3 June 2011.

28. From oral teachings given by Orgyen Tobgyal Rinpoche at Lerab Ling, 30 May 2011.

29. From oral teachings given by Orgyen Tobgyal Rinpoche at Lerab Ling, 30 May 2011 and *View, The Rigpa Journal*, July 2011.

30. *Tibetan Book of Living and Dying*, p. 270.

31. From oral teachings given by Orgyen Tobgyal Rinpoche at Lerab Ling, 30 May 2011.

GLOSSARY

To make it as easy as possible for the English reader, the Sanskrit (Skt.), Tibetan (Tib.), Japanese (Jpn.), and Pali (Pali) terms are simply rendered phonetically. Only the terms most commonly used in this volume are briefly explained here as a reference.

abhisheka (Skt.), *wang* (Tib.) Empowerment or initiation; transference of blessings and a necessary prerequisite to perform specific practices in Vajrayana

Avalokiteshwara (Skt.), Chenresig (Tib.) Buddha of Compassion

bardo (Tib.) Intermediate state

bhikshu (Skt.), *gelong* (Tib.) Fully ordained Buddhist monk

bhikshuni (Skt.), *gelongma* (Tib.) Fully ordained Buddhist nun

bodhichitta (Skt.), *changchub sem* (Tib.) "Awakened heart"; the altruistic aspiration to attain enlightenment for the sake of all sentient beings

bodhisattva (Skt.), *changchub sempa* (Tib.) Someone who has developed the altruistic intention of bodhichitta

Bon (Tib.) Once the dominant pre-Buddhist religion of Tibet, in its current form recognized as one of five Tibetan Buddhist practice traditions

Buddha (Skt.), *sangye* (Tib.) Awakened One

chöd (Tib.) "Cutting through"; practice of severing ego-clinging

dakini (Skt.), *khandro* (Tib.) Female embodiment of enlightenment

delog (Tib.) Person who lived to tell of their after-death experience

dharma (Skt.), *chö* (Tib.) Buddha's teachings; the word has a wide range of meanings, including truth, path, and phenomena

Dzogchen (Tib.) "Great Perfection" or "Great Completeness"; a practice tradition mostly associated with the Nyingma School

Gelug (Tib.) "The way of the virtuous"; one of the five main Tibetan Buddhist practice lineages

geshe (Tib.) Academic title traditionally bestowed by the three great Gelug monasteries; roughly equal to a PhD

Golok (Tib.) A region in East Tibet

guru (Skt.), lama (Tib.) Common term for a revered teacher in Hindu and Buddhist traditions

Hinayana (Skt.) "Foundational Vehicle"; a later classification of the oldest form of exoteric Buddhism

jetsun(ma) (Tib.) "Venerable"; highly honorific Tibetan term

jomo (Tib.) Honorific term for a nun or noble woman

Kagyü (Tib.) "Oral lineage"; one of the five main Tibetan Buddhist practice lineages

karma (Skt.) The principle of cause and effect

Kham (Tib.) Region in East Tibet; one of three regions traditionally considered to constitute Tibet

khenpo (Tib.) Academic title for a graduate of traditional studies in Buddhist philosophy

kyabjé (Tib.) "Lord of Refuge"; term of enormous reverence for a highly realized teacher, often translated as "His Holiness"

Mahayana (Skt.) "Great vehicle"; path of the bodhisattvas

mandala (Skt.), *kyilkhor* (Tib.) Circle and circumference; most commonly used for a physical representation or diagram of a deity along with its retinue and surroundings

Manjushri (Skt.), Jampal Yang (Tib.) Buddha of Wisdom

mantra (Skt.) Sacred syllables

Mantrayana (Skt.) "Vehicle of Mantra"; another term for Vajrayana or esoteric Buddhism

mudra (Skt.) Symbolic hand gestures

nangpa (Tib.) "Insider"; Buddhist

nirvana (Skt.) Liberation from suffering; enlightenment

Nyingma (Tib.) "Ancient School"; one of the five main Tibetan Buddhist practice lineages

Padmasambhava (Skt.) "Lotus-Born"; eighth-century pioneer of Tibetan Buddhism

phowa (Tib.) Transference of consciousness at the time of death

prajna (Skt.), *sherab* (Tib.) Wisdom, intelligence, or knowledge

Prajnaparamita (Skt.) "Perfection of Wisdom"; (1) class of scriptures; (2) female embodiment of the perfection of wisdom; (3) supreme level of spiritual realization and practice

purba (Tib.) Ceremonial dagger

Rimé (Tib.) Nonsectarian

rinpoche (Tib.) "Precious"; honorific title for a Tibetan teacher

roshi (Jpn.) Honorific title for a Zen priest

sadhana (Skt.) "Means of accomplishment"; tantric practice text

Sakya (Tib.) "Grey earth"; one of the five main Tibetan Buddhist practice lineages

samaya (Skt.) Tantric commitment

samsara (Skt.) "Wandering"; the continuous cycle of birth, life, death, and rebirth

sangha (Skt.), *gedün* (Tib.) Buddhist community

sangyum (Tib.) "Sacred consort"; honorific term for a revered master's consort

Shakyamuni (Skt.) Name of the historical Buddha who lived around the fifth century BCE

shamatha (Skt.), *shyiné* (Tib.) "Calm abiding" meditation

shunyata (Skt.) Emptiness; the lack of true, inherent existence of all phenomena

siddha (Skt.) Accomplished master

stupa (Skt.), *chörten* (Tib.) Reliquary or monument of enlightenment

Sutra (Skt.) Discourses of the Buddha; one of three categories of Buddhist teachings

Sutrayana (Skt.) "Vehicle of Sutra"; exoteric Buddhism

Tantra (Skt.), *gyü* (Tib.) "Loom, thread"; class of esoteric texts and practices that originated in India in the early centuries CE

Tantrayana (Skt.) "Vehicle of Tantra"; another term for Vajrayana or esoteric Buddhism

Tara (Skt.), Drolma (Tib.) "Liberator"; female buddha

terma (Tib.) Hidden treasure

terton (Tib.) Treasure revealer

thangka (Tib.) Tibetan cloth painting

Theravada (Pali) "Ancient teachings"; earliest surviving Buddhist school, predominant in Southeast Asia

togden (Tib.) "Endowed with realization"; a realized yogi; more specifically refers to a yogi-monk in the Drukpa Kagyü tradition

tonglen (Tib.) "Sending and taking"; compassion practice

tsa lung (Tib.) "Channels and wind"; advanced yogic exercises, which include breath work, meditation, visualization, and specific movements

tsa tsa (Tib.) Small clay icon of a stupa, buddha, or deity

tukdam (Tib.) Honorific term for a meditation practice frequently used to refer to the period after an accomplished master's physical death

tulku (Tib.), *nirmanakaya* (Skt.) "Emanation body"; reincarnation of a master who intentionally chooses to return

upaya (Skt.) Skillful means

vajra (Skt.), *dorje* (Tib.) A ritual scepter or thunderbolt, symbolizing indestructibility

Vajrayana (Skt.), *dorje tekpa* (Tib.) "Diamond Vehicle"; the tantric branch of Mahayana Buddhism widely practiced in Tibet, also called Tantrayana or Mantrayana

Vajrayogini (Skt.), Dorje Naljorma (Tib.) Important female meditational deity

Vinaya (Skt.) Monastic codex

vipashyana (Skt.), *lhaktong* (Tib.) "Clear seeing"; advanced form of meditation that includes a direct recognition of the nature of reality

yidam (Tib.) Meditational deity

yoga (Skt.), *naljor* (Tib.) "Union"; guru yoga is the practice of merging one's mind with the mind of the teacher

yogi (Skt.), *naljorpa* (Tib.) Practitioner of yoga

yogini (Skt.), *naljorma* (Tib.) Dedicated female practitioner

Zen (Jpn.) School of Mahayana Buddhism

SELECTED BIBLIOGRAPHY

Allione, Tsultrim. *Feeding Your Demons: Ancient Wisdom for Resolving Inner Conflict.* New York: Little, Brown and Company, 2008.

————. *The Mandala of the Enlightened Feminine* [audio recording]. 5 compact discs. Louisville, CO: Sounds True, 2003.

————. *Women of Wisdom.* Ithaca, NY: Snow Lion Publications, 2000.

Chagdud Tulku. *Lord of the Dance.* Junction City, CA: Padma Publishing, 1992.

Changchub, Gyalwa, and Namkhai Nyingpo. *Lady of the Lotus-Born: The Life and Enlightenment of Yeshe Tsogyal.* Boston: Shambhala Publications, 2002.

Chödrön, Pema. *No Time to Lose.* Boston: Shambhala Publications, 2007.

————. *The Places That Scare You: A Guide to Fearlessness in Difficult Times.* Boston: Shambhala Publications, 2007.

————. *Start Where You Are: A Guide to Compassionate Living.* Boston: Shambhala Publications, 2004.

————. *When Things Fall Apart: Heart Advice for Difficult Times.* Boston: Shambhala Publications, 2002.

————. *The Wisdom of No Escape.* Boston: Shambhala Publications, 2001.

Chodron, Thubten. *Buddhism for Beginners.* Ithaca, NY: Snow Lion Publications, 2001.

————. *Don't Believe Everything You Think.* Boston & London: Snow Lion/Shambhala Publications, 2012.

————. *How to Free Your Mind: Tara the Liberator.* Ithaca, NY: Snow Lion Publications, 2005.

————. *Open Heart, Clear Mind.* Ithaca, NY: Snow Lion Publications, 1990.

———. *Taming the Mind*. Ithaca, NY: Snow Lion Publications, 2004.

———. *Working with Anger*. Ithaca, NY: Snow Lion Publications, 2001.

Chönam, Lama, and Sangye Khandro, trans. *Key to the Precious Treasury: A Concise Commentary on the General Meaning of the "Glorious Secret Essence Tantra."* By Dodrupchen Jigme Tenpa'i Nyima. Ithaca, NY: Snow Lion Publications, 2010.

———. *The Lives and Liberation of Princess Mandarava, the Indian Consort of Padmasambhava*. Boston: Wisdom Publications, 1998.

———. *Yeshe Lama*. By Vidyadhara Jigme Lingpa. Ithaca, NY: Snow Lion Publications, 2009.

David-Neel, Alexandra. *Magic and Mystery in Tibet*. New Delhi: Rupa Publications, 1989.

———. *My Journey to Lhasa*. New York: HarperPerennial, 2005.

Diemberger, Hildegard. *When a Woman Becomes a Religious Dynasty: The Samding Dorje Phagmo of Tibet*. New York: Columbia University Press, 2007.

Dresser, Marianne, ed. *Buddhist Women on the Edge*. Berkeley, CA: North Atlantic Books, 1996.

Dowman, Keith. *Sky Dancer: The Secret Life and Songs of the Lady Yeshe Tsogyel*. London: Routledge and Kegan Paul, 1984.

Dunham, Mikel. *Buddha's Warriors*. New York: Penguin, 2004.

Edou, Jerome. *Machig Labdrön and the Foundations of Chöd*. Ithaca, NY: Snow Lion Publications, 1995.

Findly, Ellison Banks, ed. *Women's Buddhism, Buddhism's Women: Tradition, Revision, Renewal*. Boston: Wisdom Publications, 2000.

Friedman, Leonore. *Meetings with Remarkable Women: Buddhist Teachers in America*. Boston: Shambhala Publications, 2000.

Gregory, Peter N., and Susanne Mrozik, eds. *Women Practicing Buddhism: American Experiences*. Boston: Wisdom Publications, 2008.

Gross, Rita M. *Soaring and Settling. Buddhist Perspectives on Contemporary Social and Religious Issues*. London: Continuum, 1998.

———. *Buddhism After Patriarchy: A Feminist History, Analysis, and Reconstruction of Buddhism*. Albany, NY: SUNY Press, 1993.

Gyatrul Rinpoche. *Meditation, Transformation, and Dream Yoga*. Translated by B. Alan Wallace and Sangye Khandro. Ithaca, NY: Snow Lion Publications, 2002.

Gyatso, Janet, and Hanna Havnevik, eds. *Women in Tibet*. New York: Columbia University Press, 2005.

Halifax, Joan. *Being with Dying: Cultivating Compassion and Fearlessness in the Presence of Death*. Boston: Shambhala Publications, 2008.

———. *A Buddhist Life in America: Simplicity in the Complex*. New York: Paulist Press, 1998.

———. *The Fruitful Darkness: A Journey through Buddhist Practice and Tribal Wisdom*. New York: Grove Press, 2004.

———. *Shamanic Voices*. London: Penguin, 1991.

Harding, Sarah, ed. and trans. *Machik's Complete Explanation: Clarifying the Meaning of Chöd*. By Machig Labdrön. Ithaca, NY: Snow Lion Publications, 2003.

Jackson, David P. *A Saint in Seattle: The Life of the Tibetan Mystic Dezhung Rinpoche*. Boston: Wisdom Publications, 2003.

Khadro, Chagdud. *Ngondro Commentary*. Junction City, CA: Padma Publishing, 1995.

———. *P'howa*. Junction City, CA: Padma Publishing, 1998.

———. *Red Tara Commentary*. Junction City, CA: Padma Publishing, 1986.

Khandro Rinpoche. *This Precious Life: Tibetan Buddhist Teachings on the Path to Enlightenment*. Boston: Shambhala Publications, 2005.

Khyentse, Dilgo. *Brilliant Moon: The Autobiography of Dilgo Khyentse*. Boston: Shambhala Publications, 2009.

Kornman, Robin, Lama Chönam, and Sangye Khandro, trans. *The Epic of Gesar of Ling: Gesar's Magical Birth, Early Years, and Coronation as King*. Boston: Shambhala Publications, 2011.

Mackenzie, Vicki. *Cave in the Snow: Tenzin Palmo's Quest for Enlightenment*. New York: Bloomsbury, 1999.

Mattis-Namgyel, Elizabeth. *The Power of an Open Question*. Boston: Shambhala Publications, 2010.

Midal, Fabrice, ed. *Recalling Chögyam Trungpa*. Boston: Shambhala Publications, 2005.

Moyers, Bill. Interview with Pema Chödrön. "Bill Moyers on Faith and Reason," PBS, August 4, 2006. http://video.pbs.org/video/1383845135.

Mukpo, Diana. *Dragon Thunder: My Life With Chögyam Trungpa*. Boston: Shambhala Publications, 2006.

Palmo, Tenzin. *Into the Heart of Life.* Ithaca, NY: Snow Lion Publications, 2011.

——. *Reflections on a Mountain Lake: Teachings on Practical Buddhism.* Ithaca, NY: Snow Lion Publications, 2002.

Patrul Rinpoche. *The Words of My Perfect Teacher.* Boston: Shambhala Publications, 1998.

Pema, Jetsun. *Tibet: My Story.* Boston: Wisdom Publications, 1998.

Pistono, Matteo. *In the Shadow of the Buddha.* New York: DuttonPenguin, 2011.

Sakya, Jamyang, and Julie Emory. *Princess in the Land of Snows: The Life of Jamyang Sakya in Tibet.* Boston: Shambhala Publications, 2001.

Sakya, Jamyang Dagmo, and Tulku Yeshi Gyatso. *bDag mo 'jam dbyangs dpal mo'i mi tse'i lo rgyus* [The biography of Dagmo Jamyang Sakya]. Taipei: Kathog Rigzin Chenpo, 2009.

Scales, Sandra. *Sacred Voices of the Nyingma Masters.* Junction City, CA: Padma Publishing, 2004.

Shakya, Tsering. *The Dragon in the Land of Snows.* New York: Penguin Compass, 1999.

Shaw, Miranda. *Passionate Enlightenment.* Princeton, NJ: Princeton University Press, 1994.

Sidor, Ellen S., ed. *A Gathering of Spirit: Women Teaching in American Buddhism.* Cumberland, RI: Primary Point Press, 1987.

Simmer-Brown, Judith. *Dakini's Warm Breath: The Feminine Principle in Tibetan Buddhism.* Boston: Shambhala Publications, 2002.

Sogyal Rinpoche. *The Tibetan Book of Living and Dying.* New York: HarperCollins, 1994.

Thondup, Tulku. *Masters of Meditation and Miracles: Lives of the Great Buddhist Masters of India and Tibet.* Boston: Shambhala Publications, 1999.

Trungpa, Chögyam. *Born in Tibet.* Boston: Shambhala Publications, 1995.

——. *Cutting Through Spiritual Materialism.* Boston: Shambhala Publications, 1987.

——. *Smile at Fear.* Boston: Shambhala Publications, 2009.

Tsomo, Karma Lekshe, ed. *Buddhism Through American Women's Eyes.* Ithaca, NY: Snow Lion Publications, 1995.

———, ed. *Buddhist Women Across Cultures*. Albany, NY: SUNY Press, 1999.

———, ed. *Buddhist Women and Social Justice: Ideas, Challenges, and Achievements*. Albany, NY: SUNY Press, 2004.

———, ed. *Sakyadhita: Daughters of the Buddha*. Ithaca, NY: Snow Lion Publications, 1988.

———. *Sisters in Solitude: Two Traditions of Buddhist Monastic Ethics for Women*. Albany, NY: SUNY Press, 1996.

Urgyen Tulku. *Blazing Splendor: The Memoirs of Tulku Urgyen Rinpoche*. Berkeley, CA: North Atlantic Books, 2005.